S0-BOD-789

GREAT RECIPES COLLECTION

# chicken

Grand Avenue Books
Des Moines, Iowa

Grand Avenue Books
An imprint of Meredith® Corporation

*Great Recipes Collection: Chicken*
Contributing Editors: Sharyl Heiken, Rosemary Hutchinson
   (Spectrum Communication Services)
Senior Associate Art Director: Ken Carlson
Copy and Production Editor: Victoria Forlini
Contributing Designer: Joline Rivera
Copy Chief: Terri Fredrickson
Contributing Proofreaders: Sheila Mauck, Gretchen Kauffman
Editorial Operations Manager: Karen Schirm
Manager, Book Production: Rick von Holdt
Electronic Production Coordinator: Paula Forest
Editorial and Design Assistants: Kaye Chabot, Mary Lee Gavin, Patricia Loder

**Grand Avenue Books**
Editor In Chief: Linda Raglan Cunningham
Design Director: Matt Strelecki
Managing Editor: Gregory H. Kayko
Executive Editor, Grand Avenue Books: Dan Rosenberg

Publisher: James D. Blume
Executive Director, New Business Development: Todd M. Davis
Director, Production: Douglas M. Johnston
Executive Director, Marketing: Jeffrey Myers
Director, Operations: George A. Susral
Executive Director, Sales: Ken Zagor
Vice President and General Manager: Douglas J. Guendel

**Meredith Publishing Group**
President, Publishing Group: Stephen M. Lacy
Vice President-Publishing Director: Bob Mate

**Meredith Corporation**
Chairman and Chief Executive Officer: William T. Kerr
Chairman of the Executive Committee: E.T. Meredith III

All of us at
Grand Avenue Books
are dedicated to
providing you with the
information you need to create
delicious foods. If for any
reason you are not satisfied
with this book, or if you have
other comments or suggestions,
write to us at: Grand Avenue
Books, Editorial Department
LN-116, 1716 Locust Street,
Des Moines, IA 50309-3023

Copyright © 2003 by Meredith Corporation, Des Moines, Iowa.
First Edition. All rights reserved. Printed in the United States of America.
Library of Congress Control Number: 2002111438
ISBN: 0-696-21674-4

# mealtime mainstay

## From one generation to the next, cooks have relied on chicken and turkey to create satisfying meals for their families.

Looking for something for dinner tonight? Chicken or turkey is the perfect solution. Why? Because both are nutritious, terrific-tasting, and easy to fit into almost any schedule. And *Great Recipes Collection: Chicken* is your best bet for discovering creative new ideas for poultry.

Scan the pages of this book and you'll see more than 250 recipes for whole birds—including Cornish hens, chicken pieces, turkey breasts and tenderloins, and ground poultry.

You also can select from whatever type of dish suits your mood and your schedule. There are quick fixes and slow simmers. There are stove-top specialties, stir-fries, soups, roasted poultry, oven delights, grilled or broiled favorites, salads, and sandwiches. And there are recipes that start from scratch or ones based on leftovers or a roasted bird

from the deli. In addition, you'll find down-to-earth advice for carving a whole turkey or chicken and helpful charts with cooking times for roasting, broiling, and grilling poultry.

What's more, no matter what flavors you prefer, *Chicken* has something to please. Enjoy traditional favorites, such as Maryland Fried Chicken, Turkey with Cranberry Sauce, Deep-Dish Chicken Pie, and Smoked Turkey and Wild Rice Salad. Or savor ethnic-influenced dishes, such as Chicken Cacciatore, Turkey-Black Bean Chili, Asian Chicken Kabobs, and Muffuletta.

With *Chicken,* creating satisfying family meals has never been easier or more delicious. So the next time you're trying to decide how to fix chicken or turkey, turn to this exceptional collection of first-rate recipes for inspiration.

Mad-Dash Dinner Salad, page 260

# contents

# range-top dishes

*From a quick-fixing skillet supper and crispy fried chicken to a slow-simmered cassoulet, you can enjoy poultry just about any way you like it with these tantalizing top-of-the-stove ideas.*

Oregano Chicken and Vegetables, page 38

# Maryland Fried Chicken

*Be sure to serve plenty of mashed potatoes to soak up the creamy gravy that accompanies this cracker crumb-coated chicken.*

**Prep:** 25 minutes  **Cook:** 55 minutes  **Makes:** 6 servings

1 beaten egg

3 tablespoons milk

1 cup finely crushed saltine crackers (28 crackers)

1 teaspoon dried thyme, crushed

½ teaspoon paprika

⅛ teaspoon pepper

2½ to 3 pounds meaty chicken pieces (breasts, thighs, and drumsticks)

2 to 3 tablespoons cooking oil

1 cup milk

1 recipe Cream Gravy

Hot mashed potatoes (optional)

Fresh thyme sprigs (optional)

*1.* In a small bowl combine the egg and the 3 tablespoons milk. In a shallow bowl combine crushed crackers, dried thyme, paprika, and pepper. Dip chicken pieces, 1 at a time, in egg mixture, then roll in cracker mixture.

*2.* In a large skillet cook chicken, uncovered, in hot oil over medium heat for 10 to 15 minutes or until browned, turning to brown evenly. Remove chicken from skillet; drain off fat. Return chicken to skillet.

*3.* Add the 1 cup milk to skillet. Reduce heat to medium-low; cover. Cook for 35 minutes. Uncover; cook about 10 minutes more or until chicken is tender and no longer pink. Drain on paper towels. Transfer chicken to a serving platter, reserving drippings in skillet. Cover chicken and keep warm. Prepare Cream Gravy. If desired, serve with mashed potatoes and garnish with fresh thyme.

*Cream Gravy:* Skim fat from drippings in skillet. Reserve 3 tablespoons of the drippings in skillet. In a screw-top jar combine ¾ cup milk, 3 tablespoons all-purpose flour, ¼ teaspoon salt, and ⅛ teaspoon pepper; cover and shake well. Add to skillet. Stir in ¾ cup milk. Cook over medium heat, stirring constantly, until thickened and bubbly. Cook and stir for 1 minute more. (If desired, thin with additional milk.)

Nutrition Facts per serving: **409 calories, 23 g total fat, 118 mg cholesterol, 398 mg sodium, 17 g carbohydrate, 30 g protein.**

# Spanish-Style Chicken

*If you're using fresh herbs, get maximum flavor by stirring them in just before serving.*

**Prep:** 25 minutes  **Cook:** 37 minutes  **Makes:** 6 servings

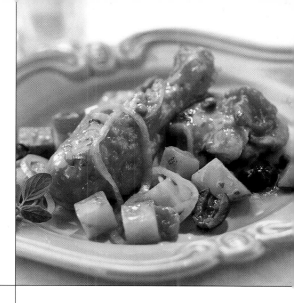

**1.** In a large plastic bag combine flour, salt, and ground red pepper. Add chicken pieces, a few pieces at a time; shake to coat. In a 4-quart Dutch oven cook chicken in hot oil over medium heat about 10 minutes or until lightly browned, turning to brown evenly.

**2.** Add undrained tomatoes, potatoes, onion, olives, wine, capers (if using), dried basil (if using), dried oregano (if using), and garlic to Dutch oven. Bring to boiling; reduce heat. Cover and simmer for 35 to 45 minutes or until chicken is tender and no longer pink. Remove chicken to a serving dish; cover and keep warm.

**3.** In a small bowl combine the cold water and cornstarch; add to chicken mixture in Dutch oven. Cook and stir until thickened and bubbly. Cook and stir for 2 minutes more. Stir in snipped fresh basil (if using) and fresh oregano (if using). Pour thickened mixture over chicken in dish. If desired, garnish with fresh basil or oregano sprigs.

Nutrition Facts per serving: 354 calories, 12 g total fat, 77 mg cholesterol, 566 mg sodium, 28 g carbohydrate, 29 g protein.

- ¼ cup all-purpose flour
- ½ teaspoon salt
- ¼ teaspoon ground red pepper
- 1 3- to 3½-pound broiler-fryer chicken, cut up and skinned
- 2 tablespoons olive oil or cooking oil
- 1 28-ounce can whole Italian-style tomatoes, cut up
- 4 medium potatoes, cut into ½-inch pieces
- 1 medium onion, sliced
- ½ cup halved pitted ripe olives
- ½ cup dry red wine
- 2 tablespoons capers (optional)
- 1 tablespoon snipped fresh basil or 1 teaspoon dried basil, crushed
- 2 teaspoons snipped fresh oregano or ½ teaspoon dried oregano, crushed
- 2 cloves garlic, minced
- 1 tablespoon cold water
- 2 teaspoons cornstarch
  Fresh basil or oregano sprigs (optional)

# Super-Crunch Batter-Fried Chicken

*Self-rising flour is the secret to a crunchy coating.*

**Prep:** 10 minutes  **Stand:** 15 minutes  **Cook:** 1 hour  **Makes:** 6 servings

1½ cups self-rising flour

1 cup low-fat buttermilk

1 3- to 3½-pound broiler-fryer
   chicken, cut up

½ teaspoon salt

½ teaspoon freshly ground
   black pepper

½ teaspoon ground nutmeg

2 cups shortening

**1.** Place the flour in a large bowl; pour the buttermilk into another large bowl. Dip the chicken in flour, then in buttermilk, shaking off any excess. Roll chicken in flour again; place, skin sides up, on a plate. Sprinkle with salt, pepper, and nutmeg. Let stand for 15 minutes.

**2.** Melt the shortening in a heavy, 10-inch skillet over medium heat; heat to 350°. Carefully add half of the chicken; cover and cook for 10 minutes.

**3.** Uncover and cook, turning once, about 20 minutes more or until crisp and juices run clear when the chicken is pierced with a fork. Drain on paper towels. Transfer to a baking pan; keep warm in a 300° oven. Repeat with remaining chicken.

Nutrition Facts per serving: **450 calories, 30 g total fat, 116 mg cholesterol, 418 mg sodium, 13 g carbohydrate, 31 g protein.**

# Autumn Chicken with Pear, Sage, and Cheese

*Plan the menu for your next dinner party around this elegant yet easy chicken dish.*

**Start to Finish:** 35 minutes **Makes:** 4 servings

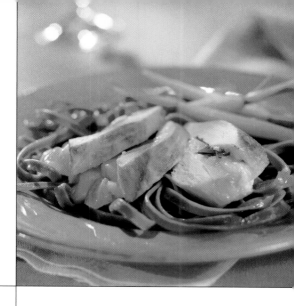

**1.** Cut a 3-inch-long pocket into the thick side of each chicken breast. Insert 2 slices of pear and 1 slice of cheese into each pocket. Place about 1 teaspoon of the sliced sage into each pocket on top of the cheese, reserving remaining sage.

**2.** Add olive oil to a medium skillet; heat over medium-high heat. Cook breasts in hot oil until browned on one side. Sprinkle lightly with salt and pepper; turn. Cook until second side is browned. Pour apple juice and reserved sliced sage over breasts. Heat to boiling; reduce heat. Cover and simmer for 7 to 10 minutes or just until tender and no longer pink. Remove chicken from skillet; cover and keep warm. Heat cooking liquid to boiling; boil gently about 5 minutes or until reduced to 1 cup. If desired, serve chicken over fettuccine. Serve cooking liquid over chicken.

Nutrition Facts per serving: **257 calories, 7 g total fat, 82 mg cholesterol, 188 mg sodium, 17 g carbohydrate, 29 g protein.**

- 4 **large skinless, boneless chicken breast halves (about 1¼ pounds total)**
- 1 **small Bartlett pear, cored and cut into 8 thin slices**
- 1 **ounce Romano or Emmentaler cheese, cut into 4 thin slices**
- 2 **tablespoons thinly sliced fresh sage leaves**
- 2 **teaspoons olive oil**
  **Salt**
  **Pepper**
- 1½ **cups apple juice or apple cider**
  **Hot cooked spinach fettuccine (optional)**

# Braised Chicken Thighs With Peppers and Olives

*Saffron contributes a sunny yellow color and exotic flavor to this chicken and rice dish.*

**Prep:** 25 minutes  **Cook:** 25 minutes  **Makes:** 6 servings

12  skinless, boneless
    chicken thighs
    (about 2 pounds total)
    Salt
    Ground black pepper
 2  tablespoons olive oil
 1  large onion, chopped
 1  medium red sweet pepper,
    cut into thin strips
 3  cloves garlic, minced
 1  cup long grain rice
¼  teaspoon thread saffron,
    crushed, or ⅛ teaspoon
    ground saffron
1½  cups water
½  cup pimiento-stuffed
    green olives, halved
½  cup dry white wine, dry
    vermouth, or chicken broth
    Lemon wedges

**1.** Sprinkle chicken with salt and black pepper. In a 12-inch skillet heat olive oil over medium-high heat. Add chicken; cook about 10 minutes or until browned, turning once. Remove chicken, reserving 1 tablespoon of the drippings in skillet.

**2.** Add onion, sweet pepper, and garlic to skillet; cook and stir for 4 to 5 minutes or until vegetables are tender. Stir in uncooked rice and saffron; add the water, olives, and wine. Bring to boiling. Return chicken to skillet; reduce heat. Cover and simmer about 25 minutes or until chicken is no longer pink and rice is tender. Serve with lemon wedges.

Nutrition Facts per serving: **328 calories, 11 g total fat, 73 mg cholesterol, 338 mg sodium, 28 g carbohydrate, 24 g protein.**

# Chicken Braised with Wine and Tomatoes

*Serve the saucy chicken thighs with hot cooked noodles or rice.*

**Prep:** 15 minutes **Cook:** 40 minutes **Makes:** 4 servings

**1.** In a large skillet cook chicken in hot oil over medium heat about 5 minutes or until browned, turning to brown evenly. Drain off fat. Add the ⅔ cup broth, the wine or additional broth, garlic, dried rosemary (if using), salt, and black pepper to chicken in skillet. Bring to boiling; reduce heat. Cover and simmer for 20 minutes.

**2.** Add tomatoes, mushrooms, and sweet peppers to skillet. Cover and simmer about 15 minutes more or until chicken is tender and no longer pink. Transfer chicken to a serving dish, reserving vegetables and cooking liquid in skillet. Cover chicken with foil to keep warm.

**3.** In a small bowl combine the cornstarch, cold water, and fresh rosemary (if using); stir into mixture in skillet. Cook and stir until thickened and bubbly. Cook and stir for 2 minutes more. Spoon vegetables and sauce around chicken. Serve with noodles or rice.

Nutrition Facts per serving: 355 calories, 10 g total fat, 117 mg cholesterol, 408 mg sodium, 34 g carbohydrate, 29 g protein.

- 8 small or 4 large chicken thighs (about 2 pounds total), skinned
- 1 tablespoon cooking oil
- ⅔ cup chicken broth
- ¼ cup dry white wine or chicken broth
- 2 cloves garlic, minced
- 2 teaspoons snipped fresh rosemary or ¾ teaspoon dried rosemary, crushed
- ¼ teaspoon salt
- ¼ teaspoon ground black pepper
- 2 cups chopped roma tomatoes (6 medium)
- 1½ cups sliced fresh mushrooms
- 1 medium yellow sweet pepper, cut into ½-inch-wide strips
- 1 medium green sweet pepper, cut into ½-inch-wide strips
- 2 tablespoons cornstarch
- 2 tablespoons cold water
  Hot cooked noodles or rice

# Chicken Curry in a Hurry

*Apple adds just the right touch of sweetness.*

**Start to Finish:** 30 minutes  **Makes:** 4 servings

2 tablespoons curry powder

2 tablespoons water

1 teaspoon ground cumin

1 teaspoon bottled minced
   garlic

1 teaspoon tomato paste

¾ teaspoon salt

¼ teaspoon freshly ground
   black pepper
   Pinch ground cloves

2 cups finely chopped onion

1 tablespoon cooking oil

8 skinless, boneless chicken
   thighs, halved (about
   1½ pounds total)

1 Golden Delicious apple,
   cored and cut into
   1-inch pieces

1 cup carrots cut into
   ½-inch pieces

¾ cup chicken broth

1 cup frozen peas, thawed
   Hot cooked rice or couscous

*1.* In a small bowl combine curry powder, water, cumin, garlic, tomato paste, salt, pepper, and cloves. Set aside.

*2.* In a Dutch oven cook onion in hot oil until tender. Stir in spice mixture; cook about 1 minute or until fragrant.

*3.* Add chicken thighs, apple, carrots, and broth. Bring to boiling; reduce heat. Cover and simmer for 12 to 14 minutes or until chicken and vegetables are tender and chicken is tender and no longer pink. Stir in peas; heat through. Serve with rice or couscous.

Nutrition Facts per serving: **485 calories, 11 g total fat, 118 mg cholesterol, 814 mg sodium, 61 g carbohydrate, 35 g protein.**

# Chicken and Mushrooms

*Dark-meat lovers take note—this poultry dish uses both chicken thighs and drumsticks.*

**Prep:** 30 minutes  **Cook:** 25 minutes  **Makes:** 4 to 6 servings

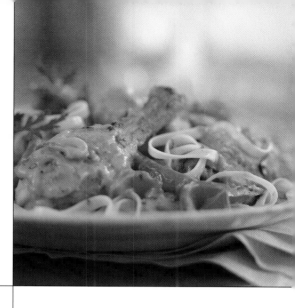

**1.** In a plastic bag combine the ¼ cup flour, the salt, black pepper, and paprika. Add chicken pieces, a few at a time, to the bag; shake to coat.

**2.** In a very large skillet cook chicken in hot oil over medium heat about 10 minutes or until well browned, turning to brown evenly. Remove chicken from skillet, reserving drippings in the skillet.

**3.** Add onion, mushrooms, sweet pepper, and garlic to skillet. Cook and stir for 2 minutes. Add red wine or beef broth and balsamic vinegar. Cook and stir for 5 minutes more.

**4.** Add undrained tomatoes and Italian seasoning. Bring to boiling, scraping up browned bits from the bottom of the skillet. Return chicken to the skillet; reduce heat. Cover and simmer about 20 minutes or until chicken is tender and no longer pink. Remove chicken; keep warm.

**5.** Stir together the half-and-half or light cream and the 1 tablespoon flour; add to skillet. Cook and stir until slightly thickened and bubbly. Cook and stir for 1 minute more. Return chicken to pan; heat through. Sprinkle with snipped parsley. If desired, serve over hot cooked pasta. If desired, garnish with parsley sprigs.

Nutrition Facts per serving: **323 calories, 13 g total fat, 89 mg cholesterol, 400 mg sodium, 21 g carbohydrate, 25 g protein.**

¼ cup all-purpose flour
¼ teaspoon salt
¼ teaspoon ground black pepper
¼ teaspoon paprika
4 chicken thighs, skinned
4 chicken drumsticks, skinned
2 tablespoons cooking oil
1 medium onion, sliced
2 cups whole or sliced small mushrooms
1 medium red sweet pepper, cut into 1-inch-wide strips
3 cloves garlic, minced
½ cup dry red wine or beef broth
2 tablespoons balsamic vinegar
1 14½-ounce can diced tomatoes
2 teaspoons dried Italian seasoning, crushed
¼ cup half-and-half or light cream
1 tablespoon all-purpose flour
¼ cup snipped fresh flat-leaf parsley
  Hot cooked pasta (optional)
  Fresh flat-leaf parsley sprigs (optional)

# Basil Chicken with Wine Sauce

*Simple ingredients—mushrooms, onion, basil, and dry white wine—merge to make an out-of-the-ordinary sauce.*

**Prep:** 30 minutes  **Cook:** 35 minutes  **Makes:** 5 servings

Nonstick cooking spray

2 cups sliced fresh
   mushrooms

1 small onion, chopped

2 tablespoons snipped fresh
   basil or 2 teaspoons dried
   basil, crushed

1 clove garlic, minced

⅓ cup reduced-sodium
   chicken broth

⅓ cup dry white wine

¼ teaspoon salt

¼ teaspoon pepper

2 pounds meaty chicken
   pieces (breasts, thighs,
   and drumsticks), skinned

1 tablespoon cornstarch

1 tablespoon cold water

**1.** Coat an unheated large skillet with nonstick cooking spray. Preheat over medium heat. Add mushrooms, onion, dried basil (if using), and garlic. Cook until onion is tender.

**2.** Stir in fresh basil (if using), chicken broth, wine, salt, and pepper. Arrange chicken in skillet. Bring to boiling; reduce heat. Cover and cook over low heat about 30 minutes or until chicken is tender and no longer pink. Transfer chicken and vegetables to a serving platter; keep warm.

**3.** Measure cooking liquid. If necessary, add water to measure 1 cup total liquid. Pour into skillet.

**4.** In a small bowl stir together cornstarch and water. Stir into cooking liquid in skillet. Cook and stir until thickened and bubbly. Cook and stir for 2 minutes more. Serve over chicken.

Nutrition Facts per serving: **184 calories, 6 g total fat, 74 mg cholesterol, 217 mg sodium, 4 g carbohydrate, 25 g protein.**

# Chicken with Artichokes

*Trim the prep time by taking advantage of convenience products. Check your supermarket for sliced fresh mushrooms, cut-up dried tomatoes, bottled minced garlic, and canned chicken broth.*

**Prep:** 30 minutes  **Cook:** 30 minutes  **Makes:** 4 servings

**1.** Sprinkle chicken pieces with salt and pepper. Using scissors, cut dried tomatoes into thin strips. Set aside.

**2.** In a large skillet cook mushrooms, leek or onion, garlic, and dried rosemary (if using) in hot oil until leek is tender. Remove with slotted spoon; set aside. Add chicken pieces to the skillet; cook over medium heat about 10 minutes or until browned, turning to brown evenly. Add dried tomatoes, leek mixture, broth, lemon peel, and lemon juice to the skillet. Bring to boiling; reduce heat. Cover and simmer for 20 minutes.

**3.** Meanwhile, thaw artichoke hearts under cold running water just enough to separate them. Drain. Halve or quarter any large artichokes. Add to skillet along with the snipped fresh rosemary (if using). Return to boiling; reduce heat. Cover and simmer for 10 to 15 minutes or until chicken is tender and no longer pink. If desired, serve chicken and vegetables with hot cooked pasta. If desired, garnish with lemon wedges and rosemary sprigs.

Nutrition Facts per serving: **286 calories, 13 g total fat, 70 mg cholesterol, 427 mg sodium, 18 g carbohydrate, 26 g protein.**

- 1½ pounds meaty chicken pieces (breasts, thighs, and drumsticks), skinned
- ¼ teaspoon salt
- ⅛ teaspoon pepper
- ½ cup dried tomatoes (not oil-pack)
- 2 cups sliced fresh mushrooms
- 1 large leek, thinly sliced, or ⅓ cup chopped onion
- 2 cloves garlic, minced
- ½ teaspoon dried rosemary, crushed, or 2 teaspoons snipped fresh rosemary
- 2 tablespoons olive oil
- ¾ cup chicken broth
- 1 teaspoon finely shredded lemon peel
- 3 tablespoons lemon juice
- 1 9-ounce package frozen artichoke hearts
  Hot cooked pasta (optional)
  Lemon wedges (optional)
  Fresh rosemary sprigs (optional)

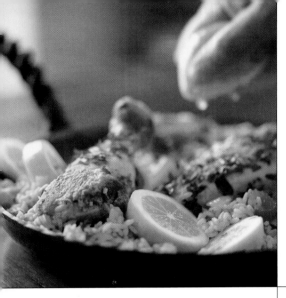

# Citrus Chicken

*Grating fresh ginger is easy. Just rub a piece of gingerroot over a grater until you get the desired amount. There's no need to peel the root before grating.*

**Prep:** 20 minutes  **Cook:** 50 minutes  **Makes:** 4 servings

¼ cup all-purpose flour
¾ teaspoon salt
¼ teaspoon pepper
2 to 2½ pounds meaty
    chicken pieces (breasts,
    thighs, and drumsticks),
    skinned
2 tablespoons cooking oil
1 cup chopped onion
½ cup chopped celery
2 cups water
1 cup long grain rice
1 tablespoon grated fresh
    ginger or 1 teaspoon
    ground ginger
½ teaspoon salt
¼ teaspoon ground allspice
¼ teaspoon ground turmeric
1 lemon, cut into thick slices
3 tablespoons snipped fresh
    flat-leaf parsley

*1.* In a shallow dish combine flour, the ¾ teaspoon salt, and the pepper. Coat chicken with flour mixture. Discard any remaining flour mixture.

*2.* In a 12-inch skillet cook chicken in hot oil over medium heat for 20 minutes, turning occasionally. Remove from skillet, reserving drippings. Set chicken aside. Add onion and celery to drippings in skillet. Cook and stir for 3 to 4 minutes or until vegetables are just tender.

*3.* Carefully stir the water, the uncooked rice, ginger, the ½ teaspoon salt, the allspice, and turmeric into vegetables in skillet. Bring to boiling; add chicken pieces. Reduce heat. Cover and simmer for 20 to 25 minutes or until rice is tender and chicken is tender and no longer pink. Top with lemon slices for the last 5 minutes of cooking.

*4.* To serve, sprinkle parsley over chicken mixture. For additional citrus flavor, squeeze warm lemon juice from the slices in pan over the chicken.

Nutrition Facts per serving: 470 calories, 15 g total fat, 92 mg cholesterol, 832 mg sodium, 48 g carbohydrate, 34 g protein.

# Italian Chicken With Artichokes

*Either frozen or canned artichoke hearts work well in this saucy dish. However, don't use marinated artichoke hearts—found in jars—they'll add a pickled flavor.*

**Prep:** 35 minutes   **Cook:** 40 minutes   **Makes:** 6 servings

**1.** In a 12-inch skillet cook onion, mushrooms, sweet pepper, carrot, and garlic in 1 tablespoon of the hot oil until tender. Remove vegetables from skillet; set aside.

**2.** In a plastic bag combine flour, salt, and black pepper. Add chicken pieces, a few at a time, shaking to coat. Cook chicken in remaining hot oil over medium heat about 10 minutes or until browned, turning to brown evenly (sprinkle any remaining flour mixture over chicken before browning). Drain off fat.

**3.** Return vegetables to skillet; add undrained tomatoes, artichoke hearts, tomato sauce, wine, and Italian seasoning. Bring to boiling; reduce heat. Cover and simmer for 35 to 40 minutes or until chicken is tender and no longer pink, stirring once or twice. Transfer chicken to serving platter; keep warm. Boil sauce gently, uncovered, about 5 minutes or until desired consistency. Serve chicken and sauce over hot cooked pasta or rice.

Nutrition Facts per serving: 508 calories, 14 g total fat, 61 mg cholesterol, 593 mg sodium, 62 g carbohydrate, 31 g protein.

1 large onion, chopped (1 cup)
1 cup sliced fresh mushrooms
¼ cup chopped green sweet pepper
¼ cup chopped carrot
1 clove garlic, minced
3 tablespoons olive oil or cooking oil
¼ cup all-purpose flour
½ teaspoon salt
¼ teaspoon ground black pepper
2 pounds meaty chicken pieces (breasts, thighs, and drumsticks), skinned
1 14½-ounce can stewed tomatoes
1 9-ounce package frozen artichoke hearts, cut up, or one 14-ounce can artichoke hearts, drained and quartered
1 8-ounce can tomato sauce
½ cup dry white wine
1 teaspoon dried Italian seasoning, crushed
Hot cooked fettuccine or rice

# Paella

*A little saffron, the costly spice harvested from purple crocus, flavors and colors this classic chicken and rice dish.*

**Prep:** 30 minutes   **Cook:** 35 minutes   **Makes:** 6 servings

---

8 ounces fresh or frozen
   medium shrimp
   Nonstick cooking spray
1 cup chopped onion
1 clove garlic, minced
1½ pounds meaty chicken
   pieces (breasts, thighs,
   and drumsticks)
1 14-ounce can reduced-
   sodium chicken broth
1 7½-ounce can tomatoes,
   cut up
1 teaspoon snipped fresh
   thyme or ¼ teaspoon
   dried thyme, crushed
¼ teaspoon ground saffron
⅛ to ¼ teaspoon ground
   red pepper
1 cup long grain rice
1 medium red or green sweet
   pepper, coarsely chopped
1 cup frozen peas

**1.** Thaw shrimp, if frozen. Peel and devein shrimp. Rinse shrimp; pat dry with paper towels. Cover and refrigerate shrimp until needed.

**2.** Coat an unheated Dutch oven with nonstick cooking spray. Preheat over medium heat. Add onion and garlic; cook until onion is tender.

**3.** Add chicken pieces, chicken broth, undrained tomatoes, thyme, saffron, and ground red pepper. Bring to boiling; reduce heat. Cover and simmer for 15 minutes.

**4.** Stir in uncooked rice. Cover and simmer about 15 minutes more or until rice is nearly tender. Stir in shrimp, sweet pepper, and peas. Cover and simmer about 5 minutes more or until the rice and chicken are tender and shrimp turn opaque.

Nutrition Facts per serving: **274 calories, 5 g total fat, 90 mg cholesterol, 363 mg sodium, 33 g carbohydrate, 24 g protein.**

# Braised Chicken With Mushrooms

*Like other braised dishes, this chicken cooks slowly in a small amount of liquid.*

**Prep:** 25 minutes **Cook:** 35 minutes **Makes:** 4 servings

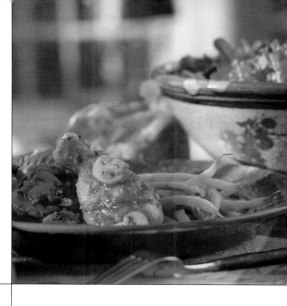

**1.** In a heavy, 12-inch skillet cook chicken in hot oil over medium-high heat about 15 minutes or until well browned, turning to brown evenly. Remove chicken from skillet. Drain off fat, reserving 1 tablespoon of the drippings in skillet.

**2.** In the same skillet cook mushrooms, onion, garlic, the dried basil, crushed red pepper, salt, and black pepper over medium heat until vegetables are tender. Stir in broth, red wine, and tomato paste. Return chicken to skillet. Bring to boiling; reduce heat. Cover and simmer for 30 to 40 minutes or until chicken is tender and no longer pink. Transfer the chicken to a platter, reserving sauce in skillet. Keep chicken warm.

**3.** In a small bowl combine cold water and flour. Stir into sauce. Cook and stir until thickened and bubbly. Cook and stir for 1 minute more. Stir in parsley; pour sauce over the chicken. If desired, garnish with basil sprigs.

Nutrition Facts per serving: **458 calories, 20 g total fat, 130 mg cholesterol, 498 mg sodium, 17 g carbohydrate, 47 g protein.**

2½ to 3 pounds meaty chicken
    pieces (breasts, thighs,
    and drumsticks)
2 tablespoons cooking oil
8 ounces mushrooms, sliced
    (3 cups)
1 large onion, chopped
2 cloves garlic, minced
2 teaspoons dried basil,
    crushed
1 teaspoon crushed red pepper
¼ teaspoon salt
¼ teaspoon ground black
    pepper
1 cup chicken broth
½ cup dry red wine
1 6-ounce can tomato paste
2 tablespoons cold water
1 tablespoon all-purpose flour
¼ cup snipped fresh parsley
    Fresh basil sprigs (optional)

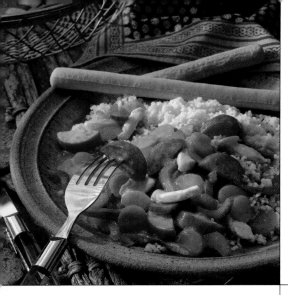

# Chicken and Sausage Couscous

*Round out the meal with crisp breadsticks and a refreshing dessert such as lemon or orange sherbet or slices of cold, crisp melon.*

**Start to Finish:** 40 minutes **Makes:** 4 servings

6 ounces cooked smoked sausage (such as Polish sausage or kielbasa), halved lengthwise and sliced into ½-inch-thick pieces

2 stalks celery, sliced

2 medium carrots, thinly sliced

1⅓ cups chicken broth

1 cup quick-cooking couscous

4 ounces skinless, boneless chicken breast, cut into bite-size strips

1 medium green sweet pepper, cut into strips

1 cup chicken broth

1 tablespoon cornstarch

**1.** In a 10-inch skillet cook and stir sausage, celery, and carrots over medium-high heat about 5 minutes or until sausage is browned. Reduce heat. Cover and cook for 3 to 5 minutes more or until carrots are nearly tender. Drain off fat.

**2.** Meanwhile, in a medium saucepan bring the 1⅓ cups broth to boiling. Stir in couscous. Cover and remove from heat. Let stand while preparing chicken and vegetable mixture.

**3.** Add chicken and sweet pepper to skillet; cook and stir over medium-high heat for 3 to 5 minutes or until chicken is no longer pink. Combine the 1 cup broth and the cornstarch; stir into mixture in skillet. Cook and stir over medium heat until thickened and bubbly; cook and stir for 2 minutes more. Fluff couscous with a fork. Serve sausage-chicken mixture over hot cooked couscous.

Nutrition Facts per serving: **400 calories, 15 g total fat, 44 mg cholesterol, 900 mg sodium, 44 g carbohydrate, 21 g protein.**

# Chicken and Vegetable Skillet

*Serve the savory chicken and vegetable medley with your choice of hot cooked orzo or rice.*

**Prep:** 35 minutes  **Cook:** 25 minutes  **Makes:** 4 to 6 servings

**1.** If desired, skin chicken. In a plastic bag combine flour, salt, paprika, and black pepper. Add chicken, a few pieces at a time, shaking to coat well.

**2.** In a 12-inch skillet cook the chicken pieces in hot oil over medium heat about 10 minutes or until lightly browned, turning to brown evenly. Remove the chicken. If necessary, add 1 tablespoon additional oil to skillet.

**3.** Add the chopped onion, garlic, and ginger to skillet. Cook for 4 to 5 minutes or until onion is tender. Carefully stir in chicken broth. Return chicken to skillet.

**4.** Bring to boiling; reduce heat. Cover and simmer about 15 minutes or until chicken is tender and no longer pink. Spoon off fat.

**5.** Add asparagus, squash, mushrooms, and sweet peppers. Stir together dry sherry, soy sauce, and cornstarch; stir into the chicken mixture.

**6.** Return to boiling; reduce heat. Cover and simmer for 5 to 10 minutes more or until vegetables are crisp-tender. Serve with cooked orzo or rice.

Nutrition Facts per serving: **621 calories, 31 g total fat, 134 mg cholesterol, 1,069 mg sodium, 33 g carbohydrate, 51 g protein.**

1  2½- to 3-pound broiler-fryer chicken, cut up
¼  cup all-purpose flour
½  teaspoon salt
½  teaspoon paprika
¼  teaspoon ground black pepper
2  tablespoons cooking oil
½  cup chopped onion
2  cloves garlic, minced
1  tablespoon grated fresh ginger
¾  cup chicken broth
1  pound fresh asparagus, cut into 1-inch pieces
3  yellow summer squash and/or zucchini, cut into 1-inch chunks
8  ounces fresh mushrooms, thickly sliced (3 cups)
2  red or green sweet peppers, cut into 1-inch strips
¼  cup dry sherry
2  tablespoons soy sauce
2  teaspoons cornstarch
   Hot cooked orzo or rice

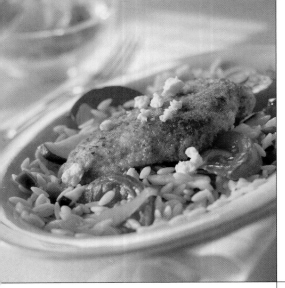

# Grecian-Style Chicken

*Olive oil, garlic, tomatoes, and feta cheese give this 30-minute main dish its Mediterranean flair.*

**Start to Finish:** 30 minutes  **Makes:** 4 servings

¼ cup toasted wheat germ or fine dry bread crumbs

4 medium skinless, boneless chicken breast halves (about 1 pound total)

2 tablespoons olive oil or cooking oil

1 small zucchini, halved lengthwise and sliced

½ of a medium green sweet pepper, chopped

½ of a medium onion, sliced and separated into rings

2 cloves garlic, minced

⅛ teaspoon salt
Dash ground black pepper

2 medium tomatoes, cut into wedges

2 tablespoons water

4 teaspoons lime juice or lemon juice
Hot cooked orzo, couscous, or rice

½ cup crumbled feta cheese (2 ounces)

**1.** Place wheat germ or bread crumbs in a shallow bowl; coat chicken with the wheat germ or bread crumbs. In a large skillet cook chicken in 1 tablespoon of the hot oil over medium heat for 10 to 12 minutes or until tender and no longer pink, turning once. Remove chicken from skillet; keep warm.

**2.** In the same skillet cook zucchini, sweet pepper, onion, garlic, salt, and black pepper in remaining hot oil for 3 minutes. Add tomato wedges, the water, and lime or lemon juice; cook for 1 minute more. Remove from heat.

**3.** To serve, spoon vegetable mixture over orzo; place chicken on top of vegetables. Sprinkle feta cheese over chicken.

Nutrition Facts per serving: 418 calories, 13 g total fat, 78 mg cholesterol, 299 mg sodium, 38 g carbohydrate, 36 g protein.

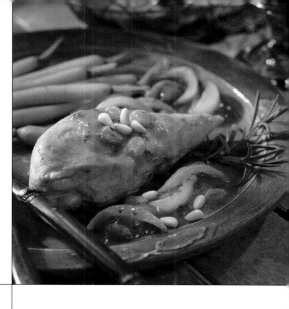

# Chicken with Golden Raisins and Pine Nuts

*To toast the pine nuts (also called pignoli), bake them in a 400° oven for 7 to 8 minutes or until lightly browned, stirring often.*

**Prep:** 30 minutes   **Cook:** 35 minutes   **Makes:** 4 servings

**1.** In a large nonstick skillet cook onion and garlic in hot oil over medium heat for 1 minute. Add chicken pieces; cook for 10 to 15 minutes or until lightly browned, turning to brown evenly. Drain well.

**2.** Add the vinegar, salt, and pepper to skillet. Bring to boiling. Cook, uncovered, over high heat about 5 minutes or until vinegar is nearly evaporated, turning chicken once. Carefully add broth, raisins, thyme, and rosemary to the skillet. Bring to boiling; reduce heat. Cover and simmer for 30 to 35 minutes or until chicken is tender and no longer pink. Transfer chicken to a serving platter. In a small bowl combine cold water and cornstarch. Add to skillet. Cook and stir until thickened and bubbly; cook and stir for 2 minutes more. Spoon some of the sauce over chicken; pass remaining sauce. Sprinkle chicken with pine nuts.

Nutrition Facts per serving: **269 calories, 10 g total fat, 71 mg cholesterol, 334 mg sodium, 22 g carbohydrate, 24 g protein.**

- 1 **medium onion, cut into thin slivers**
- 2 **cloves garlic, minced**
- 1 **tablespoon olive oil**
- 1½ **pounds meaty chicken pieces (breasts, thighs, and drumsticks), skinned**
- ½ **cup white wine vinegar**
- ¼ **teaspoon salt**
- ⅛ **teaspoon pepper**
- 1 **cup reduced-sodium chicken broth**
- ½ **cup golden raisins**
- 2 **teaspoons snipped fresh thyme or ½ teaspoon dried thyme, crushed**
- 1 **teaspoon snipped fresh rosemary or ¼ teaspoon dried rosemary, crushed**
- 1 **tablespoon cold water**
- 1½ **teaspoons cornstarch**
- 2 **tablespoons pine nuts, toasted**

# Marinated Chicken Breasts With Mozzarella

*Packaged marinated chicken breasts make this dish super easy.*

**Start to Finish:** 30 minutes  **Makes:** 4 servings

1 **6-ounce package long grain and wild rice pilaf mix**
¼ **cup thinly sliced green onions**
½ **cup water**
1 **cup broccoli flowerets**
4 **purchased marinated chicken breast halves\* (about 1 pound total)**
2 **teaspoons olive oil**
1 **medium tomato, halved and thinly sliced**
2 **slices part-skim mozzarella cheese, halved (3 ounces)**

*1.* Prepare rice pilaf mix according to package directions, adding green onions for the last 5 minutes of cooking. Meanwhile, in a medium saucepan bring the water to boiling and add broccoli flowerets. Cover and cook about 3 minutes or until crisp-tender; drain and set aside.

*2.* In a large, cast-iron skillet cook chicken breasts in hot oil over medium heat for 8 to 10 minutes or until no longer pink, turning once. Overlap the halved tomato slices on top of the chicken breasts. Spoon cooked broccoli on top of tomato slices; cover each with a half-slice of mozzarella.

*3.* Broil the chicken breasts 3 to 4 inches from the heat about 1 minute or until cheese is melted and bubbly. Serve atop hot rice pilaf.

Nutrition Facts per serving: **377 calories, 12 g total fat, 22 mg cholesterol, 1,532 mg sodium, 38 g carbohydrate, 31 g protein.**

*\*Note:* If you can't find marinated chicken breasts at your supermarket, substitute 4 medium skinless, boneless chicken breasts (about 1 pound total). Pour your favorite bottled clear Italian salad dressing over the chicken breasts and marinate in the refrigerator for at least 4 hours or up to 6 hours.

# Chicken a l'Orange

*Round out a meal featuring this citrusy chicken dish with steamed pea pods and quick-cooking brown rice.*

**Start to Finish:** 30 minutes  **Makes:** 4 servings

**1.** Sprinkle chicken with salt and black pepper. In a large skillet cook chicken in hot oil over medium heat for 8 to 10 minutes or until tender and no longer pink, turning once. Transfer to a platter; cover and keep warm.

**2.** Add ½ cup of the green onions to skillet; cook about 3 minutes or until tender. In a small bowl stir together broth and cornstarch. Add to skillet with orange sections, reserved juice, and liqueur. Cook and stir until thickened and bubbly; cook and stir for 1 minute more. Spoon over chicken. Sprinkle with remaining green onions. Sprinkle with ground red pepper.

Nutrition Facts per serving: **275 calories, 6 g total fat, 99 mg cholesterol, 481 mg sodium, 12 g carbohydrate, 40 g protein.**

- **4 medium skinless, boneless chicken breast halves (about 1 pound total)**
- **½ teaspoon salt**
- **¼ teaspoon ground black pepper**
- **1 tablespoon cooking oil**
- **¾ cup sliced green onions**
- **⅓ cup chicken broth**
- **1 teaspoon cornstarch**
- **2 navel oranges, peeled and sectioned (reserve juice)**
- **1 tablespoon orange-flavored liqueur**
- **Pinch ground red pepper**

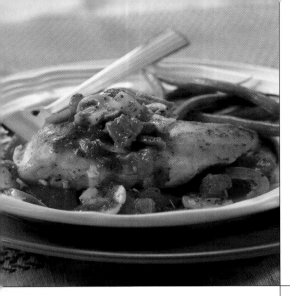

# Chicken Cacciatore

*The combination of tomatoes, mushrooms, onion, and herbs distinguishes this classic dish.*

**Prep:** 25 minutes  **Cook:** 20 minutes  **Makes:** 4 servings

Nonstick cooking spray
4 small skinless, boneless
   chicken breast halves
   (about 12 ounces total)
1 14½-ounce can stewed
   tomatoes
1 medium green sweet pepper,
   cut into thin strips
½ cup sliced fresh mushrooms
¼ cup chopped onion
¼ cup water or dry red wine
2 teaspoons dried Italian
   seasoning, crushed
⅛ teaspoon ground black
   pepper

**1.** Coat an unheated large skillet with nonstick cooking spray. Preheat over medium heat. Add chicken and cook about 6 minutes or until lightly browned, turning to brown evenly.

**2.** Stir in undrained tomatoes, sweet pepper, mushrooms, onion, water or wine, Italian seasoning, and black pepper. Bring to boiling; reduce heat. Cover and simmer about 15 minutes or until chicken is tender and no longer pink. Remove chicken from skillet; cover and keep warm. Simmer tomato mixture, uncovered, about 5 minutes or until desired consistency. Spoon over chicken.

Nutrition Facts per serving: **134 calories, 3 g total fat, 45 mg cholesterol, 309 mg sodium, 10 g carbohydrate, 18 g protein.**

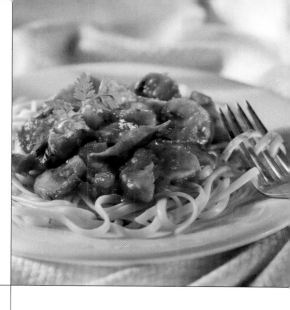

# Chicken Marinara With Mushrooms

*Here's a cooking hint worth remembering—stirring a little sugar into tomato-based sauces helps mellow the flavor.*

**Start to Finish:** 25 minutes   **Makes:** 6 servings

**1.** In a large skillet cook garlic in hot margarine for 30 seconds. Add half of the chicken and half of each of the herbs. Cook and stir for 3 to 4 minutes or until chicken is no longer pink. Remove chicken, reserving drippings in skillet. Repeat with the remaining chicken and herbs.

**2.** Add mushrooms to drippings in skillet. Cook and stir about 3 minutes or until tender. Add spaghetti sauce, wine, and, if desired, sugar. Return chicken to skillet; heat through. Serve over hot cooked pasta. If desired, garnish with parsley sprigs.

Nutrition Facts per serving: 426 calories, 7 g total fat, 40 mg cholesterol, 128 mg sodium, 64 g carbohydrate, 25 g protein.

- 4 **cloves garlic, minced**
- 2 **tablespoons lower-fat margarine**
- 1 **pound skinless, boneless chicken breasts, cut into thin, bite-size strips**
- ½ **teaspoon dried chervil, crushed**
- ½ **teaspoon dried basil, crushed**
- ¼ **teaspoon dried thyme, crushed**
- 6 **ounces assorted fresh mushrooms (such as shiitake, crimini, porcini, and button), sliced**
- 1 **27½-ounce jar light spaghetti sauce**
- ½ **cup dry white wine**
- 2 **teaspoons sugar (optional) Hot cooked pasta Fresh parsley sprigs (optional)**

# Fiesta Chicken

*Orange juice gives this Mexican-style chicken dish a delightful boost of citrus flavor.*

**Start to Finish:** 40 minutes   **Makes:** 4 servings

1 8-ounce can tomato sauce
½ cup orange juice
½ cup finely chopped onion
2 tablespoons raisins
2 tablespoons chopped
   pimiento
1½ teaspoons snipped fresh
   oregano or ½ teaspoon
   dried oregano, crushed
½ teaspoon chili powder
1 clove garlic, minced
   Several dashes bottled
   hot pepper sauce
12 ounces skinless, boneless
   chicken breasts, cut into
   2-inch pieces
1 tablespoon cold water
2 teaspoons cornstarch
2 cups hot cooked rice
¼ cup snipped fresh parsley

*1.* In a large skillet combine tomato sauce, orange juice, onion, raisins, pimiento, oregano, chili powder, garlic, and hot pepper sauce. Bring to boiling; reduce heat. Cover and simmer for 5 minutes.

*2.* Stir chicken pieces into skillet. Return to boiling; reduce heat. Cover and simmer for 12 to 15 minutes more or until chicken is tender and no longer pink.

*3.* In a small bowl combine cold water and cornstarch. Stir into mixture in skillet. Cook and stir until thickened and bubbly. Cook and stir for 2 minutes more.

*4.* Toss rice with parsley. Serve chicken mixture over hot rice mixture.

Nutrition Facts per serving: **255 calories, 3 g total fat, 45 mg cholesterol, 392 mg sodium, 37 g carbohydrate, 20 g protein.**

# French Farmhouse Garlic Chicken

*That's right—this recipe uses 40 cloves of garlic. As it cooks, the garlic mellows to give the chicken a robust but pleasing flavor.*

**Start to Finish:** 25 minutes  **Makes:** 4 servings

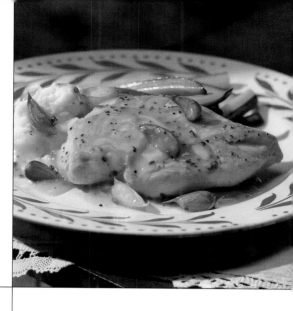

**1.** Season chicken with salt and pepper. In a 10-inch skillet cook chicken and garlic cloves in hot oil over medium-high heat for 4 to 6 minutes or just until browned, turning once. Slowly add the ½ cup wine or broth, the ½ cup broth, the lemon juice, basil, and oregano. Bring to boiling; reduce heat. Cover and simmer for 6 to 8 minutes or until chicken is tender and no longer pink.

**2.** Using a slotted spoon, transfer chicken and garlic to a warm serving platter; keep warm.

**3.** In a small bowl stir together the 2 tablespoons wine or broth and the flour. Stir into pan juices. Bring to boiling. Cook and stir for 1 minute more. Spoon over chicken. If desired, serve with mashed potatoes or rice.

**Nutrition Facts per serving:** 327 calories, 7 g total fat, 48 mg cholesterol, 755 mg sodium, 40 g carbohydrate, 22 g protein.

***Note:*** As you eat the cooked cloves, simply slip the skins off with the tip of your dinner knife. Or if you prefer, peel the garlic cloves before cooking (use the flat side of a large knife to mash them slightly, then peel off the skins).

- 4 small skinless, boneless chicken breast halves (about 12 ounces total)
- ¼ teaspoon salt
- ¼ teaspoon pepper
- 40 small cloves unpeeled garlic*
- 1 tablespoon cooking oil
- ½ cup dry white wine or chicken broth
- ½ cup chicken broth
- 1 tablespoon lemon juice
- 1 teaspoon dried basil, crushed
- ½ teaspoon dried oregano, crushed
- 2 tablespoons dry white wine or chicken broth
- 4 teaspoons all-purpose flour
  Hot mashed potatoes or cooked rice (optional)

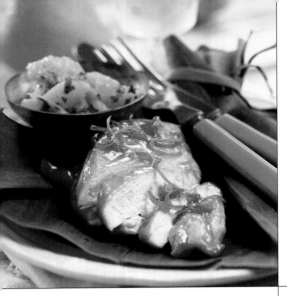

# Fusion Chicken

*This combination of flavors is a little bit Asian and a little bit South American. That's why it's labeled "fusion."*

**Start to Finish:** 40 minutes **Makes:** 4 servings

¼ cup water

3 tablespoons hoisin sauce

2 tablespoons peach
  preserves

1 tablespoon sugar

2 teaspoons soy sauce

4 medium tangerines or
  2 large oranges

3 tablespoons snipped
  fresh cilantro

4 medium skinless, boneless
  chicken breast halves
  (about 1 pound total)

1 tablespoon cooking oil
  Shredded tangerine or
  orange peel (optional)

*1.* In a small bowl combine the water, hoisin sauce, peach preserves, sugar, and soy sauce. Finely shred 1 teaspoon peel from 1 of the tangerines or oranges. Stir finely shredded peel into hoisin mixture; set aside. Peel and coarsely chop tangerines or oranges; remove seeds. In a medium bowl gently toss chopped tangerines or oranges and cilantro; set aside.

*2.* In a large skillet cook chicken in hot oil over medium heat for 3 to 5 minutes or until chicken is browned, turning once. Drain off fat. Carefully pour hoisin mixture over chicken. Bring to boiling; reduce heat. Cover and simmer for 8 to 10 minutes or until chicken is tender and no longer pink.

*3.* Remove chicken from skillet. Boil sauce gently, uncovered, about 5 minutes or until reduced to ⅓ cup. Return chicken to skillet. Heat through, turning once to coat with glaze. To serve, spoon glaze over chicken. If desired, sprinkle with additional shredded tangerine or orange peel. Serve tangerine mixture alongside the chicken.

Nutrition Facts per serving: **270 calories, 8 g total fat, 59 mg cholesterol, 446 mg sodium, 27 g carbohydrate, 23 g protein.**

# North American Chicken Couscous

*Partially freezing the chicken before cutting into pieces makes it easier to get consistent sizes.*

**Start to Finish:** 20 minutes  **Makes:** 4 servings

**1.** In a large saucepan cook onions and garlic in hot oil about 3 minutes or until crisp-tender. Add chicken pieces and carrots. Cook over medium heat for 5 minutes, stirring frequently. Stir in ½ cup of the chicken broth, the zucchini, raisins, curry powder, ½ teaspoon of the cinnamon, and the salt. Cover and cook for 3 to 4 minutes or until chicken is no longer pink and vegetables are crisp-tender.

**2.** Meanwhile, in a medium saucepan combine the remaining chicken broth and the remaining cinnamon; bring to boiling. Stir in couscous; cover. Remove from heat; let stand for 5 minutes. Fluff couscous lightly with a fork. Serve couscous with chicken and vegetable mixture. If desired, garnish with toasted almonds.

Nutrition Facts per serving: **500 calories, 8 g total fat, 60 mg cholesterol, 833 mg sodium, 72 g carbohydrate, 34 g protein.**

- **2** medium onions, cut into thin wedges
- **1** teaspoon bottled minced garlic or 2 cloves garlic, minced
- **1** tablespoon olive oil
- **1** pound skinless, boneless chicken breasts, cut into bite-size pieces
- **16** packaged peeled baby carrots (about ¾ cup)
- **2½** cups chicken broth
- **2** medium zucchini, quartered and cut into 2-inch pieces
- **½** cup raisins
- **2 to 3** teaspoons curry powder
- **1** teaspoon ground cinnamon
- **½** teaspoon salt
- **1⅓** cups quick-cooking couscous
- **¼** cup slivered almonds, toasted (optional)

# Southwest Chicken Skillet

*Use your favorite salsa as the basis for this saucy chicken dish.*

**Start to Finish:** 20 minutes  **Makes:** 4 servings

12 ounces skinless, boneless chicken breasts, cut into 1-inch pieces
1 tablespoon cooking oil
1 15-ounce jar salsa
¾ cup chicken broth
½ cup chopped green sweet pepper
¼ cup sliced pitted ripe olives (optional)
1 cup quick-cooking rice
½ cup shredded cheddar cheese or Monterey Jack cheese (2 ounces)
  Green sweet pepper strips (optional)

**1.** In a large skillet cook and stir chicken pieces in hot oil over medium heat for 2 to 3 minutes or until no longer pink.

**2.** Stir in salsa, chicken broth, chopped sweet pepper, and olives (if desired). Bring to boiling. Stir in uncooked rice. Remove from heat. Sprinkle with cheese. Cover and let stand about 5 minutes or until rice is tender. If desired, garnish with sweet pepper strips.

Nutrition Facts per serving: 344 calories, 15 g total fat, 60 mg cholesterol, 1,012 mg sodium, 34 g carbohydrate, 25 g protein.

# Stuffed Chicken Spirals

*If you don't have a meat mallet, use the bottom of a heavy saucepan or skillet to pound the chicken breasts.*

**Prep:** 35 minutes  **Cook:** 30 minutes  **Makes:** 4 servings

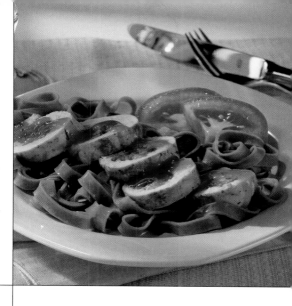

**1.** In a covered small saucepan cook mushrooms, carrot, green onion, and celery in a small amount of boiling water about 5 minutes or until tender. Drain. Stir in tomato, 1½ teaspoons of the lemon juice, half of the thyme, and the ⅛ teaspoon pepper.

**2.** Place each chicken breast half, boned side up, between 2 pieces of plastic wrap. Pound each lightly with the flat side of a meat mallet to ⅛-inch thickness. Remove plastic wrap. Spoon one-fourth of the carrot mixture onto each chicken piece. Fold in sides; roll up. Secure with wooden toothpicks. Sprinkle with salt and the few dashes pepper.

**3.** Coat an unheated skillet with nonstick cooking spray. Preheat over medium heat. Add chicken; cook for 8 to 10 minutes or until browned, turning to brown evenly. Add remaining lemon juice, remaining thyme, the ½ cup water, and the bouillon granules. Bring to boiling; reduce heat. Cover and simmer about 15 minutes or until chicken is no longer pink. Remove from skillet; keep warm.

**4.** For sauce, if desired, strain cooking liquid; return to skillet. In a small bowl combine milk and cornstarch. Add to skillet. Cook and stir until bubbly. Cook and stir for 2 minutes more. Remove toothpicks from chicken. Serve chicken with sauce. If desired, serve over spinach fettuccine.

Nutrition Facts per serving: **154 calories, 4 g total fat, 60 mg cholesterol, 354 mg sodium, 7 g carbohydrate, 23 g protein.**

1½ cups sliced fresh mushrooms
2 tablespoons shredded carrot
2 tablespoons sliced green onion
2 tablespoons finely chopped celery
1 medium tomato, peeled, seeded, and chopped
2½ teaspoons lemon juice
½ teaspoon dried thyme, crushed
⅛ teaspoon pepper
4 medium skinless, boneless chicken breast halves (about 1 pound total)
⅛ teaspoon salt
Few dashes pepper
Nonstick cooking spray
½ cup water
1 teaspoon instant chicken bouillon granules
¼ cup fat-free milk
1 tablespoon cornstarch
Hot cooked spinach fettuccine (optional)

# Thyme Chicken Marsala

*Next time you want a special dinner for two, plan the menu around this luscious entrée.*

**Start to Finish:** 30 minutes  **Makes:** 2 servings

2 medium skinless, boneless
    chicken breast halves
    (about 8 ounces total)
1 tablespoon all-purpose flour
1 medium carrot, cut into thin,
    bite-size strips
2 tablespoons olive oil
1 small red or yellow sweet
    pepper, cut into thin,
    bite-size strips
1 teaspoon bottled minced
    garlic or 2 cloves garlic,
    minced
¼ teaspoon salt
¼ teaspoon ground black
    pepper
⅓ cup dry Marsala
1 tablespoon snipped fresh
    thyme or ¼ teaspoon dried
    thyme, crushed
    Hot cooked linguine or
    other pasta (optional)

**1.** Place each chicken breast half, boned side up, between 2 pieces of plastic wrap. Pound lightly with the flat side of a meat mallet to ¼-inch thickness. Remove plastic wrap. Coat chicken breasts lightly with flour; shake off excess. Set aside.

**2.** In a large skillet cook carrot strips in 1 tablespoon of the hot oil for 3 minutes. Add the pepper strips, garlic, salt, and black pepper. Cook and stir about 5 minutes or until crisp-tender. Arrange on 2 dinner plates. Cover and keep warm.

**3.** In the same skillet cook chicken in remaining hot oil over medium heat for 4 to 6 minutes or until no longer pink, turning once. Place chicken on top of vegetables.

**4.** Add the Marsala and thyme to the skillet. Cook and stir for 1 minute, scraping up any browned bits from skillet. Pour mixture over chicken. If desired, serve with linguine or other hot cooked pasta.

Nutrition Facts per serving: **311 calories, 17 g total fat, 59 mg cholesterol, 350 mg sodium, 10 g carbohydrate, 23 g protein.**

# Rosemary Chicken With Pasta

*Put your crockery cooker to good use by cooking up this well-seasoned dish.*

**Prep:** 15 minutes  **Cook:** 3½ or 7 hours  **Makes:** 4 servings

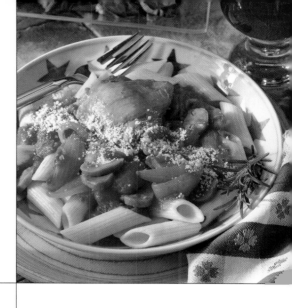

**1.** In a 3½- or 4½-quart electric crockery cooker place the onions and garlic. Add chicken to cooker.

**2.** In a medium bowl combine undrained tomatoes, tomato paste, vinegar, bay leaves, sugar, dried rosemary, salt, and pepper. Pour over chicken.

**3.** Cover and cook on low-heat setting for 7 hours or on high-heat setting for 3½ hours.

**4.** When ready to serve, discard bay leaves. Stir mushrooms into chicken mixture; cook for 5 to 10 minutes more or until heated through. Serve the chicken and sauce over the hot cooked pasta; sprinkle with Parmesan cheese. If desired, garnish with fresh oregano.

Nutrition Facts per serving: 415 calories, 5 g total fat, 47 mg cholesterol, 568 mg sodium, 65 g carbohydrate, 29 g protein.

- 2 medium onions, cut into thin wedges
- 2 teaspoons bottled minced garlic or 4 cloves garlic, minced
- 12 ounces skinless, boneless chicken breasts or thighs
- 1 16-ounce can diced tomatoes
- 1 6-ounce can tomato paste
- 2 tablespoons wine vinegar
- 2 bay leaves
- 1 teaspoon sugar
- ½ teaspoon dried rosemary, crushed
- ¼ teaspoon salt
- ¼ teaspoon pepper
- 1 4-ounce can sliced mushrooms, drained
  Hot cooked pasta
  Grated Parmesan cheese
  Fresh oregano sprigs (optional)

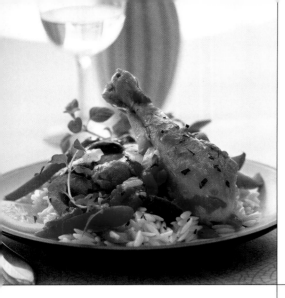

# Oregano Chicken and Vegetables

*For added color, use a combination of green and red sweet peppers.*

**Prep:** 35 minutes   **Cook:** 20 minutes   **Makes:** 4 servings

1½ to 2 pounds meaty chicken
   pieces (breasts, thighs, and
   drumsticks), skinned
¼ teaspoon salt
⅛ teaspoon ground black
   pepper
   Nonstick cooking spray
1 clove garlic, minced
1 lemon, thinly sliced
1 large tomato, peeled and
   chopped (¾ cup)
½ cup pitted ripe olives, halved
¼ cup chopped onion
¼ cup snipped fresh parsley
1 tablespoon snipped fresh
   oregano or 1 teaspoon
   dried oregano, crushed
⅛ teaspoon ground red pepper
¾ cup chicken broth
¼ cup dry white wine or
   chicken broth
2 medium green and/or
   red sweet peppers, cut
   into strips
   Fresh herb sprigs (optional)

**1.** Sprinkle chicken with salt and pepper. Lightly coat an unheated nonstick skillet with nonstick cooking spray. Preheat over medium heat. Add chicken and cook about 15 minutes or until lightly browned, turning once. Reduce heat.

**2.** Place the garlic, half of the lemon slices, half of the chopped tomato, the olives, onion, snipped parsley, and snipped or dried oregano over chicken pieces in skillet. Sprinkle with ground red pepper. Add the ¾ cup broth and the ¼ cup wine or broth. Bring to boiling; reduce heat. Cover and simmer for 15 minutes.

**3.** Add the remaining tomato and the sweet peppers. Cook, covered, for 5 to 10 minutes more or until sweet peppers are crisp-tender and chicken is tender and no longer pink. Transfer the chicken and vegetables to a platter. Top with remaining lemon slices. If desired, garnish with fresh herb.

Nutrition Facts per serving: **208 calories, 9 g total fat, 69 mg cholesterol, 425 mg sodium, 7 g carbohydrate, 24 g protein.**

# Quick Chicken Fajitas

*Serve an assortment of bottled salsa and other toppings so fajita lovers can take their choice.*

**Start to Finish:** 25 minutes **Makes:** 4 servings

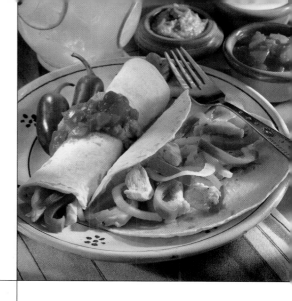

**1.** Wrap tortillas in foil. Heat in a 350° oven for 10 to 15 minutes or until heated through. [Or wrap tortillas in waxed paper and heat in a microwave oven on 100% power (high) for 15 to 20 seconds.]

**2.** Meanwhile, in a medium bowl combine lime or lemon juice, cumin, coriander, and oregano. Stir in chicken or turkey; set chicken mixture aside.

**3.** In a large skillet heat the salad dressing over medium-high heat. Add chicken mixture. Cook and stir about 2 minutes or until chicken is no longer pink. With a slotted spoon, remove the chicken from skillet.

**4.** Add sweet pepper and sliced onion to skillet; cook and stir for 2 to 3 minutes or until vegetables are crisp-tender. Return the chicken to skillet; heat through.

**5.** Spoon the chicken mixture onto warm tortillas; roll up. Serve with assorted toppings. If desired, garnish with whole jalapeño peppers.

Nutrition Facts per serving: 425 calories, 17 g total fat, 51 mg cholesterol, 600 mg sodium, 45 g carbohydrate, 23 g protein.

***Note:*** Because chile peppers, such as jalapeños, contain volatile oils that can burn your skin and eyes, avoid direct contact with them as much as possible. When working with chile peppers, wear plastic or rubber gloves. If your bare hands do touch the chile peppers, wash your hands well with soap and warm water.

**8 7-inch flour tortillas**

**1 tablespoon lime juice or lemon juice**

**½ teaspoon ground cumin**

**½ teaspoon ground coriander**

**¼ teaspoon dried oregano, crushed**

**12 ounces skinless, boneless chicken breasts or turkey breast tenderloin, cut into bite-size strips**

**¼ cup bottled clear Italian salad dressing (do not use reduced-fat dressing)**

**¾ cup red and/or green sweet pepper strips**

**1 small onion, halved lengthwise and sliced Assorted toppings (such as bottled salsa, guacamole, dairy sour cream, and chopped fresh jalapeño peppers\*)**
**Fresh whole jalapeño peppers (optional)**

# Skillet Chicken Paella

*This adaptation of paella, a classic Spanish rice dish, features chicken breasts.*

**Prep:** 20 minutes  **Cook:** 25 minutes  **Makes:** 6 servings

1¼ pounds skinless, boneless chicken breasts, cut into bite-size strips
1 tablespoon olive oil or cooking oil
1 medium onion, chopped
2 cloves garlic, minced
2¼ cups reduced-sodium chicken broth
1 cup long grain rice
1 teaspoon dried oregano, crushed
½ teaspoon paprika
¼ teaspoon salt
¼ teaspoon ground black pepper
⅛ teaspoon ground saffron or ground turmeric
1 14½-ounce can low-sodium stewed tomatoes
1 medium red sweet pepper, cut into strips
¾ cup frozen peas

**1.** In a 10-inch skillet cook chicken strips, half at a time, in hot oil for 2 to 3 minutes or until no longer pink. Remove chicken from skillet. Set aside.

**2.** Add onion and garlic to skillet; cook until tender. Add broth, uncooked rice, oregano, paprika, salt, black pepper, and saffron or turmeric to skillet. Bring to boiling; reduce heat. Cover and simmer for 15 minutes.

**3.** Add the undrained tomatoes, sweet pepper, and frozen peas to skillet. Cover and simmer about 5 minutes more or until rice is tender. Stir in cooked chicken. Cook and stir about 1 minute more or until heated through.

Nutrition Facts per serving: **285 calories, 6 g total fat, 50 mg cholesterol, 415 mg sodium, 35 g carbohydrate, 23 g protein.**

# Chicken in Peanut Sauce

*Slightly nutty, slightly sweet, and slightly hot—that's what you get in this saucy main dish that combines chicken breasts with peanut butter, coconut milk, curry powder, jalapeño pepper, and cilantro.*

**Prep:** 20 minutes  **Cook:** 12 minutes  **Makes:** 6 servings

**1.** In a large skillet heat oil over medium-high heat. Meanwhile, in a medium bowl toss chicken with curry powder and jalapeño pepper. Add to skillet; cook and stir for 2 minutes. Carefully add green beans and the water. Bring to boiling; reduce heat. Cover and simmer for 5 minutes.

**2.** In a medium bowl stir together coconut milk, peanut butter, and soy sauce. Add to the skillet. Return to boiling; reduce heat. Simmer, uncovered, about 5 minutes more or until chicken is no longer pink and green beans are tender, stirring occasionally. Stir in cilantro. Serve chicken mixture over noodles or rice.

Nutrition Facts per serving: 448 calories, 22 g total fat, 44 mg cholesterol, 524 mg sodium, 39 g carbohydrate, 27 g protein.

***Note:*** Adding nutty sweetness to Thai-inspired dishes such as the one above is as easy as opening a can of coconut milk. However, be sure to choose the right product. Canned coconut milk is made from equal parts of water and coconut and has been strained. You can usually find it in the international sections of supermarkets. Coconut milk is not the milky liquid you find when you open a fresh coconut, nor should it be confused with cream of coconut, a sweetened coconut concoction that's often used for desserts and mixing drinks such as piña coladas.

**1 tablespoon cooking oil**
**1 pound skinless, boneless chicken breasts, cut into bite-size strips**
**2 teaspoons curry powder**
**1 fresh jalapeño pepper, seeded and finely chopped (see note on page 39)**
**1 pound fresh green beans, trimmed and cut into 2-inch pieces, or 3 cups frozen cut green beans**
**¾ cup water**
**1 cup bottled light unsweetened coconut milk***
**¾ cup chunky peanut butter**
**2 tablespoons soy sauce**
**¼ cup snipped fresh cilantro**
**Hot cooked cellophane noodles or rice**

# Chicken and Dumplings

*Skinning the chicken thighs before cooking lowers the fat in this all-time favorite stew.*

**Prep:** 30 minutes  **Cook:** 50 minutes  **Makes:** 4 servings

4 **chicken thighs (about 1½ pounds total), skinned**
2½ **cups water**
1 **cup sliced carrot**
1 **cup sliced celery**
½ **cup chopped onion**
2 **teaspoons instant chicken bouillon granules**
¾ **teaspoon snipped fresh sage or ¼ teaspoon dried sage, crushed**
2 **tablespoons cold water**
4 **teaspoons cornstarch**
1 **recipe Dumplings**

*1.* In a large saucepan combine chicken, the 2½ cups water, the carrot, celery, onion, bouillon granules, and sage. Bring to boiling; reduce heat. Cover and simmer for 35 minutes.

*2.* Remove chicken pieces from saucepan; set aside. Skim fat from broth.

*3.* In a small bowl combine the 2 tablespoons cold water and the cornstarch. Stir into broth in saucepan. Cook and stir until thickened and bubbly. Return chicken to the saucepan.

*4.* Meanwhile, prepare Dumplings. Drop dough from a tablespoon, making 8 mounds on top of the hot chicken mixture. Cover saucepan tightly; simmer about 10 minutes or until a wooden toothpick inserted into centers of dumplings comes out clean.

*Dumplings:* In a medium bowl stir together 1 cup all-purpose flour, 1 tablespoon snipped fresh parsley, 2 teaspoons baking powder, and ⅛ teaspoon salt. In a small bowl combine 1 beaten egg, ¼ cup fat-free milk, and 2 tablespoons cooking oil; stir into flour mixture with a fork just until combined.

Nutrition Facts per serving: 341 calories, 14 g total fat, 103 mg cholesterol, 808 mg sodium, 33 g carbohydrate, 20 g protein.

# Caraway Chicken And Noodles

*Release the flavor of the caraway seeds by crushing them slightly using a mortar and pestle.*

**Prep:** 25 minutes   **Cook:** 35 minutes   **Makes:** 4 servings

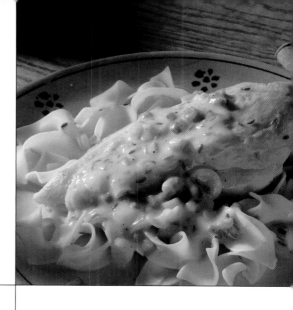

**1.** Coat an unheated large skillet with nonstick cooking spray. Preheat over medium heat. Add chicken and cook for 10 minutes, turning to brown evenly.

**2.** Carefully add the water, caraway seeds, bouillon granules, and pepper. Bring to boiling; reduce heat. Cover and simmer for 30 to 35 minutes or until chicken is tender and no longer pink. Remove chicken; cover and keep warm.

**3.** For sauce, in a small bowl combine milk and cornstarch. Stir into skillet along with the green onions. Cook and stir for 2 minutes more. Serve sauce with chicken over noodles.

Nutrition Facts per serving: **271 calories, 7 g total fat, 95 mg cholesterol, 303 mg sodium, 23 g carbohydrate, 27 g protein.**

Nonstick cooking spray
1½ pounds meaty chicken pieces (breasts, thighs, and drumsticks), skinned
¾ cup water
1 teaspoon caraway seeds, slightly crushed
1 teaspoon instant chicken bouillon granules
⅛ teaspoon pepper
⅔ cup fat-free milk
1 tablespoon cornstarch
½ cup sliced green onions
Hot cooked noodles

# Crunchy Crimson Chicken

*For a dramatic presentation, carefully spoon the bright red Raspberry Sauce over each serving.*

**Prep:** 20 minutes   **Bake:** 2 minutes   **Cook:** 20 minutes   **Makes:** 4 servings

1 recipe Raspberry Sauce
4 medium skinless, boneless
  chicken breast halves
  (about 1 pound total)
1 egg
2 tablespoons milk
1 6-ounce can smoked
  almonds, coarsely ground
2 tablespoons olive oil
3 ounces Brie cheese, cut into
  slices (rind removed,
  if desired)
  Shredded orange peel
  (optional)

*1.* Prepare Raspberry Sauce; cover and keep warm. Place each chicken breast half, boned side up, between 2 pieces of plastic wrap. Pound lightly with the flat side of a meat mallet into a rectangle about ⅛ inch thick. Remove plastic wrap.

*2.* In a medium bowl beat together egg and milk. Place almonds in a shallow dish. Dip chicken into the egg mixture, then coat both sides with almonds, pressing the nuts gently into chicken.

*3.* In a large skillet cook 2 pieces of the chicken in hot oil over medium heat for 10 to 12 minutes or until almond coating is golden brown and chicken is no longer pink; turn chicken once halfway through cooking time. Place chicken on a baking sheet; keep warm in a 350° oven. Repeat with remaining chicken. Place all chicken on the baking sheet. Top with Brie slices.

*4.* Bake in the 350° oven for 2 to 3 minutes or until cheese is softened. Place chicken, cheese sides up, on 4 dinner plates. Top with Raspberry Sauce. If desired, garnish with orange peel.

*Raspberry Sauce:* In a medium saucepan combine 1½ cups loose-pack frozen red raspberries, ½ cup water, and ⅓ cup honey; bring to boiling. Cook over medium heat for 3 to 4 minutes or until raspberries begin to break up. In a small bowl combine 2 tablespoons cold water and 1 tablespoon cornstarch; stir into raspberry mixture. Cook and stir until thickened and bubbly. Cook and stir for 2 minutes more. Remove from heat. Season to taste with salt and pepper.

Nutrition Facts per serving: 647 calories, 38 g total fat, 140 mg cholesterol, 255 mg sodium, 40 g carbohydrate, 36 g protein.

# Down-Home Chicken 'n' Greens

*For the greens in this flavorful dish, choose mustard, beet, kale, kohlrabi, collard, or turnip greens—or use 1 pound of mixed greens.*

**Start to Finish:** 40 minutes  **Makes:** 4 servings

**1.** Sprinkle chicken breasts with ¼ teaspoon black pepper and the salt. Coat an unheated large skillet with nonstick cooking spray. Preheat over medium heat. Add chicken to hot skillet and brown quickly on both sides. Reduce heat slightly. Cover and cook for 10 to 12 minutes or until chicken is tender and no longer pink.

**2.** Meanwhile, in a Dutch oven combine broth, garlic, crushed red pepper, and ¼ teaspoon black pepper. Bring to boiling. Add greens; reduce heat. Cover and cook for 9 to 12 minutes or just until greens are tender, stirring once or twice.

**3.** Remove chicken from skillet and slice. Spoon greens and their juices onto 4 dinner plates. Place chicken breast slices on top of greens. If desired, drizzle lightly with balsamic vinegar and garnish with red sweet pepper slices.

Nutrition Facts per serving: **124 calories, 3 g total fat, 45 mg cholesterol, 238 mg sodium, 5 g carbohydrate, 20 g protein.**

- **4 small skinless, boneless chicken breast halves (about 12 ounces total)**
- **¼ teaspoon coarsely ground black pepper**
- **⅛ teaspoon salt**
  **Nonstick cooking spray**
- **⅔ cup reduced-sodium chicken broth**
- **6 to 8 cloves garlic, minced**
- **¼ teaspoon crushed red pepper**
- **¼ teaspoon coarsely ground black pepper**
- **1 pound fresh greens (such as mustard, beet, kohlrabi, kale, collard, and/or turnip greens), torn (about 8 cups)**
  **Balsamic vinegar (optional)**
  **Red sweet pepper slices (optional)**

# Chicken with Apricots And Prunes

*Dress up the hot cooked rice accompaniment by stirring in some toasted slivered almonds and snipped fresh parsley.*

**Prep:** 25 minutes  **Cook:** 40 minutes  **Makes:** 6 servings

2 to 2½ pounds meaty chicken pieces (breasts, thighs, and drumsticks)
½ teaspoon salt
½ teaspoon garlic powder
¼ teaspoon pepper
2 tablespoons cooking oil
1 6-ounce package dried apricots
1 cup pitted dried plums (prunes), cut into halves
1 cup chicken broth
¾ cup dry white wine
¼ cup white wine vinegar
1 tablespoon brown sugar
3 inches stick cinnamon
4 whole cloves
3 tablespoons Dijon-style mustard
3 tablespoons cold water
4 teaspoons all-purpose flour
Hot cooked rice
Thinly sliced green onion (optional)

**1.** If desired, skin chicken. Sprinkle chicken with salt, garlic powder, and pepper.

**2.** In a 4½-quart Dutch oven cook chicken in hot oil over medium heat about 15 minutes or until lightly browned, turning to brown evenly. Drain off fat.

**3.** Add apricots, dried plums, chicken broth, white wine, wine vinegar, brown sugar, stick cinnamon, and whole cloves. Bring to boiling; reduce heat. Cover and simmer for 35 to 40 minutes or until chicken is tender and no longer pink.

**4.** Using a slotted spoon, transfer the chicken and fruit to a serving platter; keep warm. Discard cinnamon and cloves.

**5.** For sauce, in a small bowl stir together the mustard, cold water, and flour. Stir into the broth mixture. Cook and stir until thickened and bubbly. Cook and stir for 1 minute more.

**6.** Serve chicken and fruit over cooked rice. Top with some of the sauce. If desired, garnish with sliced green onion. Pass remaining sauce.

Nutrition Facts per serving: **570 calories, 13 g total fat, 69 mg cholesterol, 580 mg sodium, 82 g carbohydrate, 29 g protein.**

# Chicken with Garlic

*A slightly sweet garlic-sherry sauce complements the chicken in this elegant yet easy dish.*

**Start to Finish:** 25 minutes  **Makes:** 3 servings

**1.** In plastic bag combine flour, salt, and pepper. Add chicken; shake to coat. Shake excess flour off chicken.

**2.** In a large skillet cook chicken in hot oil until browned, turning to brown evenly. Stir in garlic and parsley. Cook and stir until garlic is tender.

**3.** Carefully add the sherry. Reduce heat to medium-low. Cover and simmer about 15 minutes or until chicken is tender and no longer pink. If desired, serve with rice. If desired, garnish with rosemary sprigs and sprinkle with paprika.

Nutrition Facts per serving: 337 calories, 14 g total fat, 89 mg cholesterol, 439 mg sodium, 8 g carbohydrate, 45 g protein.

- 2 tablespoons all-purpose flour
- ½ teaspoon salt
- ¼ teaspoon pepper
- 3 6-ounce skinless, boneless chicken breast halves
- 2 tablespoons olive oil
- 3 cloves garlic, finely chopped
- 2 tablespoons snipped fresh parsley
- ½ cup dry sherry or chicken broth
  Hot cooked rice (optional)
  Fresh rosemary sprigs (optional)
  Paprika (optional)

# Asparagus-Stuffed Turkey Rolls

*Select turkey breast tenderloin steaks, which are cut lengthwise from the turkey tenderloin, for these turkey bundles.*

**Start to Finish:** 40 minutes **Makes:** 4 servings

4 turkey breast tenderloin steaks* (about 1 pound total)

16 fresh asparagus spears
Nonstick cooking spray

⅔ cup reduced-sodium chicken broth

2 tablespoons lemon juice

2 tablespoons orange juice

¼ teaspoon salt-free seasoning blend

⅛ teaspoon pepper

1 tablespoon cold water

2 teaspoons cornstarch
Slivered orange or lemon peel (optional)
Hot cooked pasta or rice (optional)

*1.* Place each turkey breast tenderloin steak between 2 pieces of plastic wrap. Pound with the flat side of a meat mallet into a rectangle ¼ inch thick. Remove plastic wrap. Trim asparagus spears, breaking off woody ends. Arrange 4 asparagus spears on the short end of each turkey piece. Roll up turkey; secure with wooden toothpicks, if necessary.

*2.* Coat an unheated large nonstick skillet with nonstick cooking spray. Preheat over medium heat. Add turkey rolls and cook until browned on all sides, turning to brown evenly. Add broth, lemon juice, orange juice, seasoning blend, and pepper. Bring to boiling; reduce heat. Cover and simmer for 8 to 10 minutes or until turkey is tender and no longer pink.

*3.* Transfer turkey to a serving platter; discard toothpicks. Keep turkey warm.

*4.* In a small bowl combine cold water and cornstarch; add to liquid in skillet. Cook and stir until thickened and bubbly. Cook and stir for 2 minutes more. Spoon over turkey. If desired, sprinkle with slivered orange or lemon peel and serve with hot cooked pasta or rice.

Nutrition Facts per serving: **137 calories, 3 g total fat, 50 mg cholesterol, 154 mg sodium, 4 g carbohydrate, 23 g protein.**

*Note:* If you can't find turkey breast tenderloin steaks, buy two turkey breast tenderloins and split them in half lengthwise.

# Turkey-Mushroom Marsala

*Shiitake mushrooms give the sauce a pleasant, earthy flavor. If shiitakes aren't available, substitute brown or button mushrooms.*

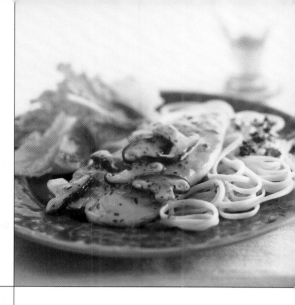

**Prep:** 15 minutes   **Marinate:** 30 minutes to 2 hours   **Cook:** 15 minutes
**Makes:** 4 servings

*1.* Place turkey in a heavy, large self-sealing plastic bag set in a shallow dish. For marinade, in a small bowl combine the mushrooms, Marsala, the ⅓ cup water, the snipped or dried thyme, rosemary, salt, and pepper. Pour over turkey; seal bag. Marinate in the refrigerator for at least 30 minutes or up to 2 hours, turning bag occasionally.

*2.* Drain turkey, reserving marinade. Pat turkey dry with paper towels. In a large skillet cook turkey in hot oil over medium heat for 8 to 10 minutes or until tender and no longer pink, turning once. Remove turkey from skillet; cover and keep warm.

*3.* Pour the reserved marinade into skillet. Bring to boiling; reduce heat. Cover and simmer for 2 minutes.

*4.* In a small bowl combine the 2 teaspoons cold water and the cornstarch; stir into marinade in skillet. Cook and stir over medium heat until thickened and bubbly. Cook and stir for 2 minutes more. If desired, serve the turkey and mushroom mixture over linguine. If desired, garnish with thyme sprigs.

Nutrition Facts per serving: **151 calories, 5 g total fat, 50 mg cholesterol, 114 mg sodium, 1 g carbohydrate, 22 g protein.**

*\*Note:* If you can't find turkey breast tenderloin steaks, buy two turkey breast tenderloins and split them in half lengthwise.

- 4 4-ounce turkey breast tenderloin steaks\*
- 1 cup sliced fresh shiitake mushrooms
- ⅓ cup dry Marsala
- ⅓ cup water
- 1½ teaspoons snipped fresh thyme or ½ teaspoon dried thyme, crushed
- 1 teaspoon snipped fresh rosemary or ¼ teaspoon dried rosemary, crushed
- ⅛ teaspoon salt
- ⅛ teaspoon pepper
- 2 teaspoons olive oil or cooking oil
- 2 teaspoons cold water
- 1 teaspoon cornstarch
  Hot cooked linguine (optional)
  Fresh thyme sprigs (optional)

# Turkey Burritos with Citrus Salsa

*A chopped jalapeño pepper adds just the right hint of hotness to the refreshing salsa.*

**Start to Finish:** 30 minutes **Makes:** 4 servings

8 8-inch fat-free flour tortillas
8 ounces uncooked ground
   turkey
1 16-ounce can fat-free
   refried beans
½ of a 15-ounce can chunky
   salsa tomato sauce
   (about ¾ cup)
½ teaspoon ground cumin
2 cups shredded lettuce
1 recipe Citrus Salsa
   Fat-free dairy sour cream
   (optional)

**1.** Wrap tortillas in foil. Heat tortillas in a 350° oven for 10 minutes to soften.

**2.** Meanwhile, for filling, in a medium skillet cook turkey over medium heat until browned. Remove from heat; drain off fat. Stir in beans, tomato sauce, and cumin. Simmer, uncovered, over medium heat about 5 minutes or until slightly thickened.

**3.** Spoon one-eighth of the filling onto each heated tortilla just below center. Fold bottom edge of tortilla up and over filling. Fold opposite sides of tortilla in, just until they meet. Roll up from the bottom. Serve over shredded lettuce with the Citrus Salsa. If desired, serve with sour cream.

***Citrus Salsa:*** Peel, seed, and chop 2 oranges. In a bowl combine oranges; 3 tablespoons chopped green sweet pepper; 1 fresh jalapeño pepper, seeded, and finely chopped;* 2 tablespoons lime juice; 1 tablespoon sliced green onion; and 1 tablespoon snipped fresh cilantro. Cover and chill until serving time. Makes about 1½ cups.

Nutrition Facts per serving: **436 calories, 5 g total fat, 21 mg cholesterol, 1,423 mg sodium, 77 g carbohydrate, 19 g protein.**

***Note:*** Because chile peppers, such as jalapeños, contain volatile oils that can burn your skin and eyes, avoid direct contact with them as much as possible. When working with chile peppers, wear plastic or rubber gloves. If your bare hands do touch the chile peppers, wash your hands and nails well with soap and warm water.

# Spaghetti with Turkey Meatballs

*Using ground turkey instead of ground beef updates this all-time favorite pasta dish.*

**Prep:** 30 minutes **Bake:** 20 minutes **Cook:** 30 minutes **Makes:** 6 servings

**1.** For sauce, in a Dutch oven cook onion, sweet pepper, carrot, and celery in hot oil until tender. Stir in fresh or undrained canned tomatoes, tomato paste, Italian seasoning, sugar, salt, and garlic powder. Bring to boiling.

**2.** Add the Turkey Meatballs; reduce heat. Cover and simmer for 30 minutes. If necessary, uncover and simmer for 10 to 15 minutes more or until sauce is desired consistency, stirring sauce occasionally.

**3.** To serve, spoon meatballs and sauce over hot cooked pasta.

**Turkey Meatballs:** In a medium bowl combine 1 beaten egg and 2 tablespoons milk. Stir in ¼ cup fine dry bread crumbs; ½ teaspoon salt; ½ teaspoon dried Italian seasoning, crushed; and ½ teaspoon ground black pepper. Add 1 pound uncooked ground turkey; mix well. Using wet hands, shape mixture into twenty-four 1-inch meatballs. Place the meatballs in a greased 13×9×2-inch baking pan. Bake in a 375° oven about 20 minutes or until meatballs are done (165°).* Drain off fat.

Nutrition Facts per serving: **442 calories, 11 g total fat, 64 mg cholesterol, 686 mg sodium, 65 g carbohydrate, 22 g protein.**

***Note:*** The internal color of ground poultry meatballs is not a reliable doneness indicator. Turkey or chicken meatballs cooked to 165°, regardless of color, are safe. Use an instant-read thermometer to check the internal temperature. To measure the doneness of meatballs, insert an instant-read thermometer into the center of a meatball.

1 large onion, chopped
1 medium green sweet pepper, coarsely chopped
1 medium carrot, coarsely chopped
1 stalk celery, sliced
1 tablespoon cooking oil
4 large ripe tomatoes, peeled and chopped (4 cups), or two 14½-ounce cans tomatoes, cut up
1 6-ounce can tomato paste
2 teaspoons dried Italian seasoning, crushed
½ teaspoon sugar
½ teaspoon salt
½ teaspoon garlic powder
1 recipe Turkey Meatballs
   Hot cooked spaghetti or mostaccioli

# Mediterranean-Style Chicken

*The pairing of tomato, wine, basil, and garlic is a traditional flavor combination in Mediterranean cooking.*

**Prep:** 25 minutes  **Cook:** 40 minutes  **Makes:** 4 servings

Nonstick cooking spray

1½ to 2 pounds meaty chicken pieces (breasts, thighs, and drumsticks), skinned

1 14½-ounce can tomatoes, cut up

¼ cup dry red wine

1 tablespoon snipped fresh basil or 1 teaspoon dried basil, crushed

1 teaspoon sugar

1 clove garlic, minced

1 bay leaf

1 tablespoon cold water

2 teaspoons cornstarch
Hot cooked spaghetti (optional)

¼ cup sliced pimiento-stuffed olives or pitted ripe olives

**1.** Coat an unheated 10-inch skillet with nonstick cooking spray. Preheat over medium heat. Add chicken and cook for 10 to 15 minutes or until browned, turning to brown evenly.

**2.** Add undrained tomatoes, wine, basil, sugar, garlic, and bay leaf. Bring to boiling; reduce heat. Cover and simmer about 35 minutes or until chicken is tender and no longer pink. Remove chicken from skillet; keep warm.

**3.** In a small bowl stir together cold water and cornstarch. Stir into tomato mixture in skillet. Cook and stir until thickened and bubbly. Cook and stir for 2 minutes more. Discard bay leaf.

**4.** If desired, serve chicken and tomato mixture over hot cooked spaghetti. Sprinkle with olives.

Nutrition Facts per serving: **194 calories, 7 g total fat, 69 mg cholesterol, 401 mg sodium, 8 g carbohydrate, 23 g protein.**

# Smoked Turkey and Wild Rice Pilaf

*Another time, chill the cooked mixture—it's delicious served as a main-dish salad.*

**Prep:** 20 minutes  **Cook:** 43 minutes  **Makes:** 4 servings

**1.** In a large skillet cook celery and onion in hot margarine over medium heat about 10 minutes or until tender. Add uncooked wild rice; cook and stir for 3 minutes. Add broth. Bring to boiling; reduce heat. Cover and simmer for 20 minutes. Stir in uncooked long grain rice. Return to boiling; reduce heat. Cover and simmer about 20 minutes more or until wild rice and long grain rice are tender and most of the liquid is absorbed.

**2.** Stir in turkey, apples, and carrot. Cook, uncovered, for 3 to 4 minutes or until heated through and liquid is absorbed. Stir in parsley. If desired, serve pilaf on lettuce leaves.

Nutrition Facts per serving: **289 calories, 7 g total fat, 44 mg cholesterol, 1,231 mg sodium, 37 g carbohydrate, 21 g protein.**

- 1 cup sliced celery
- ¼ cup chopped onion
- 1 tablespoon margarine or butter
- ⅓ cup wild rice, rinsed and drained
- 1 14-ounce can reduced-sodium chicken broth
- ⅓ cup long grain rice
- 12 ounces cooked smoked turkey, cubed
- 2 medium red-skinned apples, coarsely chopped
- 1 large carrot, peeled and cut into thin, bite-size strips
- 2 tablespoons snipped fresh parsley
- Lettuce leaves (optional)

# Turkey Jambalaya

*Although this Cajun classic varies from cook to cook, jambalaya always contains long grain rice, a spicy sausage, and the seasoning trio of onion, celery, and green pepper.*

**Prep:** 35 minutes  **Cook:** 15 minutes  **Makes:** 4 servings

1½ teaspoons garlic powder

1½ teaspoons paprika

½ teaspoon salt

½ teaspoon ground white
   pepper

½ teaspoon dried thyme,
   crushed

¼ teaspoon ground black
   pepper

¼ teaspoon ground cumin

⅛ to ¼ teaspoon ground
   red pepper

3 medium onions, chopped

2 medium green sweet
   peppers, chopped

2 stalks celery, chopped

1 cup cooked turkey andouille
   sausage links or cooked
   smoked turkey sausage
   links cut into ¼-inch
   rounds

1 teaspoon cooking oil

1 14-ounce can reduced-
   sodium chicken broth

⅓ cup water

1 cup chopped cooked turkey
   (about 5 ounces)

1 cup long grain rice

2 tomatoes, chopped
   Celery leaves (optional)

**1.** In a small bowl combine garlic powder, paprika, salt, white pepper, thyme, black pepper, cumin, and ground red pepper. Set aside.

**2.** In a heavy, large saucepan cook onions, sweet peppers, celery, turkey sausage, and the garlic powder mixture in hot oil over medium-high heat for 10 minutes, stirring frequently. Carefully add chicken broth, the water, chopped cooked turkey, and uncooked rice. Bring to boiling; reduce heat. Cover and simmer for 15 to 20 minutes or until rice is tender. Stir in the tomatoes and heat through. If desired, garnish jambalaya with celery leaves.

Nutrition Facts per serving: 377 calories, 8 g total fat, 56 mg cholesterol, 921 mg sodium, 53 g carbohydrate, 23 g protein.

# Take-It-Easy Cassoulet

*Using canned beans and broth shortcuts the preparation of this full-flavored variation of the French country classic.*

**Prep:** 20 minutes  **Cook:** 1 hour 20 minutes  **Makes:** 5 servings

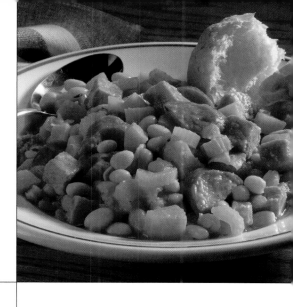

**1.** Coat an unheated large saucepan with nonstick cooking spray. Preheat over medium heat. Add the turkey sausage, pork, onion, carrot, celery, and garlic. Cook and stir until pork is browned on all sides and vegetables are nearly tender.

**2.** Stir in the chicken broth, tomato sauce, thyme, and bay leaf. Bring to boiling; reduce heat. Cover and simmer about 1 hour or until pork is tender, stirring occasionally.

**3.** Stir in beans. Simmer, uncovered, for 20 to 30 minutes more or until of desired consistency. Discard bay leaf.

Nutrition Facts per serving: 315 calories, 5 g total fat, 25 mg cholesterol, 1,266 mg sodium, 47 g carbohydrate, 23 g protein.

Nonstick cooking spray
4 ounces cooked smoked turkey sausage links, cut into bite-size pieces
4 ounces lean boneless pork, cubed
1 cup chopped onion
1 cup chopped carrot
1 cup sliced celery
2 cloves garlic, minced
1 14-ounce can reduced-sodium chicken broth
1 8-ounce can low-sodium tomato sauce
½ teaspoon dried thyme, crushed
1 bay leaf
2 15-ounce cans navy beans, rinsed and drained

# stir-fries

*Create a fabulous meal by stir-frying one of these chicken or turkey medlies. No matter whether the seasonings are Asian, Mediterranean, or All-American, the results are spectacular.*

Asian Primavera Stir-Fry, page 60

# Chicken Chop Suey

*Serve this saucy chicken-vegetable mixture over crispy chow mein noodles or hot cooked rice.*

**Start to Finish:** 25 minutes   **Makes:** 4 servings

1¼ cups chicken broth or
   beef broth

2 tablespoons cornstarch

2 tablespoons soy sauce

1 tablespoon molasses

½ teaspoon ground ginger

1 tablespoon cooking oil

2 cups sliced celery

1 medium onion, chopped

2 cups fresh bean sprouts or
   one 16-ounce can bean
   sprouts, drained

1 pound skinless, boneless
   chicken breasts, cut into
   ½-inch pieces

   Chow mein noodles or hot
   cooked rice

   Tomato wedges (optional)

*1.* For sauce, in a small bowl stir together the broth, cornstarch, soy sauce, molasses, and ginger; set aside.

*2.* In a wok or large skillet heat oil over medium-high heat. (Add more oil as necessary during cooking.) Stir-fry the celery and onion in hot oil for 2 minutes. Add fresh bean sprouts, if using, and stir-fry for 1 to 2 minutes more or until celery and onion are crisp-tender. Remove vegetables from wok.

*3.* Add half of the chicken to hot wok; stir-fry for 3 to 4 minutes or until no longer pink. Remove chicken from the wok. Repeat with remaining chicken. Return all chicken and cooked vegetables to the wok; push from the center of the wok. Stir sauce; add to the center of the wok. Cook and stir until thickened and bubbly. Add canned bean sprouts, if using. Stir all ingredients together to coat with sauce. Cook and stir about 1 minute more or until heated through. Serve immediately over chow mein noodles or hot cooked rice. If desired, garnish with tomato wedges.

Nutrition Facts per serving: 384 calories, 14 g total fat, 66 mg cholesterol, 1,025 mg sodium, 30 g carbohydrate, 34 g protein.

# Chicken, Long Beans, And Tomato Stir-Fry

*Chinese long beans are dark green, pencil-thin legumes that average about 1½ feet long. Look for them in the produce section of your supermarket or at an Asian market.*

**Start to Finish:** 30 minutes **Makes:** 4 servings

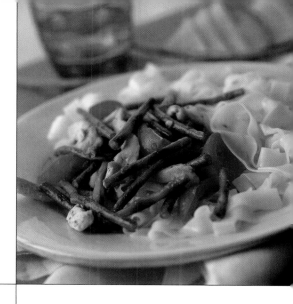

**1.** In a medium saucepan cook rice sticks in boiling, lightly salted water for 3 to 5 minutes or until tender. (Or cook egg noodles according to package directions.) Drain noodles; keep warm.

**2.** Meanwhile, in a wok or large skillet heat 2 teaspoons of the oil over medium-high heat. (Add more oil as necessary during cooking.) Add garlic and stir-fry for 15 seconds. Add beans; stir-fry for 2 minutes. Carefully add the water to wok. Reduce heat to low; cover and simmer for 6 to 8 minutes or until beans are crisp-tender. Remove beans from wok.

**3.** Toss chicken with Cajun seasoning. Add the remaining cooking oil to wok. Add chicken; stir-fry for 3 to 4 minutes or until no longer pink. Stir in beans, tomatoes, and vinegar; heat through. Serve over rice sticks or noodles.

Nutrition Facts per serving: 361 calories, 5 g total fat, 45 mg cholesterol, 334 mg sodium, 54 g carbohydrate, 25 g protein.

6 ounces wide rice sticks or
   dried egg noodles
4 teaspoons cooking oil
2 cloves garlic, minced
1 pound Chinese long beans
   or whole green beans, cut
   into 3-inch pieces
¼ cup water
12 ounces skinless, boneless
   chicken breasts, cut into
   bite-size strips
1 teaspoon Cajun seasoning or
   other spicy seasoning blend
2 medium tomatoes, cut into
   thin wedges
2 tablespoons raspberry
   vinegar

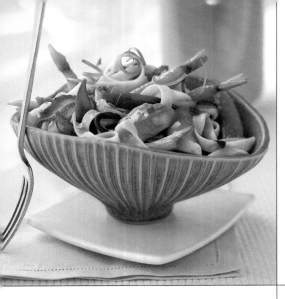

# Asian Primavera Stir-Fry

*A medley of vegetables, fettuccine, and chicken breasts combines to make a hearty one-dish meal.*

**Start to Finish:** 40 minutes  **Makes:** 4 servings

1 cup warm water
1 ounce dried shiitake
    mushrooms
1 tablespoon cornstarch
6 ounces dried fettuccine
12 ounces skinless, boneless
    chicken breasts, cut into
    bite-size pieces
2 tablespoons dry sherry
2 tablespoons light soy sauce
1 tablespoon grated fresh
    ginger
2 cloves garlic, minced
    Nonstick cooking spray
1 cup sugar snap peas, strings
    and tips removed
8 ounces tiny whole carrots
    with tops (about 12),
    trimmed
4 green onions, bias-sliced
    into 1-inch pieces
    Green onion curls (optional)

**1.** In a small bowl combine the warm water and dried shiitake mushrooms; let stand for 15 minutes. Drain mushrooms, reserving liquid; squeeze out excess liquid. Slice mushroom caps; discard stems. Stir the cornstarch into the reserved mushroom liquid.

**2.** Meanwhile, cook pasta according to package directions. Drain; keep warm.

**3.** In a small bowl combine the chicken, sherry, soy sauce, ginger, and garlic; set aside.

**4.** Lightly coat an unheated wok or large skillet with nonstick cooking spray. Preheat wok or skillet over medium-high heat. Add sugar snap peas and carrots; stir-fry for 3 to 4 minutes or until crisp-tender. Add green onion pieces and stir-fry 1 minute more. Remove vegetables from wok; set aside. Add chicken mixture to hot wok; stir-fry for 2 to 4 minutes or until chicken is no longer pink. Push chicken from center of wok. Stir cornstarch mixture; add to center of wok. Cook and stir until thickened and bubbly.

**5.** Return vegetables to wok. Add mushrooms and pasta. Stir all ingredients together to coat with sauce. Cook and stir about 1 minute or until heated through. If desired, garnish with green onion curls.

Nutrition Facts per serving: **333 calories, 3 g total fat, 45 mg cholesterol, 324 mg sodium, 48 g carbohydrate, 25 g protein.**

# Chicken and Apple Stir-Fry

*Savory and sweet seasonings meld into an irresistible sauce in this colorful stir-fry.*

**Prep:** 20 minutes **Soak:** 30 minutes **Cook:** 10 minutes **Makes:** 4 servings

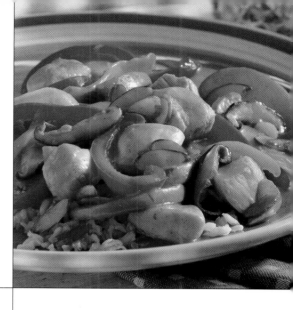

**1.** In a small bowl cover mushrooms with warm water. Let soak for 30 minutes. Rinse and squeeze mushrooms to drain thoroughly. Discard stems. Thinly slice mushrooms; set aside.

**2.** For sauce, in a small bowl stir together the cold water, juice concentrate, soy sauce, cornstarch, ginger, cinnamon, and ground red pepper; set aside.

**3.** Preheat a wok or large skillet over medium-high heat. Add almonds; stir-fry for 2 to 3 minutes or until golden. Remove almonds from wok. Let wok cool.

**4.** Pour cooking oil into the cooled wok; heat over medium-high heat. (Add more oil as necessary during cooking.) Add mushrooms, sweet peppers, and apples; stir-fry for 1 to 2 minutes or until peppers and apples are crisp-tender. Remove apple mixture from the wok.

**5.** Add chicken or turkey to the hot wok; stir-fry for 3 to 4 minutes or until no longer pink. Push chicken or turkey from the center of the wok.

**6.** Stir sauce. Add sauce to the center of the wok; cook and stir until thickened and bubbly. Return apple mixture to the wok. Stir all ingredients together to coat with sauce. Cook and stir 1 to 2 minutes more or until heated through. Stir in toasted almonds. Serve immediately over hot cooked brown rice.

Nutrition Facts per serving: 370 calories, 11 g total fat, 45 mg cholesterol, 563 mg sodium, 48 g carbohydrate, 22 g protein.

- 6 dried mushrooms (such as shiitake or wood ear mushrooms)
- ¾ cup cold water
- 3 tablespoons frozen orange, apple, or pineapple juice concentrate, thawed
- 2 tablespoons soy sauce
- 2 teaspoons cornstarch
- ¼ teaspoon ground ginger
- ¼ teaspoon ground cinnamon
- ⅛ to ¼ teaspoon ground red pepper
- ¼ cup sliced or slivered almonds
- 1 tablespoon cooking oil
- 2 medium green, red, orange, and/or yellow sweet peppers, cut into thin strips
- 2 medium apples, thinly sliced
- 12 ounces skinless, boneless chicken breasts or turkey breast tenderloin, cut into 1-inch pieces
  Hot cooked brown rice

# Stir-Fry Chicken with Feta

*A sprinkling of feta adds a pleasant salty tang to each serving.*

**Start to Finish:** 25 minutes  **Makes:** 4 servings

1 cup dried orzo (rosamarina)
    or 1 cup quick-cooking
    couscous
⅓ cup chicken broth
2 tablespoons wine vinegar
1 tablespoon cornstarch
    Nonstick cooking spray
1 cup chopped onion
1 teaspoon bottled minced
    garlic or 2 cloves garlic,
    minced
1 tablespoon olive oil
12 ounces skinless, boneless
    chicken breasts, cut into
    bite-size strips
1 14½-ounce can Italian-style
    stewed tomatoes
1 teaspoon sugar
½ cup crumbled feta cheese
    (2 ounces)
    Snipped fresh basil or
    chopped ripe olives
    (optional)

**1.** Prepare orzo or couscous according to package directions. For sauce, in a small bowl stir together broth, wine vinegar, and cornstarch. Set aside.

**2.** Meanwhile, coat an unheated wok or large skillet with nonstick cooking spray. Preheat over medium-high heat. Stir-fry onion and garlic over medium-high heat for 2 minutes. Remove from wok. Add oil to wok. Add chicken; stir-fry for 3 to 4 minutes or until no longer pink. Stir in undrained tomatoes, sugar, and onion mixture; push from center of wok. Stir sauce; add to center of wok. Cook and stir until thickened and bubbly. Cook and stir for 2 minutes more. Stir all ingredients together to coat with sauce.

**3.** Drain orzo or fluff couscous with a fork. Serve chicken mixture over hot orzo or couscous. Top each serving with feta cheese. If desired, sprinkle with basil or olives.

Nutrition Facts per serving: 345 calories, 9 g total fat, 62 mg cholesterol, 489 mg sodium, 35 g carbohydrate, 27 g protein.

# Mango Chicken

*Add a Caribbean flair to the rice by cooking it with a bit of fresh ginger and chopped fresh mint.*

**Start to Finish:** 30 minutes   **Makes:** 4 servings

**1.** For sauce, in a small bowl stir together broth, lime juice, finely shredded lime peel, brown sugar, curry powder, and cornstarch; set aside.

**2.** In a wok or large skillet heat oil over medium-high heat. (Add more oil as necessary during cooking.) Add garlic and stir-fry for 30 seconds. Add onion slices; stir-fry for 3 minutes. Remove onion from wok. Add chicken to hot wok; stir-fry for 2 to 3 minutes or until no longer pink. Push chicken from center of wok.

**3.** Stir sauce mixture. Pour sauce into center of wok; cook and stir until thickened and bubbly. Return onion to the wok. Add mango or papaya. Stir all ingredients together to coat with sauce. Cook about 2 minutes more or until heated through. Serve chicken mixture over rice. If desired, garnish with lime peel strips.

**Nutrition Facts per serving:** 301 calories, 5 g total fat, 45 mg cholesterol, 125 mg sodium, 44 g carbohydrate, 20 g protein.

½ cup reduced-sodium
   chicken broth
2 tablespoons lime juice
2 teaspoons finely shredded
   lime peel or orange peel
2 teaspoons brown sugar
2 teaspoons curry powder
1 teaspoon cornstarch
2 teaspoons peanut oil or
   cooking oil
2 cloves garlic, minced
1 cup sliced red onion
12 ounces skinless, boneless
   chicken breasts or thighs,
   cut into bite-size strips
2 cups chopped, peeled mango
   or papaya
   Hot cooked rice
   Lime peel strips (optional)

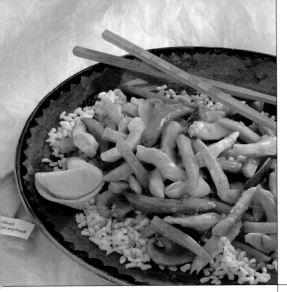

# Brown Rice with Sweet-Sour Chicken and Veggies

*Pass bottled hot pepper sauce so lovers of spicy food can add a little extra pizzazz to their portions.*

**Start to Finish:** 45 minutes  **Makes:** 4 servings

2 cups water
¼ teaspoon salt
1 cup brown rice
½ cup chicken broth
½ teaspoon finely shredded
   orange peel
¼ cup orange juice
2 tablespoons vinegar
2 tablespoons reduced-sodium
   soy sauce
1 tablespoon cornstarch
1 tablespoon brown sugar
   Few dashes bottled hot
   pepper sauce
2 teaspoons cooking oil
½ teaspoon toasted
   sesame oil
1 16-ounce package frozen
   sugar snap pea, carrot,
   onion, and mushroom
   stir-fry vegetable mix
10 ounces skinless, boneless
   chicken breasts, cut into
   bite-size strips

*1.* In a medium saucepan bring water and salt to boiling. Add uncooked brown rice; return to boiling. Cover and simmer about 35 minutes or just until tender. Remove from heat. Let stand 5 minutes.

*2.* Meanwhile, for sauce, in a small bowl stir together broth, orange peel, orange juice, vinegar, soy sauce, cornstarch, brown sugar, and hot pepper sauce; set aside.

*3.* In a wok or large skillet heat cooking oil and sesame oil over medium-high heat. (Add more oil as necessary during cooking.) Carefully add vegetable mix; stir-fry about 5 minutes or until crisp-tender. Remove vegetables from wok. Add chicken to hot wok; stir-fry for 2 to 3 minutes or until no longer pink. Push chicken from center of wok.

*4.* Stir sauce. Pour sauce into center of wok; cook and stir over medium heat until thickened and bubbly. Return vegetables to wok. Stir all ingredients together to coat with sauce. Cook and stir about 1 minute or until heated through. Serve over hot cooked brown rice.

Nutrition Facts per serving: 347 calories, 7 g total fat, 37 mg cholesterol, 559 mg sodium, 51 g carbohydrate, 20 g protein.

# Basil Chicken in Coconut Sauce

*A medley of eight spices seasons the chicken in this luscious stir-fry.*

**Prep:** 20 minutes  **Chill:** 1 to 2 hours  **Cook:** 10 minutes  **Makes:** 4 servings

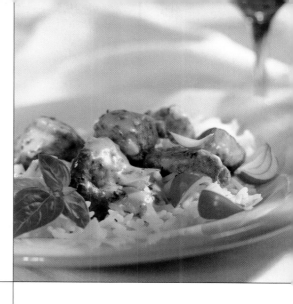

**1.** Place chicken in a medium bowl. In a small bowl stir together the salt, cardamom, cinnamon, cloves, coriander, cumin, cracked pepper, turmeric, and chili powder. Sprinkle spice mixture over chicken, tossing to coat. Cover and chill in refrigerator for 1 to 2 hours.

**2.** In a nonstick wok or large skillet heat oil over medium-high heat. (Add more oil as necessary during cooking.) Add onion, garlic, and jalapeño peppers; stir-fry for 2 minutes. Remove onion mixture from wok. Add half of the chicken to hot wok; stir-fry about 2 minutes or until no longer pink. Remove chicken from the wok. Repeat with remaining chicken.

**3.** In a small bowl stir together coconut milk and cornstarch. Carefully add to wok. Cook and stir until bubbly. Return chicken and onion mixture to wok. Stir in snipped basil and ginger. Cook and stir about 2 minutes more or until heated through. Serve over rice. If desired, garnish with basil sprigs.

Nutrition Facts per serving: 468 calories, 24 g total fat, 66 mg cholesterol, 383 mg sodium, 31 g carbohydrate, 31 g protein.

***Note:*** Because chile peppers, such as jalapeños, contain volatile oils that can burn your skin and eyes, avoid direct contact with them as much as possible. When working with chile peppers, wear plastic or rubber gloves. If your bare hands do touch the chile peppers, wash your hands and nails well with soap and warm water.

- 1 pound skinless, boneless chicken breasts, cut into 1-inch pieces
- ½ teaspoon salt
- ½ teaspoon ground cardamom
- ½ teaspoon ground cinnamon
- ½ teaspoon ground cloves
- ½ teaspoon ground coriander
- ½ teaspoon ground cumin
- ½ teaspoon cracked black pepper
- ¼ teaspoon ground turmeric
- ¼ teaspoon chili powder
- 1 tablespoon olive oil
- 1 small red onion, cut into wedges
- 5 cloves garlic, minced
- 2 fresh jalapeño peppers, seeded and finely chopped*
- 1 14-ounce can unsweetened coconut milk
- 2 teaspoons cornstarch
- 3 tablespoons snipped fresh basil
- 1 tablespoon finely chopped fresh ginger
- Hot cooked rice
- Fresh basil sprigs (optional)

# Spicy Stir-Fried Chicken With Cashews

*Control the heat in this dynamite dish by using 2 to 4 fresh red chile peppers to suit your taste.*

**Start to Finish:** 25 minutes  **Makes:** 4 servings

2 tablespoons oyster-flavored
    sauce
1 tablespoon fish sauce or
    soy sauce
1 tablespoon brown sugar
2 teaspoons cornstarch
⅓ cup water
2 tablespoons cooking oil
1 medium onion, sliced
2 to 4 fresh red chili peppers,
    seeded and cut into
    thin strips*
½ teaspoon bottled minced
    garlic or 1 clove garlic,
    minced
12 ounces skinless, boneless
    chicken breasts, cut into
    bite-size strips
½ cup unsalted or lightly
    salted roasted cashews
    Hot cooked rice
    Whole fresh red chili
    peppers (optional)

**1.** For sauce, in a small bowl stir together the oyster-flavored sauce, fish sauce or soy sauce, brown sugar, and cornstarch. Stir in the water; set aside.

**2.** In a wok or large skillet heat oil over medium-high heat. Add onion and stir-fry for 1 minute. Add chili pepper strips and garlic; stir-fry for 1 to 2 minutes or until onion is crisp-tender. Remove with slotted spoon; set aside.

**3.** Add chicken to hot wok; stir-fry for 3 to 4 minutes or until no longer pink. Push chicken from center of wok. Stir sauce. Add to center of wok; cook and stir until thickened and bubbly. Return onion mixture to wok. Cook and stir 1 minute more. Stir in cashews. Serve over rice. If desired, garnish with whole red chili peppers.

Nutrition Facts per serving: **444 calories, 18 g total fat, 47 mg cholesterol, 549 mg sodium, 48 g carbohydrate, 23 g protein.**

*__Note:__* Because chile peppers, such as jalapeños, contain volatile oils that can burn your skin and eyes, avoid direct contact with them as much as possible. When working with chile peppers, wear plastic or rubber gloves. If your bare hands do touch the chile peppers, wash your hands and nails well with soap and warm water.

# Country Chicken Stir-Fry

*With chunks of potato and sliced carrots, this satisfying chicken stir-fry resembles a hearty stew.*

**Start to Finish:** 35 minutes  **Makes:** 4 servings

**1.** In a covered medium saucepan cook potatoes and carrots in enough boiling water to cover about 10 minutes or just until tender. Drain. Set aside.

**2.** For sauce, in a small bowl stir together the ¾ cup cold water, the cornstarch, chicken bouillon granules, thyme, salt, and pepper. Set aside.

**3.** In a wok or large skillet heat oil over medium-high heat. (Add more oil as necessary during cooking.) Add onion and stir-fry about 2 minutes or until crisp-tender. Add chicken to hot wok; stir-fry for 2 to 3 minutes or until no longer pink.

**4.** Push chicken from the center of the wok. Stir sauce. Add to center of wok; cook and stir until thickened and bubbly. Add cooked potatoes and carrots. Stir all ingredients together to coat with sauce. Cover and cook about 2 minutes more or until heated through. Stir in parsley.

**Nutrition Facts per serving:** 323 calories, 6 g total fat, 45 mg cholesterol, 583 mg sodium, 47 g carbohydrate, 21 g protein.

- 4 **medium potatoes, cut into ¾-inch pieces**
- 4 **medium carrots, thinly sliced**
- ¾ **cup cold water**
- 1 **teaspoon cornstarch**
- 1 **teaspoon instant chicken bouillon granules**
- 1 **teaspoon dried thyme, crushed**
- ½ **teaspoon salt**
- ⅛ **teaspoon pepper**
- 1 **tablespoon cooking oil**
- 1 **large onion, chopped**
- 12 **ounces skinless, boneless chicken breasts, cut into bite-size strips**
- 3 **tablespoons snipped fresh parsley**

# Honey-Glazed Chicken Stir-Fry

*For this hearty dish, choose your favorite combination from the multitude of loose-pack frozen vegetable mixtures available.*

**Start to Finish:** 25 minutes  **Makes:** 4 servings

2 tablespoons honey
2 tablespoons vinegar
2 tablespoons orange juice
1 tablespoon soy sauce
1 teaspoon cornstarch
2 tablespoons cooking oil
2 cups loose-pack frozen
    vegetable combination
12 ounces skinless, boneless
    chicken breasts or
    skinless, boneless
    chicken thighs, cut into
    1-inch pieces
    Hot cooked rice

*1.* For sauce, in a small bowl stir together honey, vinegar, orange juice, soy sauce, and cornstarch; set aside.

*2.* In a wok or large skillet heat oil over medium-high heat. (Add more oil as necessary during cooking.) Add vegetables; stir-fry about 3 minutes or until vegetables are crisp-tender. Remove vegetables from wok. Add chicken to hot wok; stir-fry for 3 to 4 minutes or until no longer pink. Push chicken from center of wok. Stir sauce. Add to center of wok; cook and stir until thickened and bubbly.

*3.* Return cooked vegetables to wok. Stir all ingredients together to coat with sauce. Cook and stir about 1 minute more or until heated through. Serve over hot cooked rice.

Nutrition Facts per serving: 443 calories, 10 g total fat, 45 mg cholesterol, 333 mg sodium, 66 g carbohydrate, 23 g protein.

# Kung Pao Chicken

*Serve mounds of hot cooked rice with this delicious homemade version of a restaurant favorite.*

**Start to Finish:** 30 minutes  **Makes:** 4 servings

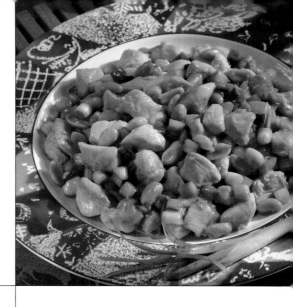

**1.** In a medium bowl stir together chicken, sherry, and the 1 teaspoon cornstarch; let stand for 15 minutes.

**2.** For sauce, in a small bowl stir together water, soy sauce, the 4 teaspoons cornstarch, the sugar, vinegar, and hot pepper sauce; set aside.

**3.** In a wok or large skillet heat oil over medium-high heat. (Add more oil as necessary during cooking.) Add ginger and garlic; stir-fry for 15 seconds. Add chicken mixture; stir-fry for 3 to 4 minutes or until no longer pink.

**4.** Push chicken from center of wok. Stir sauce. Add to center of wok; cook and stir until thickened and bubbly. Add green onion pieces and peanuts. Stir all ingredients together to coat with sauce. Cook and stir for 1 to 2 minutes more or until heated through. Serve with hot cooked rice. If desired, garnish with green onion fans.

Nutrition Facts per serving: 374 calories, 15 g total fat, 45 mg cholesterol, 1,220 mg sodium, 35 g carbohydrate, 24 g protein.

12 ounces skinless, boneless chicken breasts, cut into ¾-inch pieces
1 tablespoon dry sherry
1 teaspoon cornstarch
¼ cup cold water
¼ cup soy sauce
4 teaspoons cornstarch
1 tablespoon sugar
1 teaspoon vinegar
　Few dashes bottled hot pepper sauce
1 tablespoon cooking oil
2 teaspoons grated fresh ginger
2 cloves garlic, minced
6 green onions, cut into ½-inch pieces
½ cup dry-roasted peanuts
　Hot cooked rice
　Green onion fans (optional)

# Quick Chicken Asian

*Using the orange juice option instead of chicken broth gives the gingery sauce a pleasant citrus flavor.*

**Start to Finish:** 25 minutes  **Makes:** 4 servings

⅓ cup chicken broth or
    orange juice
2 tablespoons soy sauce
2 teaspoons cornstarch
1 teaspoon brown sugar
½ teaspoon ground ginger
1 tablespoon cooking oil
1 16-ounce package fresh
    cut-up Oriental stir-fry
    vegetables or one
    16-ounce package frozen
    vegetable combination,
    thawed and drained
12 ounces skinless, boneless
    chicken breasts or turkey
    breast tenderloins, cut into
    ¼-inch-wide strips
Hot cooked rice

*1.* For sauce, in a small bowl stir together broth or juice, soy sauce, cornstarch, brown sugar, and ginger; set aside.

*2.* In a wok or large skillet heat oil over medium-high heat. (Add more oil as necessary during cooking.) Add fresh or thawed vegetables; stir-fry for 2 to 3 minutes or until crisp-tender. Remove vegetables. Add the chicken to hot wok; stir-fry for 2 to 3 minutes or until no longer pink. Push chicken from center of wok. Stir sauce. Add to center of wok; cook and stir until thickened and bubbly.

*3.* Return cooked vegetables to wok. Stir all ingredients together to coat with sauce. Cook and stir about 1 minute more or until heated through. Serve with hot cooked rice.

Nutrition Facts per serving: 374 calories, 10 g total fat, 76 mg cholesterol, 642 mg sodium, 39 g carbohydrate, 30 g protein.

# Sweet-and-Sour Chicken

*Check the supermarket's Asian food section or an Asian food
store for rice sticks (also called rice noodles or rice vermicelli).*

**Start to Finish:** 30 minutes   **Makes:** 4 servings

**1.** If using rice sticks, break them into a large bowl; cover with warm water. Let stand for 15 minutes.

**2.** Meanwhile, drain pineapple, reserving juice (you should have about ⅓ cup). For sauce, in a small bowl stir together the reserved pineapple juice, the chicken broth, vinegar, brown sugar, cornstarch, and soy sauce. Set aside.

**3.** In a wok or large skillet heat oil over medium-high heat. (Add more oil as necessary during cooking.) Add garlic; stir-fry for 15 seconds. Add celery and onion; stir-fry for 2 minutes. Add the sweet pepper; stir-fry for 2 minutes more. Remove vegetables from wok.

**4.** Add the chicken to hot wok; stir-fry for 2 to 3 minutes or until no longer pink. Push chicken from center of wok. Stir sauce. Add to center of wok; cook and stir until thickened and bubbly. Add cooked vegetables and pineapple. Cook and stir for 2 minutes more or until heated through. Drain rice sticks, if using; arrange rice sticks or hot cooked rice on 4 dinner plates. Top with chicken mixture.

Nutrition Facts per serving: 388 calories, 6 g total fat, 45 mg cholesterol,
706 mg sodium, 64 g carbohydrate, 19 g protein.

- **6 ounces rice sticks or 2 cups hot cooked rice**
- **1 8-ounce can pineapple chunks (juice pack)**
- **¾ cup chicken broth**
- **¼ cup vinegar**
- **3 tablespoons brown sugar**
- **2 tablespoons cornstarch**
- **2 tablespoons soy sauce**
- **1 tablespoon cooking oil**
- **½ teaspoon bottled minced garlic or 1 clove garlic, minced**
- **1 cup sliced celery**
- **1 medium onion, sliced**
- **1 small red or green sweet pepper, cut into thin, bite-size strips**
- **12 ounces skinless, boneless chicken breasts, cut into bite-size pieces**

# Easy Chicken and Vegetable Stir-Fry

*Using several purchased convenience products—a frozen vegetable mixture; skinless, boneless chicken; chow mein noodles; and fruit jam—makes this stir-fry truly easy.*

**Start to Finish:** 25 minutes **Makes:** 4 servings

1 3-ounce can chow mein noodles
2 tablespoons soy sauce
1 tablespoon apricot or peach jam or preserves
1 tablespoon vinegar
1 teaspoon cornstarch
1 tablespoon cooking oil
3 cups loose-pack frozen broccoli, green beans, onions, and red peppers
12 ounces skinless, boneless chicken thighs or skinless, boneless chicken breasts, cut into 1-inch pieces

*1.* Pour noodles into a baking pan; heat in a 350° oven for 5 minutes.

*2.* Meanwhile, for sauce, in a small bowl stir together soy sauce, jam or preserves, vinegar, and cornstarch; set aside.

*3.* In a wok or large skillet heat oil over medium-high heat. (Add more oil as necessary during cooking.) Add frozen vegetables; stir-fry for 2 to 3 minutes or until crisp-tender. Remove vegetables from wok. Add chicken to hot wok; stir-fry for 3 to 4 minutes or until no longer pink. Push chicken from center of wok. Stir sauce. Add to center of wok; cook and stir until thickened and bubbly.

*4.* Return cooked vegetables to wok. Stir all ingredients together to coat with sauce. Cook and stir about 1 minute more or until heated through. Serve over noodles.

Nutrition Facts per serving: 394 calories, 20 g total fat, 41 mg cholesterol, 842 mg sodium, 34 g carbohydrate, 19 g protein.

# Stir-Fried Chicken With Peanuts

*Look in the produce section of your supermarket for bottled grated fresh ginger as well as bottled minced garlic.*

**Start to Finish:** 30 minutes **Makes:** 4 servings

**1.** For sauce, in a small bowl stir together teriyaki sauce or soy sauce, cornstarch, ground red pepper, and water; set aside.

**2.** In a wok or large skillet heat oil over medium-high heat. (Add more oil as necessary during cooking.) Add ginger and garlic; stir-fry for 15 seconds. Add sweet peppers; stir fry about 2 minutes or until crisp-tender. Remove peppers from wok.

**3.** Add half of the chicken to hot wok; stir-fry for 2 to 3 minutes or until no longer pink. Remove chicken from wok. Repeat with remaining chicken. Return all chicken to wok. Push chicken from center of wok. Stir sauce. Add to center of wok; cook and stir until thickened and bubbly. Return vegetable mixture to wok. Stir all ingredients together to coat with sauce. Cook and stir about 1 minute more or until heated through. Serve over chow mein noodles. Sprinkle with peanuts.

Nutrition Facts per serving: **274 calories, 15 g total fat, 54 mg cholesterol, 665 mg sodium, 15 g carbohydrate, 21 g protein.**

- 3 **tablespoons bottled teriyaki sauce or soy sauce**
- 1 **teaspoon cornstarch**
- ⅛ **teaspoon ground red pepper**
- 3 **tablespoons water**
- 1 **tablespoon peanut oil or cooking oil**
- 1 **tablespoon grated fresh ginger**
- 1½ **teaspoons bottled minced garlic**
- 1 **green sweet pepper, cut into 1-inch squares**
- 1 **red or yellow sweet pepper, cut into 1-inch squares**
- 1 **pound skinless, boneless chicken thighs, cut into 1-inch pieces**
- 1 **3-ounce can chow mein noodles**
- ¼ **cup peanuts**

# Creamy Turkey Dijon

*An old favorite—turkey à la king—gets new zest with the addition of mustard, onion, and garlic.*

**Start to Finish:** 35 minutes   **Makes:** 4 servings

2 tablespoons all-purpose flour
2 tablespoons Dijon-style
   mustard
2 tablespoons dry white wine
½ teaspoon salt
⅛ teaspoon ground black
   pepper
1 cup half-and-half or light
   cream
1 tablespoon cooking oil
1 clove garlic, minced
1 medium red or green sweet
   pepper, cut into thin,
   bite-size strips
1 medium onion, chopped
1½ cups sliced fresh
   mushrooms
12 ounces turkey breast
   tenderloin, cut into
   bite-size strips
¾ cup frozen peas, thawed
   Hot cooked noodles or
   fettuccine
   Fresh whole mushrooms
   (optional)
   Fresh basil sprigs (optional)

**1.** For sauce, in a small bowl stir together flour, mustard, wine, salt, and black pepper. Slowly stir in half-and-half or light cream until well mixed; set aside.

**2.** In wok or large skillet heat oil over medium-high heat. (Add more oil as necessary during cooking.) Add garlic; stir-fry for 15 seconds. Add sweet pepper and onion; stir-fry for 2 minutes. Add sliced mushrooms; stir-fry about 2 minutes more or until crisp-tender. Remove vegetables from wok.

**3.** Add turkey to hot wok; stir-fry for 2 to 3 minutes or until no longer pink. Push turkey from center of wok.

**4.** Stir sauce. Add sauce to center of wok; cook and stir until thickened and bubbly. Return cooked vegetables to the wok. Add thawed peas. Stir all ingredients together to coat with sauce. Cook and stir for 1 to 2 minutes more or until heated through. Serve over hot cooked noodles or fettuccine. If desired, garnish with whole mushrooms and fresh basil.

Nutrition Facts per serving: 463 calories, 15 g total fat, 108 mg cholesterol, 553 mg sodium, 52 g carbohydrate, 28 g protein.

# Turkey-Apricot Stir-Fry

*Dried apricots and apricot nectar contribute a sweet-and-sour flavor that makes this hearty dish pleasantly different.*

**Start to Finish:** 35 minutes **Makes:** 4 servings

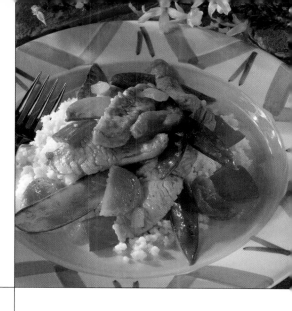

**1.** For sauce, in a small bowl stir together apricot or peach nectar, soy sauce, vinegar, cornstarch, and ground red pepper; stir in apricots. Set aside.

**2.** In a wok or large skillet heat oil over medium-high heat. (Add more oil as necessary during cooking.) Add onion; stir-fry for 1 minute. Add fresh pea pods (if using) and sweet pepper; stir-fry for 1 to 2 minutes more or until crisp-tender. Remove vegetables from wok.

**3.** Add turkey to hot wok; stir-fry for 2 to 3 minutes or until no longer pink. Push turkey from center of wok.

**4.** Stir sauce. Add sauce to center of wok; cook and stir until thickened and bubbly. Return cooked vegetables to wok. Stir in thawed frozen pea pods (if using). Stir all ingredients together to coat with sauce. Cook and stir about 1 minute more or until heated through. Serve over hot cooked couscous or rice.

Nutrition Facts per serving: **325 calories, 6 g total fat, 37 mg cholesterol, 817 mg sodium, 46 g carbohydrate, 23 g protein.**

½ cup apricot or peach nectar
3 tablespoons soy sauce
2 tablespoons rice vinegar
   or white vinegar
1 tablespoon cornstarch
¼ teaspoon ground red pepper
½ cup dried apricot halves,
   cut in half
1 tablespoon cooking oil
1 small onion, chopped
2 cups fresh pea pods, strings
   removed, or one 6-ounce
   package frozen pea pods,
   thawed
1 small red or green sweet
   pepper, cut into 1-inch
   pieces
12 ounces turkey breast
   tenderloin, cut into
   bite-size strips
   Hot cooked couscous or rice

# Pineapple-Orange Ginger Turkey

*The tangy-sweet flavors of pineapple and orange juice concentrate, plus a generous amount of fresh ginger, complement the turkey in this easy-to-fix Polynesian-style dish.*

**Prep:** 20 minutes  **Chill:** 30 minutes to 1 hour  **Cook:** 10 minutes  **Makes:** 4 servings

1 pound turkey breast tenderloin, cut into bite-size strips

2 tablespoons soy sauce

2 tablespoons dry sherry

½ of a 6-ounce can (⅓ cup) frozen orange juice concentrate, thawed

2 tablespoons soy sauce

1 tablespoon water

2 teaspoons cornstarch

½ teaspoon sugar

1 tablespoon cooking oil

2 to 3 teaspoons grated fresh ginger

1 medium red or green sweet pepper, cut into bite-size strips

1 8-ounce can pineapple chunks (juice pack), drained

Hot cooked rice

Orange slices (optional)

Fresh rosemary sprigs (optional)

**1.** In a medium bowl stir together turkey, 2 tablespoons soy sauce, and the dry sherry. Cover and chill in the refrigerator for at least 30 minutes or up to 1 hour.

**2.** For sauce, in a small bowl stir together the orange juice concentrate, 2 tablespoons soy sauce, the water, cornstarch, and sugar; set aside.

**3.** In a wok or large skillet heat oil over medium-high heat. (Add more oil as necessary during cooking.) Add ginger; stir-fry for 15 seconds. Add pepper strips; stir-fry for 1 to 2 minutes or until crisp-tender. Remove pepper strips from wok.

**4.** Add half of the turkey mixture to hot wok; stir-fry for 2 to 3 minutes or until no longer pink. Remove turkey from wok. Repeat with the remaining turkey mixture. Return all of the turkey to wok. Push turkey from center of wok.

**5.** Stir sauce. Add sauce to center of wok; cook and stir until thickened and bubbly. Return pepper strips to wok. Add pineapple. Stir all ingredients together to coat with sauce. Cook and stir about 1 minute more or until heated through. Serve with hot rice. If desired, garnish with orange slices and rosemary sprigs.

Nutrition Facts per serving: **352 calories, 6 g total fat, 50 mg cholesterol, 1,077 mg sodium, 46 g carbohydrate, 25 g protein.**

# Thai Turkey

*For a please-anyone version of this saucy dish, use the bottom of the range given for the crushed red pepper. For a spicy version, use the top of the range given.*

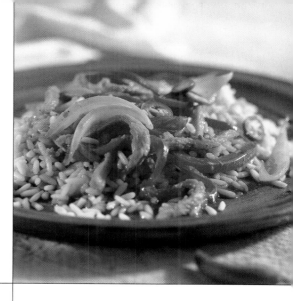

**Start to Finish:** 25 minutes **Makes:** 4 servings

**1.** For sauce, in a small bowl stir together the water, soy sauce, honey, sesame oil, curry powder, cornstarch, and crushed red pepper; set aside.

**2.** Coat an unheated wok or large skillet with nonstick cooking spray. Preheat over medium-high heat. Add the onion wedges and sweet pepper strips; stir-fry until tender. Stir in the turkey strips and garlic. Push mixture from center. Stir sauce. Add sauce to center of wok; cook and stir until thickened and bubbly. Cook and stir for 1 minute more. Serve over hot cooked rice. If desired, garnish with serrano peppers.

Nutrition Facts per serving: 335 calories, 11 g total fat, 81 mg cholesterol, 576 mg sodium, 31 g carbohydrate, 27 g protein.

***Note:*** Because chile peppers, such as serranos, contain volatile oils that can burn your skin and eyes, avoid direct contact with them as much as possible. When working with chile peppers, wear plastic or rubber gloves. If your bare hands do touch the chile peppers, wash your hands well with soap and warm water.

- ⅔ **cup water**
- 2 **tablespoons soy sauce**
- 1 **tablespoon honey**
- 2 **teaspoons toasted sesame oil**
- 2 **teaspoons curry powder**
- 1 **teaspoon cornstarch**
- ⅛ **to ¼ teaspoon crushed red pepper**
- **Nonstick cooking spray**
- 1 **small onion, cut into thin wedges**
- 1 **red sweet pepper, cut into thin strips**
- 12 **ounces cooked turkey, cut into bite-size strips (about 3 cups)**
- ½ **teaspoon bottled minced garlic or 1 clove garlic, minced**
- **Hot cooked rice**
- **Sliced fresh serrano peppers* (optional)**

# soups and stews

When it comes to homey foods, chicken soup is a hands-down favorite. Here you'll find three dozen innovative variations to satisfy your cravings for old-fashioned comfort food.

Moroccan Chicken Stew, page 90

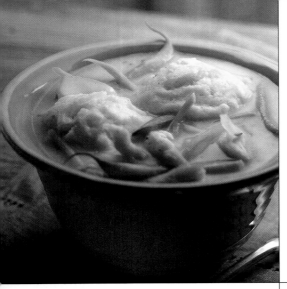

# Chicken 'n' Dumpling Soup

*Cheesy dumplings top this steaming meal in a bowl.*

**Start to Finish:** 30 minutes   **Makes:** 4 servings

12 ounces packaged boneless
  chicken strips for stir-frying

⅛ teaspoon salt

⅛ teaspoon pepper

1 tablespoon olive oil or
  cooking oil

2 tablespoons all-purpose flour

¼ teaspoon dried marjoram,
  crushed

1 14-ounce can chicken broth

1 cup water

1 medium onion, cut into
  wedges

1 cup fresh green beans
  trimmed and halved

1 cup coarsely shredded
  carrots

⅔ cup reduced-fat packaged
  biscuit mix

⅓ cup yellow cornmeal

¼ cup shredded cheddar
  cheese (1 ounce)

½ cup milk

**1.** Season chicken with salt and pepper. In a large saucepan cook and stir chicken in hot oil over medium-high heat about 2 minutes or until chicken is browned. Sprinkle flour and marjoram over chicken. Stir in broth, water, onion, beans, and carrots. Bring to boiling; reduce heat. Cover and simmer for 5 minutes.

**2.** Meanwhile, for dumplings, in a medium bowl stir together biscuit mix, cornmeal, and cheese. Stir in milk just until mixture is moistened. Drop batter onto the hot liquid, making 8 mounds. Return to boiling; reduce heat. Cover and simmer for 10 to 12 minutes or until a wooden toothpick inserted into a dumpling comes out clean. Do not lift cover while simmering.

Nutrition Facts per serving: 345 calories, 11 g total fat, 55 mg cholesterol, 716 mg sodium, 35 g carbohydrate, 25 g protein.

# Chicken Chili with Couscous

*Tomatillos, often referred to as Mexican green tomatoes, add a hint of lemon and apple flavor to this chunky chili.*

**Start to Finish:** 35 minutes  **Makes:** 4 servings

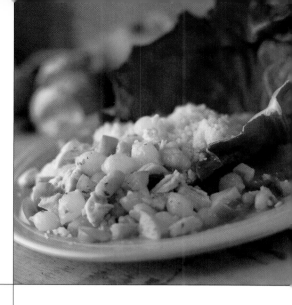

**1.** In a large saucepan cook the garlic and jalapeño pepper in hot oil for 30 seconds. Carefully stir in onions, chicken broth, chili powder, cumin, oregano, salt, white pepper, and red pepper.

**2.** Bring to boiling; reduce heat. Cover and simmer for 20 minutes. Add beans, chicken, and tomatillos; cook and stir until heated through. Serve over couscous.

Nutrition Facts per serving: **309 calories, 7 g total fat, 31 mg cholesterol, 555 mg sodium, 46 g carbohydrate, 22 g protein.**

***Note:*** Because chile peppers, such as jalapeños, contain volatile oils that can burn your skin and eyes, avoid direct contact with them as much as possible. When working with chile peppers, wear plastic or rubber gloves. If your bare hands do touch the chile peppers, wash your hands and nails well with soap and warm water.

3 cloves garlic, minced
1 fresh jalapeño pepper, seeded and finely chopped*
1 tablespoon cooking oil
2 cups frozen small whole onions
1 cup reduced-sodium chicken broth
2 teaspoons chili powder
1 teaspoon ground cumin
1 teaspoon dried oregano, crushed
¼ teaspoon salt
⅛ teaspoon ground white pepper
⅛ teaspoon ground red pepper
1 19-ounce can white kidney beans (cannellini beans), rinsed and drained
1 cup chopped cooked chicken (about 5 ounces)
1 cup chopped fresh tomatillos
Hot cooked couscous or rice

# Chicken Soup with Lentils and Barley

*Serve this mouthwatering soup with crusty bread.*

**Prep:** 20 minutes   **Cook:** 40 minutes   **Makes:** 6 servings

½ cup dry brown lentils
1 cup sliced leeks or chopped onion
½ cup chopped red or green sweet pepper
1 clove garlic, minced
2 tablespoons butter or margarine
5 cups chicken broth
1½ teaspoons snipped fresh basil or ½ teaspoon dried basil, crushed
1 teaspoon snipped fresh oregano or ¼ teaspoon dried oregano, crushed
¾ teaspoon snipped fresh rosemary or ¼ teaspoon dried rosemary, crushed
¼ teaspoon ground black pepper
1½ cups chopped cooked chicken or turkey (about 8 ounces)
1½ cups sliced carrots
½ cup quick-cooking barley
1 16-ounce can tomatoes, cut up

**1.** Rinse the lentils under cold running water. Drain; set aside. In a large saucepan or Dutch oven cook leeks or onion, sweet pepper, and garlic in hot butter until tender.

**2.** Carefully stir in chicken broth, basil, oregano, rosemary, black pepper, and lentils. Bring to boiling; reduce heat. Cover and simmer for 20 minutes.

**3.** Stir in chicken or turkey, carrots, and uncooked barley. Cover and simmer about 20 minutes more or just until carrots are tender. Stir in undrained tomatoes; heat through.

Nutrition Facts per serving: 367 calories, 13 g total fat, 51 mg cholesterol, 1,324 mg sodium, 36 g carbohydrate, 28 g protein.

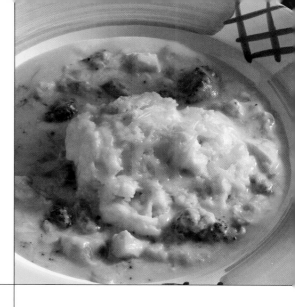

# Chicken-Broccoli Soup With Dumplings

*Stretch a little bit of chicken—1 cup cubed cooked chicken, to be exact—to feed four by making this flavorful soup.*

**Start to Finish:** 25 minutes  **Makes:** 4 or 5 servings

**1.** In a large saucepan stir together chicken, soup, milk, broccoli, carrot, mustard, and basil. Bring to boiling; reduce heat.

**2.** Meanwhile, prepare Dumplings. Drop batter onto the hot soup, making 4 or 5 mounds. Return to boiling; reduce heat. Cover and simmer for 10 to 12 minutes or until a toothpick inserted into centers of dumplings comes out clean. Sprinkle dumplings with cheese.

**Dumplings:** In a small bowl stir together ⅔ cup all-purpose flour and 1 teaspoon baking powder. Add ¼ cup milk and 2 tablespoons cooking oil. Stir just until mixture is moistened.

Nutrition Facts per serving: **493 calories, 26 g total fat, 71 mg cholesterol, 1,445 mg sodium, 38 g carbohydrate, 27 g protein.**

- 1 **cup cubed cooked chicken (about 5 ounces)**
- 2 **10¾-ounce cans condensed cream of chicken soup**
- 2 **cups milk**
- 1½ **cups loose-pack frozen cut broccoli**
- ½ **cup finely shredded carrot**
- 1 **teaspoon Dijon-style mustard**
- ½ **teaspoon dried basil, crushed**
- 1 **recipe Dumplings**
- ½ **cup shredded cheddar cheese (2 ounces)**

# Easy Cheesy Vegetable-Chicken Chowder

*Start with cooked chicken and condensed soup, add vegetables and cheese, and you've got a soup the whole family will love.*

**Start to Finish:** 30 minutes  **Makes:** 4 servings

1 cup small broccoli flowerets
1 cup loose-pack frozen whole
    kernel corn
½ cup water
¼ cup chopped onion
1½ teaspoons snipped fresh
    thyme or ½ teaspoon dried
    thyme, crushed
2 cups milk
1½ cups chopped cooked
    chicken or turkey
    (about 8 ounces)
1 10¾-ounce can condensed
    cream of potato soup
1 cup shredded cheddar
    cheese (4 ounces)
    Dash pepper

**1.** In a large saucepan combine broccoli, corn, water, onion, and thyme. Bring to boiling; reduce heat. Cover and simmer for 8 to 10 minutes or until vegetables are tender. Do not drain.

**2.** Stir milk, chicken or turkey, potato soup, ¾ cup of the cheddar cheese, and the pepper into vegetable mixture. Cook and stir over medium heat until cheese melts and mixture is heated through. Sprinkle with the remaining cheddar cheese.

Nutrition Facts per serving: **368 calories, 18 g total fat, 94 mg cholesterol, 901 mg sodium, 23 g carbohydrate, 30 g protein.**

# Easy Mulligatawny Soup

*The classic version of this curry-flavored soup hails from India.*

**Prep:** 20 minutes  **Cook:** 20 minutes  **Makes:** 4 servings

**1.** In a large saucepan combine chicken broth, water, apple, carrot, undrained tomatoes, celery, uncooked rice, onion, raisins, cilantro or parsley, curry powder, lemon juice, pepper, and mace or nutmeg. Bring to boiling; reduce heat. Cover and simmer about 20 minutes or until rice is tender. Stir in chopped cooked chicken; heat through.

Nutrition Facts per serving: **259 calories, 6 g total fat, 51 mg cholesterol, 665 mg sodium, 30 g carbohydrate, 22 g protein.**

2½ **cups chicken broth**
 1 **cup water**
 1 **cup chopped apple**
 1 **cup chopped carrot**
 1 **7½-ounce can tomatoes, cut up**
 ½ **cup chopped celery**
 ⅓ **cup long grain rice**
 ¼ **cup chopped onion**
 ¼ **cup raisins**
 1 **tablespoon snipped fresh cilantro or parsley**
 1 to 1½ **teaspoons curry powder**
 1 **teaspoon lemon juice**
 ¼ **teaspoon coarsely ground black pepper**
 ⅛ **teaspoon ground mace or nutmeg**
1½ **cups chopped cooked chicken (about 8 ounces)**

# Asian Chicken-Noodle Soup

*For an extra-special touch, substitute strips of wonton skins for the egg noodles. Use four wonton skins cut into thin strips.*

**Start to Finish:** 25 minutes  **Makes:** 3 or 4 servings

2 14-ounce cans chicken
broth

1 cup water

1 medium red sweet pepper,
cut into ¾-inch pieces

½ cup chopped carrot

½ cup fine egg noodles

⅓ cup thinly sliced green onion

1 tablespoon soy sauce

1 teaspoon grated fresh
ginger

⅛ teaspoon crushed
red pepper

1 cup chopped cooked
chicken or turkey
(about 5 ounces)

1 cup fresh pea pods, halved
crosswise, or ½ of a
6-ounce package frozen
pea pods, thawed and
halved crosswise

**1.** In a large saucepan or Dutch oven combine chicken broth, water, sweet pepper, carrot, egg noodles, green onion, soy sauce, ginger, and crushed red pepper. Bring to boiling; reduce heat. Cover and simmer for 4 to 6 minutes or until vegetables are crisp-tender and noodles are tender.

**2.** Stir in chicken or turkey and pea pods. Simmer, uncovered, for 1 to 2 minutes more or until pea pods are crisp-tender.

Nutrition Facts per serving: **217 calories, 6 g total fat, 53 mg cholesterol, 1,343 mg sodium, 15 g carbohydrate, 24 g protein.**

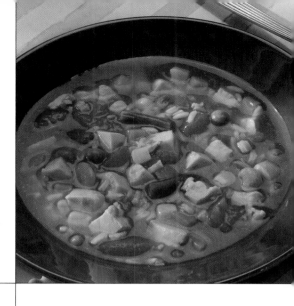

# Quick-to-Fix Turkey And Rice Soup

*Remember this no-fuss recipe the next time you have leftover cooked turkey or chicken.*

**Start to Finish:** 25 minutes **Makes:** 6 servings

**1.** In a large saucepan or Dutch oven combine chicken broth, water, rosemary, and pepper. Bring to boiling.

**2.** Stir in mixed vegetables and uncooked rice. Return to boiling; reduce heat. Cover and simmer for 10 to 15 minutes or until vegetables and rice are tender. Stir in turkey or chicken and undrained tomatoes; heat through.

Nutrition Facts per serving: 231 calories, 6 g total fat, 49 mg cholesterol, 681 mg sodium, 23 g carbohydrate, 21 g protein.

- 4 cups chicken broth
- 1 cup water
- 1 teaspoon snipped fresh rosemary or ¼ teaspoon dried rosemary, crushed
- ¼ teaspoon pepper
- 1 10-ounce package frozen mixed vegetables (2 cups)
- 1 cup quick-cooking rice
- 2 cups chopped cooked turkey or chicken (about 10 ounces)
- 1 14½-ounce can tomatoes, cut up

# Chicken, Oyster, and Sausage Gumbo

*A roux, made by slowly stirring fat and flour over heat until the mixture becomes a nutty brown, is the cornerstone of the traditional Louisiana-style stew known as gumbo.*

**Prep:** 30 minutes   **Cook:** 65 minutes   **Makes:** 6 servings

⅓ cup all-purpose flour

⅓ cup cooking oil

1 large onion, chopped

½ cup chopped green
   sweet pepper

4 cloves garlic, minced

½ teaspoon ground
   black pepper

¼ teaspoon ground red pepper

4 cups hot water

2 pounds chicken thighs,
   skinned, boned, and cut
   into bite-size pieces

12 ounces cooked andouille
   sausage links or cooked
   smoked sausage links, cut
   into ½-inch-thick slices
   and quartered

1 pint shucked oysters,
   drained

   Hot cooked rice

   Filé powder (optional)

   Snipped fresh basil
   (optional)

**1.** In a heavy, 4-quart Dutch oven stir together flour and oil until smooth. Cook and stir over medium-high heat for 5 minutes. Reduce heat to medium. Cook, stirring constantly, about 15 minutes more or until dark reddish brown.

**2.** Stir in onion, sweet pepper, garlic, black pepper, and red pepper. Cook and stir over medium heat for 3 to 5 minutes or until vegetables are tender.

**3.** Gradually stir hot water into the vegetable mixture. Stir in chicken. Bring to boiling; reduce heat. Cover and simmer for 40 minutes.

**4.** Stir in sausage. Cover and simmer about 20 minutes more or until chicken is tender. Remove from heat. Skim off fat.

**5.** Stir oysters into gumbo. Cover and simmer for 5 to 10 minutes or until edges of oysters curl and gumbo mixture is heated through.

**6.** Serve over hot cooked rice. If desired, serve ¼ to ½ teaspoon filé powder to the side of each serving to stir into gumbo. If desired, sprinkle with basil.

Nutrition Facts per serving: 572 calories, 36 g total fat, 116 mg cholesterol, 644 mg sodium, 35 g carbohydrate, 27 g protein.

# Chicken Stew With Tortellini

*Next time you roast, grill, or broil chicken, cook some extra so you'll have enough left over to make this easy-to-prepare stew.*

**Start to Finish:** 35 minutes  **Makes:** 6 servings

**1.** In a Dutch oven bring water and chicken broth to boiling. Add greens, squash, sweet pepper, tortellini, onion, carrot, rosemary, seasoning blend, and black pepper.

**2.** Return to boiling; reduce heat. Cover and simmer about 15 minutes or until pasta and vegetables are nearly tender.

**3.** Stir in chicken. Cover and cook about 5 minutes more or until pasta and vegetables are tender. Stir fresh basil into soup.

Nutrition Facts per serving: 234 calories, 6 g total fat, 45 mg cholesterol, 530 mg sodium, 22 g carbohydrate, 22 g protein.

- 2 cups water
- 1 14-ounce can reduced-sodium chicken broth
- 6 cups torn fresh beet greens, turnip greens, or spinach
- 1 medium yellow summer squash, halved lengthwise and cut into ½-inch-thick slices
- 1 green sweet pepper, coarsely chopped
- 1 cup dried cheese-filled tortellini
- 1 medium onion, cut into thin wedges
- 1 medium carrot, sliced
- 1½ teaspoons snipped fresh rosemary
- ½ teaspoon salt-free seasoning blend
- ¼ teaspoon ground black pepper
- 2 cups chopped cooked chicken (about 10 ounces)
- 1 tablespoon snipped fresh basil

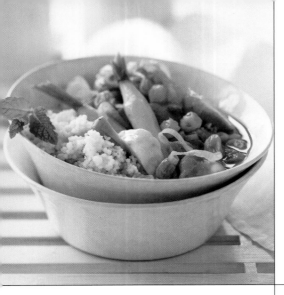

# Moroccan Chicken Stew

*This chicken and vegetable stew gets its full-bodied flavor from aromatic cumin, paprika, cinnamon, and saffron.*

**Start to Finish:** 30 minutes   **Makes:** 4 servings

1 cup quick-cooking couscous

12 ounces skinless, boneless chicken thighs or breasts, cut into 1-inch pieces

⅓ cup sliced shallots

3 cloves garlic, minced

1 tablespoon olive oil

½ teaspoon salt

½ teaspoon paprika

½ teaspoon ground cumin

¼ teaspoon ground cinnamon

¼ teaspoon ground saffron or ground turmeric

⅛ teaspoon ground red pepper

6 ounces baby pattypan squash or 1½ cups sliced zucchini

1 cup tiny whole carrots with tops or packaged peeled baby carrots

1 cup reduced-sodium chicken broth

¼ cup golden or dark raisins
    Fresh mint sprigs (optional)

**1.** Cook couscous according to package directions, except omit oil and salt; keep warm.

**2.** Meanwhile, in a large nonstick skillet cook chicken, shallots, and garlic in hot oil over medium-high heat for 2 minutes, stirring occasionally.

**3.** In a small bowl combine salt, paprika, cumin, cinnamon, saffron or turmeric, and ground red pepper; sprinkle evenly over mixture in skillet. Cook and stir about 2 minutes more or until chicken is no longer pink.

**4.** Cut any large pieces of squash and carrots in half; add to skillet along with broth and raisins. Bring to boiling; reduce heat. Cover and simmer for 6 to 8 minutes or until vegetables are crisp-tender. Serve stew over couscous. If desired, garnish with fresh mint sprigs.

Nutrition Facts per serving: 363 calories, 7 g total fat, 45 mg cholesterol, 496 mg sodium, 51 g carbohydrate, 24 g protein.

# Chicken and Shrimp Tortilla Soup

*Crispy homemade bits of tortilla add crunch to this cumin-flavored Mexican-style soup.*

**Start to Finish:** 30 minutes  **Makes:** 6 servings

**1.** Thaw shrimp, if frozen. Rinse shrimp; pat dry. Set aside.

**2.** In a large saucepan cook the onion and cumin seeds in hot oil about 5 minutes or until onion is tender. Carefully add chicken broth, undrained tomatoes, cilantro, and lime juice.

**3.** Bring to boiling; reduce heat. Cover and simmer for 8 minutes. Stir in shrimp and chicken. Cook about 3 minutes more or until shrimp turn opaque, stirring occasionally. Top with Crisp Tortilla Shreds.

***Crisp Tortilla Shreds:*** Brush four 5½-inch corn tortillas with 1 tablespoon cooking oil. In a small bowl combine ½ teaspoon salt and ⅛ teaspoon pepper; sprinkle mixture over tortillas. Cut tortillas into thin shreds. Arrange in a single layer on a baking sheet. Bake in a 350° oven about 8 minutes or until crisp.

Nutrition Facts per serving: **160 calories, 5 g total fat, 80 mg cholesterol, 794 mg sodium, 8 g carbohydrate, 21 g protein.**

- **6** ounces peeled and deveined fresh or frozen medium shrimp
- **1** large onion, chopped
- **1** teaspoon cumin seeds
- **1** tablespoon cooking oil
- **4½** cups reduced-sodium chicken broth
- **1** 14½-ounce can Mexican-style stewed tomatoes
- **3** tablespoons snipped fresh cilantro
- **2** tablespoons lime juice
- **1⅔** cups shredded cooked chicken breast (about 8 ounces)
- **1** recipe Crisp Tortilla Shreds

# Chicken Stew with Gremolata

*Pass the gremolata—a medley of fresh parsley, garlic, and lemon peel—and let diners sprinkle it on each serving of this chicken-and-vegetable stew.*

**Prep:** 25 minutes **Cook:** 30 minutes **Makes:** 4 servings

Nonstick cooking spray

1¼ to 1½ pounds meaty chicken pieces (breasts, thighs, and drumsticks), skinned

1 pound tiny new potatoes

2 cups packaged peeled baby carrots

1 cup frozen small whole onions

2 stalks celery, cut into 1-inch pieces

1 cup reduced-sodium chicken broth

½ cup dry white wine or reduced-sodium chicken broth

½ teaspoon dried oregano, crushed

¼ teaspoon dried thyme, crushed

1 medium zucchini, halved lengthwise and cut into ½-inch-thick pieces

½ cup evaporated fat-free milk

3 tablespoons all-purpose flour

1 recipe Gremolata

**1.** Coat an unheated very large saucepan or 4½-quart Dutch oven with nonstick cooking spray. Preheat pan over medium heat. Cook chicken in hot pan about 10 minutes or until lightly browned, turning to brown evenly. If necessary, drain off fat.

**2.** Cut any large potatoes in half. Add potatoes, carrots, onions, celery, the 1 cup broth, the wine or additional broth, oregano, and thyme. Bring to boiling; reduce heat. Cover and simmer for 20 minutes. Add zucchini; cook about 5 minutes more or until chicken and vegetables are tender. Remove chicken pieces; keep warm.

**3.** Stir together milk and flour. Stir into hot mixture. Cook and stir until thickened and bubbly. Cook and stir for 1 minute more. Return chicken to mixture. Heat through. Serve with Gremolata.

***Gremolata:*** In a small bowl combine 3 tablespoons snipped fresh parsley; 1 large clove garlic, minced; and 1 teaspoon finely shredded lemon peel. Toss to mix.

Nutrition Facts per serving: **348 calories, 5 g total fat, 59 mg cholesterol, 248 mg sodium, 45 g carbohydrate, 27 g protein.**

# Mexican Chicken-Tortilla Soup

*Cilantro, a parsleylike fresh herb, gives a distinctive flavor to this soup and many other Mexican dishes.*

**Prep:** 30 minutes  **Cook:** 35 minutes  **Makes:** 4 servings

**1.** In a large saucepan or Dutch oven combine chicken and chicken broth. Bring to boiling; reduce heat. Cover and simmer about 15 minutes or until chicken is tender and no longer pink. Remove chicken. Set aside to cool. Skin, bone, and shred chicken. Set chicken aside. Discard skin and bones. Strain broth through a large sieve or colander lined with two layers of 100%-cotton cheesecloth. Skim fat from broth; set broth aside.

**2.** In the same saucepan cook onion, garlic, and cumin in the 1 tablespoon hot oil until onion is tender. Stir in strained broth, undrained tomatoes, tomato sauce, chili peppers, cilantro or parsley, and oregano. Bring to boiling; reduce heat. Cover and simmer for 20 minutes. Stir in shredded chicken. Heat through.

**3.** Meanwhile, cut tortillas in half, then cut crosswise into ½-inch-wide strips. In a heavy, medium skillet heat ¼ inch cooking oil. Cook tortilla strips in hot oil, half at a time, about 1 minute or until crisp and lightly browned. Remove with a slotted spoon; drain on paper towels.

**4.** Divide fried tortilla strips among 4 soup bowls. Ladle soup over tortilla strips. Sprinkle with shredded cheese. Serve soup immediately.

**Nutrition Facts per serving: 496 calories, 24 g total fat, 85 mg cholesterol, 1,658 mg sodium, 33 g carbohydrate, 38 g protein.**

1½ pounds whole chicken breasts
3½ cups chicken broth
½ cup chopped onion
1 clove garlic, minced
½ teaspoon ground cumin
1 tablespoon cooking oil
1 14½-ounce can tomatoes, cut up
1 8-ounce can tomato sauce
1 4-ounce can whole green chili peppers, rinsed, seeded, and cut into thin, bite-size strips
¼ cup snipped fresh cilantro or parsley
1 tablespoon snipped fresh oregano or 1 teaspoon dried oregano, crushed
6 6-inch corn tortillas
Cooking oil
1 cup shredded cheddar or Monterey Jack cheese (4 ounces)

# Cajun Jambalaya

*Chicken andouille sausage or smoked turkey sausage gives the desired spicy flavor to this hearty stew, with less fat than traditional pork andouille sausage.*

**Prep:** 30 minutes  **Cook:** 15 minutes  **Makes:** 4 servings

8 ounces fresh or frozen
   medium shrimp, peeled
   and deveined
1 large onion, chopped
1 stalk celery, thinly sliced
4 cloves garlic, minced
2 teaspoons olive oil
2 tablespoons all-purpose flour
1 14½-ounce can low-sodium
   stewed tomatoes
1 cup reduced-sodium
   chicken broth
8 ounces cooked chicken
   andouille sausage links or
   cooked smoked turkey
   sausage links, halved
   lengthwise and cut into
   ½-inch-thick slices
1 medium yellow or green
   sweet pepper, cut into
   ½-inch pieces
1 teaspoon dried basil,
   crushed
1 teaspoon dried thyme,
   crushed
¾ to 1 teaspoon bottled
   hot pepper sauce
1 bay leaf
   Hot cooked rice
   Fresh parsley sprigs
   (optional)

**1.** Thaw shrimp, if frozen. Rinse shrimp; pat dry. Set aside.

**2.** In a large saucepan cook onion, celery, and garlic in hot oil for 10 minutes, stirring occasionally. Add flour; cook 1 minute, stirring constantly. Stir in undrained tomatoes and broth. Add sausage, sweet pepper, basil, thyme, hot pepper sauce, and bay leaf. Bring to boiling; reduce heat. Simmer, uncovered, for 10 minutes. Stir in shrimp. Simmer, uncovered, about 5 minutes more or until shrimp turn opaque. Discard bay leaf. Ladle into shallow bowls; top each serving with a scoop of rice. If desired, garnish with parsley.

Nutrition Facts per serving: 350 calories, 11 g total fat, 117 mg cholesterol, 849 mg sodium, 40 g carbohydrate, 23 g protein.

# Catalan Chicken Chowder

*A sprinkling of toasted almonds adds a delightful crunch to each serving of this flavor-packed soup.*

**Start to Finish:** 30 minutes  **Makes:** 4 servings

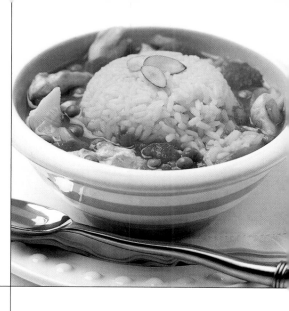

**1.** Prepare rice mix according to package directions; set aside and keep warm. Meanwhile, in a large saucepan cook chicken, onion, and garlic in hot oil about 5 minutes or until chicken is no longer pink.

**2.** Add undrained tomatoes, broth, and artichoke hearts to chicken mixture. Bring to boiling; reduce heat. Simmer, uncovered, for 10 minutes, stirring occasionally. Add peas and roasted red sweet peppers. Cook for 3 to 4 minutes more or until heated through.

**3.** To serve, ladle chowder into 4 soup bowls. Spoon a mound of the cooked rice into the center of each serving. Sprinkle with toasted slivered almonds.

Nutrition Facts per serving: 321 calories, 10 g total fat, 30 mg cholesterol, 1,099 mg sodium, 42 g carbohydrate, 19 g protein.

- 1 5-ounce package saffron-flavored yellow rice mix
- 8 ounces skinless, boneless chicken breasts, cut into bite-size pieces
- ½ cup chopped onion
- 1 clove garlic, minced
- 2 teaspoons olive oil
- 1 14½-ounce can diced tomatoes
- 1 14-ounce can reduced-sodium chicken broth
- ½ of a 14-ounce can artichoke hearts, drained and quartered
- ½ cup loose-pack frozen baby sweet peas
- ½ of a 7-ounce jar roasted red sweet peppers, drained and cut into strips
- 2 tablespoons toasted slivered almonds

# Chipotle Pepper Soup

*This chicken-and-tomato-based soup gets its smoky flavor from chipotle peppers, which are smoked jalapeños.*

**Start to Finish:** 35 minutes  **Makes:** 3 servings

1 large onion, finely chopped

4 cloves garlic, minced

1 tablespoon olive oil or cooking oil

12 ounces skinless, boneless chicken breasts, cut into bite-size pieces

1 14-ounce can chicken broth

2 teaspoons chopped canned chipotle peppers in adobo sauce

½ teaspoon sugar

¼ teaspoon salt

2 cups chopped tomatoes or one 14½-ounce can low-sodium diced tomatoes

¼ cup snipped fresh cilantro

**1.** In a Dutch oven cook the onion and garlic in hot oil about 4 minutes or until tender. Add the chicken; cook for 2 minutes. Stir in the chicken broth, chipotle peppers in adobo sauce, sugar, and salt.

**2.** Bring to boiling; reduce heat. Simmer, uncovered, for 15 minutes. Remove from heat. Stir in the chopped tomatoes or undrained diced tomatoes and cilantro.

Nutrition Facts per serving: 246 calories, 9 g total fat, 60 mg cholesterol, 735 mg sodium, 14 g carbohydrate, 26 g protein.

# Chicken and Salsa Soup

*Vary the heat in this Mexican-inspired soup by using mild, medium, or hot salsa to suit your taste.*

**Start to Finish:** 30 minutes  **Makes:** 4 servings

**1.** In a 3-quart saucepan combine the water, broth, chicken, and chili powder. Bring to boiling; reduce heat. Cover and simmer for 8 minutes. Add corn. Simmer, uncovered, for 5 minutes more. Stir in salsa; heat through.

**2.** To serve, ladle into 4 soup bowls. Top with tortilla chips and sprinkle with cheese.

Nutrition Facts per serving: **319 calories, 9 g total fat, 42 mg cholesterol, 989 mg sodium, 32 g carbohydrate, 20 g protein.**

1¾ cups water

1 14-ounce can reduced-sodium chicken broth

8 ounces skinless, boneless chicken, cut into bite-size pieces

1 to 2 teaspoons chili powder

1 11-ounce can whole kernel corn with sweet peppers, drained

1 cup chunky garden-style salsa

3 cups broken baked tortilla chips

2 ounces Monterey Jack cheese with jalapeño peppers, shredded (½ cup)

# Chicken-Pasta Soup

*Skinning the chicken before cooking reduces the fat in this chock-full-of-chicken soup.*

**Prep:** 30 minutes  **Cook:** 35 minutes  **Makes:** 4 servings

1 pound chicken thighs,
    skinned
2 14-ounce cans
    chicken broth
½ cup water
2 stalks celery
1 onion, quartered
¼ to ½ teaspoon pepper
1 bay leaf
1½ cups bias-sliced carrots
½ cup dried bow-tie pasta
    or medium noodles
1 teaspoon dried basil,
    crushed

**1.** Place chicken in a Dutch oven; add broth and water. Cut tops off celery stalks; slice stalks and set aside. Add celery tops, onion, pepper, and bay leaf to Dutch oven. Bring to boiling; reduce heat. Cover and simmer about 25 minutes or until chicken is tender and no longer pink.

**2.** Remove chicken from Dutch oven, reserving broth. Strain broth, discarding mixture in sieve. Cool chicken slightly. Remove meat from bones and discard bones; chop meat and set aside. Skim fat from broth. Return broth to Dutch oven. Add sliced celery, carrots, pasta, and basil to broth. Bring to boiling; reduce heat. Simmer, uncovered, for 10 to 15 minutes or until vegetables and pasta are tender. Stir in chicken; heat through.

Nutrition Facts per serving: **226 calories, 9 g total fat, 59 mg cholesterol, 770 mg sodium, 14 g carbohydrate, 21 g protein.**

# Mexican Chicken Posole

*This quick-fixin' version of the hearty Mexican stew known as posole features chicken rather than the traditional pork.*

**Start to Finish:** 20 minutes  **Makes:** 4 servings

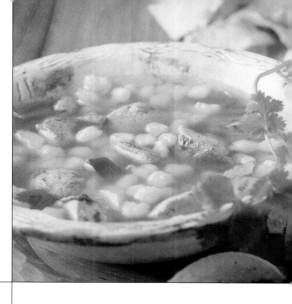

**1.** Sprinkle chicken pieces with Mexican seasoning; toss to coat evenly. In a large saucepan cook and stir seasoned chicken in hot oil over medium-high heat for 3 minutes. Add sweet pepper; cook and stir about 1 minute more or until chicken is no longer pink.

**2.** Carefully add broth and hominy or black-eyed peas. Bring to boiling; reduce heat. Cover and simmer about 3 minutes or until heated through. If desired, serve with salsa, sour cream, lime wedges, and/or broken tortilla chips. If desired, garnish with cilantro sprigs.

Nutrition Facts per serving: 192 calories, 8 g total fat, 41 mg cholesterol, 905 mg sodium, 14 g carbohydrate, 15 g protein.

12 ounces skinless, boneless chicken thighs or breasts, cut into 1-inch pieces

3 to 4 teaspoons Mexican seasoning or chili powder

2 teaspoons cooking oil or olive oil

1 red or yellow sweet pepper, cut into bite-size pieces

2 14-ounce cans reduced-sodium or regular chicken broth

1 15-ounce can hominy or black-eyed peas, rinsed and drained

Salsa, light dairy sour cream, lime wedges, and/or broken tortilla chips (optional)

Fresh cilantro sprigs (optional)

# Thai Chicken-Coconut Soup

*Look for fish sauce in the Asian foods section of your supermarket or at an Asian foods market.*

**Start to Finish:** 30 minutes  **Makes:** 4 servings

1 pound skinless, boneless chicken breasts or skinless, boneless chicken thighs, cut into bite-size strips

4 cups chicken broth

2 tablespoons fish sauce (optional)

2 tablespoons lemon juice or lime juice

1 tablespoon grated fresh ginger

1 teaspoon ground cumin

1½ cups broccoli flowerets

1 cup thin red, yellow, or green sweet pepper strips

1 fresh jalapeño pepper, seeded and chopped*

3 green onions, sliced into ½-inch pieces

2 tablespoons snipped fresh cilantro

1 14-ounce can unsweetened coconut milk

**1.** In a Dutch oven stir together chicken, broth, fish sauce (if using), lemon or lime juice, ginger, and cumin.

**2.** Bring to boiling; reduce heat. Cover and simmer for 10 minutes. Stir in broccoli, sweet pepper, jalapeño pepper, green onions, and cilantro. Cover and simmer about 10 minutes more or until vegetables are tender. Stir in coconut milk; heat through, but do not boil.

Nutrition Facts per serving: 461 calories, 33 g total fat, 60 mg cholesterol, 857 mg sodium, 9 g carbohydrate, 31 g protein.

***Note:*** Because chile peppers, such as jalapeños, contain volatile oils that can burn your skin and eyes, avoid direct contact with them as much as possible. When working with chile peppers, wear plastic or rubber gloves. If your bare hands do touch the chile peppers, wash your hands and nails well with soap and warm water.

# Chunky Chicken Chili

*Gutsy in flavor, but low in fat, this chicken and vegetable meal-in-a-bowl is sure to please.*

**Start to Finish:** 40 minutes  **Makes:** 6 servings

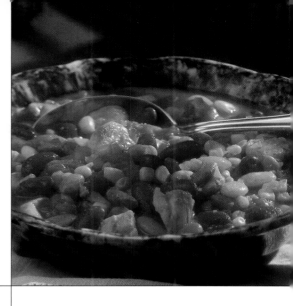

**1.** In a large saucepan heat ½ teaspoon of the oil over high heat. Add half of the chicken cubes and cook until browned, turning to brown evenly. Remove chicken. Repeat with remaining oil and remaining chicken.

**2.** Add onion to saucepan; cover and cook over medium heat about 5 minutes or until tender. Stir in garlic, chili powder, cumin, and cinnamon; cook for 30 seconds. Add tomatoes; bring to boil. Add beans, broth, and succotash. Bring to boiling; reduce heat. Simmer, uncovered, for 10 minutes. Add chicken; simmer for 5 minutes more.

Nutrition Facts per serving: 263 calories, 4 g total fat, 44 mg cholesterol, 736 mg sodium, 30 g carbohydrate, 27 g protein.

- 1 teaspoon cooking oil
- 1 pound skinless, boneless chicken breasts or turkey breast, cut into 1-inch cubes
- 1 cup chopped onion
- 1 tablespoon bottled minced garlic
- 2 teaspoons chili powder
- ½ teaspoon ground cumin
- ⅛ teaspoon ground cinnamon
- 1 14½- or 16-ounce can tomatoes, chopped
- 1 15-ounce can pinto beans, rinsed and drained
- 1 15-ounce can red kidney beans, rinsed and drained
- 1 14-ounce can chicken broth
- 1 10-ounce package frozen succotash

# Herbed Cream of Chicken Soup

*Basil, thyme, bay leaf, and whole black peppercorns season this rich soup to perfection.*

**Prep:** 20 minutes  **Cook:** 25 minutes  **Makes:** 4 to 6 servings

12 ounces skinless, boneless chicken breasts or skinless, boneless chicken thighs
5 cups chicken broth
1 bay leaf
¼ teaspoon whole black peppercorns
1½ cups carrots cut into thin, bite-size strips
¾ cup chopped onion
¾ cup sliced celery
1 teaspoon dried basil, crushed
1 teaspoon dried thyme, crushed
¼ teaspoon salt
½ cup long grain rice
1 cup half-and-half or light cream
1 tablespoon all-purpose flour
1 egg yolk

**1.** In a Dutch oven combine chicken, broth, bay leaf, and peppercorns. Bring to boiling; reduce heat. Simmer for 10 to 15 minutes or until chicken is tender and no longer pink. Remove chicken and cool. Strain broth through a double thickness of 100%-cotton cheesecloth; discard bay leaf and peppercorns. Return broth to Dutch oven. Skim fat from broth. Add carrots, onion, celery, basil, thyme, and salt to Dutch oven. Bring to boiling; stir in uncooked rice. Reduce heat. Cover and simmer about 20 minutes or until rice is tender.

**2.** Meanwhile, cut cooked chicken into thin strips. In a small bowl whisk together half-and-half or light cream, flour, and egg yolk. Add egg yolk mixture to soup. Stir in the chicken strips. Cook and stir until soup mixture thickens slightly and comes to a boil.

Nutrition Facts per serving: **468 calories, 24 g total fat, 165 mg cholesterol, 1,237 mg sodium, 34 g carbohydrate, 28 g protein.**

# Hearty Chicken and Noodles

*A bevy of simple ingredients turns into real comfort food in this satisfying chicken and vegetable stew.*

**Prep:** 20 minutes **Cook:** 70 minutes **Makes:** 6 servings

**1.** In a 4½-quart Dutch oven combine chicken, water, celery leaves, parsley, bay leaf, thyme, salt, and pepper. Bring to boiling; reduce heat. Cover and simmer for 30 minutes.

**2.** Add the onion, carrots, and sliced celery. Cover and simmer about 30 minutes more or until chicken is tender and no longer pink. Remove from heat. Remove chicken; cool slightly. Discard the bay leaf. Remove meat from bones; discard bones. Chop chicken and set aside.

**3.** Heat vegetable mixture to boiling. Add noodles; cook for 5 minutes. Stir in 1½ cups of the milk and the peas.

**4.** In a screw-top jar combine remaining milk and the flour. Cover and shake until smooth. Stir into noodle mixture. Cook and stir until thickened and bubbly. Stir in chicken. Cook for 1 to 2 minutes more or until heated through.

Nutrition Facts per serving: 321 calories, 8 g total fat, 83 mg cholesterol, 535 mg sodium, 38 g carbohydrate, 24 g protein.

3 chicken legs (drumstick-thigh piece) (about
   2 pounds total), skinned
4 cups water
½ cup chopped celery leaves
2 tablespoons snipped
   fresh parsley
1 bay leaf
1 teaspoon dried thyme,
   crushed
1 teaspoon salt
¼ teaspoon pepper
1½ cups chopped onion
2 cups sliced carrots
1 cup sliced celery
3 cups dried wide noodles
2 cups milk
1 cup loose-pack frozen peas
2 tablespoons all-purpose flour

# Chicken and Vegetable Stew

*If fresh green beans aren't available, use frozen cut green beans.*

**Prep:** 20 minutes  **Cook:** 40 minutes  **Makes:** 4 servings

8 small chicken thighs (about
    2 pounds total), skinned
2 tablespoons cooking oil
2 cups water
8 small new potatoes, halved
4 medium carrots, sliced into
    1-inch pieces
2 stalks celery, bias-sliced
    into ¾-inch pieces
1 cup fresh green beans cut
    into 1½-inch pieces, or
    frozen cut green beans
1 small onion, chopped
2 tablespoons tomato paste
1 bay leaf
¾ teaspoon salt
½ teaspoon dried rosemary,
    crushed
1 medium zucchini, quartered
    lengthwise and cut into
    ½-inch-thick slices
    (1¼ cups)
¼ cup cold water
2 tablespoons all-purpose flour
    Snipped fresh parsley
    (optional)

**1.** In a 4½-quart Dutch oven cook chicken in hot oil over medium heat for 10 to 15 minutes or until chicken is lightly browned, turning to brown evenly. Drain off fat.

**2.** Add the 2 cups water, the potatoes, carrots, celery, fresh green beans (if using), onion, tomato paste, bay leaf, salt, and rosemary. Bring to boiling; reduce heat. Cover and simmer for 25 minutes.

**3.** Add zucchini and frozen green beans (if using). Cover and cook for 10 to 15 minutes more or until chicken is tender and no longer pink. Discard bay leaf.

**4.** Combine the ¼ cup cold water and the flour. Add to chicken mixture. Cook and stir until thickened and bubbly. Cook and stir for 1 minute more. If desired, sprinkle with parsley.

Nutrition Facts per serving: 424 calories, 15 g total fat, 93 mg cholesterol, 581 mg sodium, 43 g carbohydrate, 31 g protein.

# Cincinnati-Style Chicken Chili

*Seasoned with a little cinnamon and served over pasta, this distinctive chili is sure to please the whole family.*

**Prep:** 20 minutes **Cook:** 55 minutes **Makes:** 4 servings

**1.** In a 4½-quart Dutch oven cook ground chicken, onion, and garlic over medium heat for 5 to 7 minutes or until chicken is browned. Drain off fat, if necessary.

**2.** Add chili powder, paprika, cumin, salt, cinnamon, cloves, red pepper, and bay leaf. Cook and stir over medium heat for 3 minutes more. Stir in undrained stewed tomatoes, tomato sauce, water, red wine vinegar, and molasses. Bring to boiling; reduce heat. Cover; simmer for 45 minutes, stirring occasionally.

**3.** Uncover and simmer to desired consistency. Discard bay leaf. In a medium saucepan heat undrained kidney beans; drain. To serve, spoon chicken mixture and beans over hot spaghetti.

Nutrition Facts per serving: 402 calories, 8 g total fat, 54 mg cholesterol, 1,223 mg sodium, 61 g carbohydrate, 30 g protein.

- 1 **pound uncooked ground chicken**
- 1 **large onion, chopped**
- 1 **clove garlic, minced**
- 3 **tablespoons chili powder**
- 2 **teaspoons paprika**
- 1 **teaspoon ground cumin**
- ½ **teaspoon salt**
- ½ **teaspoon ground cinnamon**
- ⅛ **teaspoon ground cloves**
- ⅛ **teaspoon ground red pepper**
- 1 **bay leaf**
- 1 **14½-ounce can stewed tomatoes**
- 1 **8-ounce can tomato sauce**
- ½ **cup water**
- 1 **tablespoon red wine vinegar**
- 1 **tablespoon molasses**
- 1 **15½-ounce can kidney beans**
  **Hot cooked spaghetti**

# Spicy Chicken with Beans

*Plan on four servings if you're feeding big eaters or six servings for those with lighter appetites.*

**Prep:** 20 minutes   **Cook:** 25 minutes   **Makes:** 4 to 6 servings

1 pound uncooked
  ground chicken
1 large onion, chopped
2 cloves garlic, minced
1 tablespoon cooking oil
1 teaspoon ground cumin
½ teaspoon salt
½ teaspoon ground
  black pepper
1 28-ounce can tomatoes,
  cut up
1 15-ounce can tomato sauce
4 pickled jalapeño peppers,
  seeded and chopped*
  (optional)
1 15-ounce can black beans,
  rinsed and drained
1 15-ounce can Great
  Northern beans, rinsed
  and drained
¼ cup dairy sour cream or
  shredded cheddar cheese
  Sliced green onion
  (optional)

**1.** In a large saucepan cook chicken, onion, and garlic in hot oil over medium heat for 8 to 10 minutes or until chicken is browned and onion is tender. Drain off fat.

**2.** Add cumin, salt, and black pepper; cook and stir for 1 minute more. Stir in undrained tomatoes, tomato sauce, and, if desired, jalapeño peppers. Bring to boiling; reduce heat. Cover and simmer for 20 minutes, stirring occasionally. Stir in black beans and Great Northern beans; heat through. Serve topped with sour cream or cheese and, if desired, sliced green onion.

Nutrition Facts per serving: 438 calories, 13 g total fat, 60 mg cholesterol, 1,251 mg sodium, 54 g carbohydrate, 34 g protein.

***Note:*** Because chile peppers, such as jalapeños, contain volatile oils that can burn your skin and eyes, avoid direct contact with them as much as possible. When working with chile peppers, wear plastic or rubber gloves. If your bare hands do touch the chile peppers, wash your hands well with soap and warm water.

# Tex-Mex Cream of Chicken Soup

*If you're a fan of hot and spicy foods, use Monterey Jack cheese with jalapeño peppers.*

**Start to Finish:** 30 minutes   **Makes:** 4 servings

**1.** In a large saucepan or Dutch oven cook ground chicken or turkey, onion, and garlic until chicken or turkey is browned and onion is tender. Drain off fat.

**2.** Stir in milk, soup, corn, tomato, chili peppers, cilantro or parsley, and the ground red pepper. Bring to boiling; reduce heat. Simmer, uncovered, for 5 minutes, stirring occasionally. Add cheese; cook and stir until cheese melts.

Nutrition Facts per serving: 375 calories, 19 g total fat, 68 mg cholesterol, 1,481 mg sodium, 29 g carbohydrate, 24 g protein.

- 8 ounces uncooked ground chicken or turkey
- ¼ cup chopped onion
- 2 cloves garlic, minced
- 2 cups milk
- 1 10¾-ounce can condensed cream of chicken soup
- 1 7- or 11-ounce can whole kernel corn with sweet peppers, drained
- 1 medium tomato, chopped
- 1 4-ounce can diced green chili peppers, drained
- 2 tablespoons snipped fresh cilantro or parsley
- ¼ teaspoon ground red pepper
- 1 cup shredded Monterey Jack cheese (4 ounces)

# Sausage and Vegetable Ragoût

*Look in your supermarket's produce section for washed, packaged escarole, Swiss chard, kale, or spinach.*

**Start to Finish:** 35 minutes  **Makes:** 4 servings

1 8-ounce package cooked
   chicken andouille sausage
   links or cooked smoked
   turkey sausage links, cut
   into ½-inch-thick slices
1 medium yellow crookneck
   squash, cut into ½-inch
   pieces
1 14-ounce can reduced-
   sodium chicken broth
1 tablespoon snipped fresh
   rosemary or 1 teaspoon
   dried rosemary, crushed
2 cups coarsely chopped fresh
   escarole, Swiss chard, baby
   kale, and/or spinach leaves
1 15-ounce can white kidney
   beans (cannellini beans),
   rinsed and drained
1 cup carrots cut into thin,
   bite-size sticks
   Freshly ground black pepper
   Purchased garlic croutons
   (optional)

**1.** In a large saucepan combine sausage, squash, broth, and rosemary. Bring to boiling; reduce heat. Simmer, uncovered, for 5 minutes. Stir in escarole, beans, and carrots. Return to boiling; reduce heat. Cover and simmer about 5 minutes more or until vegetables are tender. Season to taste with freshly ground black pepper. If desired, top each serving with croutons.

Nutrition Facts per serving: **156 calories, 8 g total fat, 20 mg cholesterol, 785 mg sodium, 20 g carbohydrate, 16 g protein.**

# Turkey Soup with Barley

*Quick-cooking barley adds a slightly nutty flavor and pleasantly chewy texture to this hearty soup.*

**Prep:** 25 minutes  **Cook:** 15 minutes  **Makes:** 4 or 5 servings

**1.** In a Dutch oven cook and stir turkey or chicken in hot oil for 5 minutes. With a slotted spoon, remove turkey or chicken from Dutch oven. In the pan drippings cook onion, sweet pepper, and garlic for 3 minutes, stirring occasionally. Drain off fat.

**2.** Return turkey or chicken to Dutch oven. Add broth, beans, corn, barley, sugar, thyme, basil, salt, black pepper, and bay leaf. Bring to boiling; reduce heat. Cover and simmer for 15 to 20 minutes or until barley is cooked. Discard bay leaf.

Nutrition Facts per serving: 411 calories, 12 g total fat, 51 mg cholesterol, 1,108 mg sodium, 45 g carbohydrate, 33 g protein.

- 1 **pound turkey breast tenderloin or skinless, boneless chicken breasts or thighs, cut into bite-size strips**
- 2 **tablespoons cooking oil**
- 1 **cup chopped onion**
- 1 **cup chopped red or green sweet pepper**
- 1 **clove garlic, minced**
- 4 **cups chicken broth**
- 1 **10-ounce package frozen cut green beans**
- 1 **cup loose-pack frozen whole kernel corn or one 8-ounce can whole kernel corn, drained**
- ⅔ **cup quick-cooking barley**
- 1 **teaspoon sugar**
- 1 **teaspoon dried thyme, crushed**
- 1 **teaspoon dried basil, crushed**
- ½ **teaspoon salt**
- ¼ **teaspoon ground black pepper**
- 1 **bay leaf**

# Turkey-Black Bean Chili

*Use a food processor to make short work of chopping the green sweet pepper and onion.*

**Prep:** 30 minutes  **Cook:** 20 minutes  **Makes:** 6 servings

1 pound turkey breast tenderloin or skinless, boneless chicken breasts or thighs, cut into bite-size strips
2 tablespoons cooking oil
1 cup chopped green sweet pepper
1 cup chopped onion
2 cloves garlic, minced
2 28-ounce cans tomatoes, cut up
2 15-ounce cans black beans or Great Northern beans, rinsed and drained
1 12-ounce can beer
2 tablespoons red wine vinegar
1 tablespoon chili powder
1 teaspoon dried oregano, crushed
1 teaspoon ground cumin
¼ teaspoon bottled hot pepper sauce
1 bay leaf
1 teaspoon salt
¼ teaspoon ground black pepper
1 cup shredded Monterey Jack or cheddar cheese (4 ounces)

**1.** In a Dutch oven cook turkey or chicken in hot oil over medium heat until browned. With a slotted spoon, remove turkey or chicken from Dutch oven. In the pan drippings cook sweet pepper, onion, and garlic for 3 minutes, stirring occasionally. Drain off fat.

**2.** Return turkey or chicken to pan. Add undrained tomatoes, drained beans, beer, vinegar, chili powder, oregano, cumin, hot pepper sauce, bay leaf, salt, and black pepper. Bring to boiling; reduce heat. Cover and simmer about 20 minutes or until turkey or chicken is tender, stirring occasionally. Discard bay leaf. Sprinkle some of the cheese over each serving.

Nutrition Facts per serving: 377 calories, 13 g total fat, 50 mg cholesterol, 1,286 mg sodium, 38 g carbohydrate, 31 g protein.

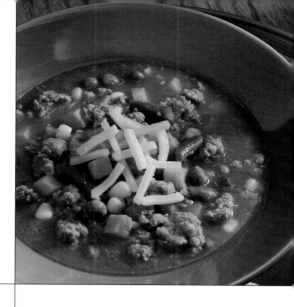

# Turkey and Vegetable Soup

*Use your favorite frozen vegetable mixture in this easy-to-fix soup.*

**Start to Finish:** 20 minutes  **Makes:** 4 servings

**1.** In a large nonstick skillet cook ground turkey and garlic until turkey is browned. Stir in chili powder; cook and stir for 1 minute. Add tomato juice, broth, and vegetables. Bring to boiling; reduce heat. Simmer, uncovered, about 5 minutes or until vegetables are tender. If desired, top with cheese. Serve with corn chips.

Nutrition Facts per serving: 275 calories, 11 g total fat, 42 mg cholesterol, 754 mg sodium, 25 g carbohydrate, 21 g protein.

1 pound uncooked
   ground turkey
1 teaspoon bottled minced
   garlic or 2 cloves garlic,
   minced
1 teaspoon chili powder
2 cups tomato juice
1 cup chicken broth
1 16-ounce package frozen
   mixed vegetables
   Shredded cheddar cheese
   (optional)
   Corn chips

# Turkey Meatball Soup

*A small ice cream scoop is handy for shaping the meatballs.*

**Prep:** 25 minutes  **Cook:** 15 minutes  **Makes:** 6 servings

1 slightly beaten egg

⅓ cup fine dry seasoned
   bread crumbs

1 pound uncooked ground
   turkey or chicken

2 tablespoons cooking oil

4 cups chicken broth

2 cups diced peeled potatoes

2 cups shredded fresh kale
   or spinach

1 10-ounce package frozen
   peas and carrots

2 teaspoons dried basil,
   crushed

½ teaspoon ground sage

¼ teaspoon pepper

**1.** In a medium bowl combine egg and bread crumbs. Add turkey and mix well. Using your hands, shape turkey mixture into 24 meatballs.

**2.** In a Dutch oven cook meatballs in hot oil until browned on all sides, turning frequently to brown evenly. Drain off fat. Add broth, potatoes, kale, peas and carrots, basil, sage, and pepper. Bring to boiling; reduce heat. Cover and simmer for 15 to 20 minutes or until vegetables are tender and meatballs are cooked through.

Nutrition Facts per serving: **249 calories, 10 g total fat, 64 mg cholesterol, 763 mg sodium, 21 g carbohydrate, 18 g protein.**

# Turkey and Black Bean Soup

*Keep canned beans, broth, and tomatoes on hand and you'll have a head start on soups such as this one.*

**Start to Finish:** 20 minutes  **Makes:** 4 or 5 servings

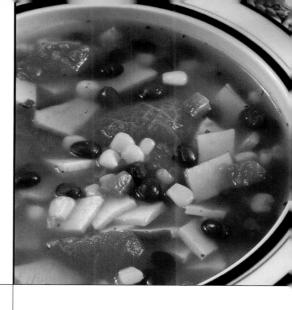

**1.** In a 3-quart saucepan combine broth, beans, undrained tomatoes, corn, wine, oregano, garlic, seasoned salt, and cumin. Bring to boiling; reduce heat. Simmer, uncovered, for 3 minutes. Stir in turkey; ladle into bowls.

Nutrition Facts per serving: **226 calories, 2 g total fat, 19 mg cholesterol, 1,874 mg sodium, 31 g carbohydrate, 22 g protein.**

2 14-ounce cans chicken broth

1 15-ounce can black beans, rinsed and drained

1 14½-ounce can Mexican-style stewed tomatoes

1 cup loose-pack frozen whole kernel corn

½ cup dry red or white wine

1 teaspoon dried oregano, crushed

1 teaspoon bottled minced garlic

½ teaspoon seasoned salt

¼ teaspoon ground cumin

6 ounces sliced cooked smoked turkey or turkey breast, cut into squares

# Turkey and Mushroom Soup

*Leftover roast turkey is ideal for this flavorful soup.*

**Start to Finish:** 35 minutes  **Makes:** 4 servings

2 cups sliced fresh
　　mushrooms (such as
　　crimini, shiitake, porcini,
　　or button)
1 stalk celery, thinly sliced
1 medium carrot, thinly sliced
1 small onion, chopped
1 tablespoon margarine
　　or butter
4½ cups water
1 tablespoon instant chicken
　　bouillon granules
⅛ teaspoon pepper
½ cup dried orzo (rosamarina)
1½ cups chopped cooked turkey
　　(about 8 ounces)
2 tablespoons snipped
　　fresh parsley
1 teaspoon snipped
　　fresh thyme

*1.* In a large saucepan cook the mushrooms, celery, carrot, and onion in hot margarine until crisp-tender. Stir in water, bouillon granules, and pepper. Bring to boiling; stir in orzo. Return to boiling; reduce heat. Simmer, uncovered, for 5 to 8 minutes or until orzo is tender but still firm. Stir in turkey, parsley, and thyme; heat through.

Nutrition Facts per serving: **199 calories, 6 g total fat, 40 mg cholesterol, 767 mg sodium, 17 g carbohydrate, 19 g protein.**

# Turkey Sausage and Bean Soup

*This soup's distinctive smoky flavor comes from turkey kielbasa.*

**Start to Finish:** 25 minutes  **Makes:** 4 servings

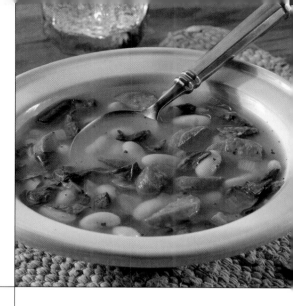

**1.** In a large saucepan or Dutch oven combine broth, beans, kielbasa, onion, basil, garlic or garlic powder, and pepper. Bring to boiling; reduce heat. Cover and simmer for 10 to 15 minutes or until onion is tender.

**2.** Meanwhile, remove stems from spinach. Stack the leaves and cut into 1-inch-wide strips. Just before serving, stir spinach strips into soup.

Nutrition Facts per serving: **257 calories, 6 g total fat, 39 mg cholesterol, 1,620 mg sodium, 35 g carbohydrate, 28 g protein.**

- 4 cups chicken broth
- 2 15-ounce cans white kidney beans (cannellini beans), Great Northern beans, or red kidney beans, rinsed and drained
- 8 ounces cooked turkey kielbasa, halved lengthwise and cut into ½-inch-thick slices
- 1 medium onion, chopped
- 1 teaspoon dried basil, crushed
- ½ teaspoon bottled minced garlic or 1 clove garlic, minced, or ⅛ teaspoon garlic powder
- ¼ teaspoon coarsely ground black pepper
- 3 cups fresh spinach

# roasted birds

Looking for an extra-special main dish? How about rich, full-flavored roasted poultry? This collection of whole birds and pieces has an idea for every occasion from Thanksgiving to an after-work dinner party.

Spring Chicken with Garlic Galore, page 121

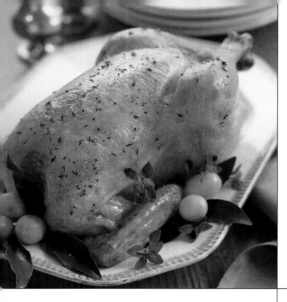

# Roasted Chicken

*Kumquats, fresh bay leaves, and fresh herbs make an attractive garnish for this succulent bird.*

**Prep:** 10 minutes   **Roast:** 1¼ hours   **Stand:** 10 minutes   **Makes:** 6 to 8 servings

1 3½- to 4-pound whole
   broiler-fryer chicken
   Salt (optional)
1 small onion, quartered
   (optional)
2 stalks celery, cut up
   (optional)
   Cooking oil
   Dried thyme or oregano,
   crushed (optional)

**1.** If desired, rub inside of chicken's body cavity with salt. If desired, place onions and celery in body cavity. Skewer neck skin to back. Tie legs to tail. Twist wing tips under back. Place chicken, breast side up, on a rack in a shallow roasting pan; brush with cooking oil and, if desired, sprinkle with herb.

**2.** Insert an oven-going meat thermometer into center of an inside thigh muscle, making sure bulb does not touch bone. Roast, uncovered, in a 375° oven for 1¼ to 1¾ hours or until meat thermometer registers 180°. At this time, drumsticks move easily in their sockets and chicken is no longer pink.

**3.** Remove chicken from oven. Cover and let stand for 10 minutes before carving.

Nutrition Facts per serving: **264 calories, 16 g total fat, 92 mg cholesterol, 85 mg sodium, 0 g carbohydrate, 29 g protein.**

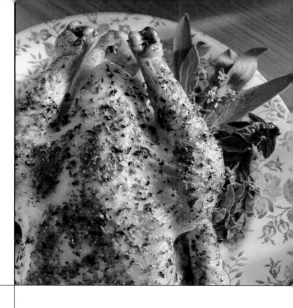

# Herb-Roasted Chicken

*The simple herb rub turns plain chicken into company fare.*

**Prep:** 15 minutes  **Roast:** 1 hour  **Stand:** 10 minutes  **Makes:** 6 servings

**1.** Skewer chicken's neck skin to back. Tie legs to tail. Twist wing tips under back. Place chicken, breast side up, on a rack in a shallow roasting pan. Brush with melted margarine or butter; rub garlic over bird. In a small bowl stir together basil, salt, sage, thyme, and lemon-pepper seasoning; rub onto bird.

**2.** Insert an oven-going meat thermometer into center of an inside thigh muscle, making sure bulb does not touch bone. Roast, uncovered, 1 to 1¼ hours or until meat thermometer registers 180°. At this time, drumsticks move easily in their sockets and chicken is no longer pink.

**3.** Remove chicken from oven. Cover and let stand for 10 minutes before carving.

Nutrition Facts per serving: **215 calories, 14 g total fat, 66 mg cholesterol, 329 mg sodium, 1 g carbohydrate, 21 g protein.**

1 2½- to 3-pound whole broiler-fryer chicken
2 tablespoons margarine or butter, melted
2 cloves garlic, minced
1 teaspoon dried basil, crushed
½ teaspoon salt
½ teaspoon ground sage
½ teaspoon dried thyme, crushed
¼ teaspoon lemon-pepper seasoning or pepper

# Garlic Chicken Italiano

*Even though this recipe uses two heads of garlic (about 16 cloves), the garlic flavor is mild because the cloves mellow as they cook.*

**Prep:** 20 minutes   **Roast:** 1¼ hours   **Stand:** 10 minutes   **Makes:** 4 servings

2 tablespoons olive oil

¼ to ½ teaspoon coarse salt

¼ teaspoon pepper

2 heads garlic

1 3- to 3½-pound whole broiler-fryer chicken

1 lemon, halved

2 cups water

½ cup dry white wine

**1.** In a small bowl combine olive oil, coarse salt, and pepper. Separate garlic into cloves; peel cloves. Mince 4 of the garlic cloves and stir into olive oil. Brush chicken with oil mixture.

**2.** Squeeze lemon over chicken. Place lemon halves inside chicken cavity. Skewer the neck skin to the back; tie the legs to the tail. Twist wing tips under back. Insert an oven-going meat thermometer into the center of an inside thigh muscle, making sure bulb does not touch bone.

**3.** Place chicken, breast side up, on a rack in a shallow roasting pan. Pour the water and wine into pan. Add remaining garlic cloves to pan.

**4.** Roast, uncovered, in a 400° oven for 1¼ to 1½ hours or until meat thermometer registers 180°. At this time, drumsticks move easily in their sockets and chicken is no longer pink.

**5.** Remove chicken from oven. Cover and let stand 10 minutes before carving. Using a slotted spoon, remove garlic from juices. Skim fat from pan juices. Carve chicken. Pour some of the pan juices over chicken. Serve garlic cloves with chicken. Pass remaining pan juices.

Nutrition Facts per serving: 432 calories, 25 g total fat, 118 mg cholesterol, 252 mg sodium, 9 g carbohydrate, 43 g protein.

# Spring Chicken with Garlic Galore

*"Galore" refers to the 40 cloves of garlic used for this flavorful bird.*

**Prep:** 25 minutes **Roast:** 1¼ hours **Stand:** 10 minutes **Makes:** 6 servings

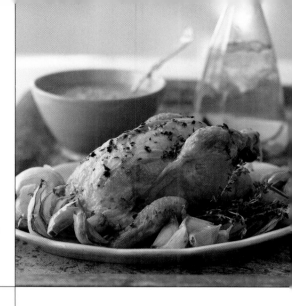

**1.** Peel papery outer leaves from garlic heads, leaving skin of cloves intact. Separate cloves. Peel and mince 4 of the cloves. Set aside remaining cloves. Combine minced garlic, 1 tablespoon of the oil, and next 3 ingredients; rub garlic mixture over chicken.

**2.** Place 6 of the garlic cloves into chicken's body cavity. Skewer neck skin to back. Tie legs to tail. Twist wing tips under back. Place onion wedges and remaining garlic cloves in shallow roasting pan. Drizzle onion and garlic with remaining oil.

**3.** Place chicken, breast side up, on onion. Insert an oven-going meat thermometer into center of an inside thigh muscle. Roast, uncovered, 1¼ to 1½ hours or until thermometer registers 180°, drumsticks move easily in sockets, and chicken is no longer pink.

**4.** Remove from oven. Using a slotted spoon, remove onion and garlic from pan. Reserve 2 or 3 onion wedges for garnish. Cover chicken; let stand 10 minutes before carving.

**5.** For gravy, squeeze 10 cloves of the roasted garlic from skins into blender container. Add remaining onion wedges and ¼ cup of the half-and-half. Cover and blend until smooth. Transfer to a saucepan. Stir in flour. Add remaining half-and-half, 1 teaspoon snipped or ¼ teaspoon dried thyme, ¼ teaspoon salt, and the ⅛ teaspoon pepper. Cook and stir over medium heat until slightly thickened and bubbly. Cook and stir for 1 minute more. Serve chicken with gravy, remaining roasted garlic cloves, and reserved onion wedges. If desired, garnish with thyme sprigs.

Nutrition Facts per serving: 282 calories, 10 g total fat, 67 mg cholesterol, 343 mg sodium, 18 g carbohydrate, 26 g protein.

- **3 heads garlic (about 40 small cloves)**
- **2 tablespoons olive oil or cooking oil**
- **1 tablespoon snipped fresh lemon thyme or thyme, or 1 teaspoon dried thyme, crushed**
- **1 teaspoon cracked black pepper**
- **¼ teaspoon salt**
- **1 3- to 3½-pound whole broiler-fryer chicken**
- **1 medium onion, cut into wedges**
- **2 cups fat-free half-and-half or regular half-and-half**
- **2 tablespoons all-purpose flour**
- **1 teaspoon snipped fresh lemon thyme or thyme, or ¼ teaspoon dried thyme, crushed**
- **¼ teaspoon salt**
- **⅛ teaspoon cracked black pepper**
- **Fresh thyme sprigs (optional)**

# Stuffed Italian-Style Chicken

*If you don't use all of the stuffing in the bird, spoon it into a small casserole and cover and bake it alongside the chicken for the last 30 minutes of roasting.*

**Prep:** 20 minutes  **Marinate:** 2 to 6 hours  **Roast:** 1¾ hours  **Stand:** 10 minutes
**Makes:** 10 to 12 servings

1 5- to 6-pound whole roasting
   chicken
⅔ cup Italian salad dressing
   Salt (optional)
1 recipe Olive Stuffing

**1.** Brush bird's body cavity with some of the salad dressing; place in deep nonmetal bowl. Pour remaining dressing over bird. Cover; marinate in the refrigerator for at least 2 hours or up to 6 hours, turning bird occasionally. Drain chicken, reserving marinade. Pat chicken dry. If desired, sprinkle cavity with salt.

**2.** Spoon Olive Stuffing loosely into body and neck cavities. Skewer neck skin to back. Tie legs to tail. Twist wing tips under back. Place bird, breast side up, on rack in shallow roasting pan.

**3.** Insert oven-going meat thermometer into center of an inside thigh muscle. Roast, uncovered, in a 325° oven for 1¾ to 2½ hours or until thermometer registers 180°, drumsticks move easily in their sockets, and chicken is no longer pink. When bird is two-thirds done, cut string between the legs so thighs will cook evenly. Baste occasionally with reserved marinade up to the last 30 minutes of roasting. Discard any remaining marinade. Remove from oven. Cover; let stand 10 minutes before carving.

*Olive Stuffing:* In a large skillet cook 1 cup chopped zucchini, 1 cup chopped red onion, and 2 cloves garlic, minced, in 2 tablespoons hot olive oil until vegetables are tender. Drain off fat. Stir in 1 cup chopped, peeled tomatoes and 2 tablespoons snipped fresh basil or 2 teaspoons dried basil, crushed. Remove from heat. Toss together 3 cups seasoned croutons and ½ cup sliced pitted ripe olives. Add vegetable mixture; toss. Moisten with water or chicken broth if mixture seems dry.

Nutrition Facts per serving: 353 calories, 23 g total fat, 70 mg cholesterol, 271 mg sodium, 10 g carbohydrate, 26 g protein.

# Fruit-Stuffed Roasted Chicken

*Orange juice blends harmoniously with apples, onion, celery, dried plums, and green grapes to make an outstanding stuffing.*

**Prep:** 45 minutes **Roast:** 1¾ hours **Stand:** 10 minutes **Makes:** 10 servings

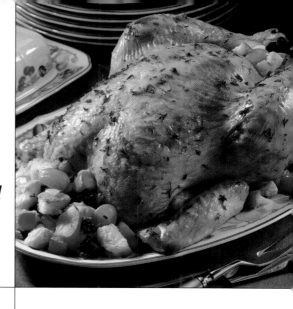

**1.** Season chicken's body cavity with salt and pepper. In small bowl combine 2 tablespoons of the margarine, 2 tablespoons of the dry sherry, 1 tablespoon of the fresh thyme or 1 teaspoon of the dried thyme, and 1 teaspoon of the orange peel; mix well. Brush bird with sherry mixture.

**2.** For stuffing, in medium skillet cook apples, onion, and celery in remaining margarine about 5 minutes or until tender. In a large bowl combine apple mixture, cubed French bread, dried plums or apricots, grapes, orange juice, remaining dry sherry, remaining fresh or dried thyme, and remaining orange peel. Mix well. (Stuffing will become more moist while cooking.) Spoon some of the stuffing loosely into the neck cavity; skewer neck skin to back. Lightly spoon the remaining stuffing into the body cavity. Tie legs to the tail. Twist wing tips under back. Place chicken, breast side up, on a rack in a shallow roasting pan.

**3.** Insert an oven-going meat thermometer into center of an inside thigh muscle, making sure bulb does not touch bone. Roast, uncovered, in a 325° oven for 1¾ to 2½ hours or until meat thermometer registers 180°, drumsticks move easily in their sockets, and chicken is no longer pink. When bird is two-thirds done, cut string between legs so thighs will cook evenly.

**4.** Remove chicken from oven. Cover and let stand 10 minutes before carving.

Nutrition Facts per serving: 393 calories, 18 g total fat, 93 mg cholesterol, 250 mg sodium, 22 g carbohydrate, 33 g protein.

1 5- to 6-pound whole roasting chicken
   Salt
   Pepper
¼ cup margarine or butter, melted
¼ cup dry sherry
4½ teaspoons snipped fresh thyme or 1½ teaspoons dried thyme, crushed
2 teaspoons finely shredded orange peel
2 medium apples, cored and chopped
1 medium onion, chopped
½ cup chopped celery
2 cups cubed French bread (¾ inch cubes)
10 pitted dried plums (prunes) or dried apricot halves, cut up
1 cup seedless green grapes, halved
2 tablespoons orange juice

# Herbed Chicken with Spinach Stuffing

*This entrée for 10 is perfect for a dinner party.*

**Prep:** 45 minutes   **Roast:** 1¾ hours   **Stand:** 10 minutes   **Makes:** 10 servings

1 5- to 6-pound whole roasting chicken

1 tablespoon olive oil or cooking oil

1 teaspoon dried basil, crushed

1 teaspoon dried oregano, crushed

1 teaspoon dried parsley flakes

¼ teaspoon garlic salt

2 10-ounce packages frozen chopped spinach, thawed and well drained

1 cup finely chopped red or green sweet pepper

4 ounces prosciutto or cooked ham, chopped

¾ cup soft bread crumbs (1 slice)

½ cup sliced green onions

⅓ cup pine nuts or slivered almonds

¼ cup margarine or butter, melted

¼ teaspoon ground black pepper

*1.* Brush chicken with oil. In a small bowl combine basil, oregano, parsley flakes, and garlic salt; sprinkle on the outside of the bird, then rub in.

*2.* For stuffing, in a large bowl combine the spinach, sweet pepper, prosciutto or ham, bread crumbs, green onions, pine nuts or almonds, melted margarine or butter, and black pepper.

*3.* Starting at the neck opening, slip your fingers between the skin and breast meat of the bird, forming a pocket. Spoon some of the stuffing into the pocket. Spoon some of the stuffing loosely into the neck cavity. Skewer neck skin to back. Lightly spoon the remaining stuffing into the body cavity. Tie legs to tail. Twist wing tips under back. Place stuffed chicken, breast side up, on a rack in a shallow roasting pan.

*4.* Insert an oven-going meat thermometer into center of an inside thigh muscle, making sure bulb does not touch bone. Roast, uncovered, in a 325° oven for 1¾ to 2½ hours or until meat thermometer registers 180°. At this time, drumsticks move easily in their sockets and chicken is no longer pink. When the bird is two-thirds done, cut the string between the legs so the thighs will cook evenly.

*5.* Remove chicken from oven. Cover and let stand 10 minutes before carving.

Nutrition Facts per serving: **514 calories, 38 g total fat, 93 mg cholesterol, 586 mg sodium, 7 g carbohydrate, 38 g protein.**

# Roast Chicken Southwestern-Style

*While the chicken roasts, prepare the black bean salsa and refrigerate it until serving time.*

**Prep:** 50 minutes **Roast:** 1¾ hours **Stand:** 10 minutes **Makes:** 10 servings

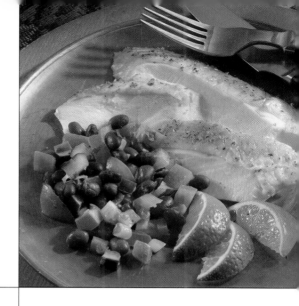

**1.** Brush chicken with 1 tablespoon oil. In a small bowl combine oregano and cumin; sprinkle over the outside of the bird, then rub into skin. Place the 6 lime wedges and the 2 cilantro sprigs in chicken's body cavity. Tie legs to tail. Twist wing tips under back. Place chicken, breast side up, on a rack in a shallow pan.

**2.** Insert an oven-going meat thermometer into center of an inside thigh muscle, making sure bulb does not touch bone. Roast, uncovered, in a 325° oven for 1¾ to 2½ hours or until meat thermometer registers 180°. At this time, the drumsticks move easily in their sockets and chicken is no longer pink. When the bird is two-thirds done, cut the string between the legs so the thighs will cook evenly.

**3.** Meanwhile, for black bean salsa, in a bowl combine black beans, tomato, cucumber, green onions, snipped cilantro or parsley, lime peel, lime juice, 1 tablespoon oil, the garlic, and salt. Cover and chill in the refrigerator until serving time.

**4.** Remove chicken from oven. Cover and let stand for 10 minutes before carving. Serve black bean salsa with chicken. If desired, garnish with additional cilantro and lime wedges.

Nutrition Facts per serving: **310 calories, 16 g total fat, 93 mg cholesterol, 214 mg sodium, 9 g carbohydrate, 35 g protein.**

- **1** 5- to 6-pound whole roasting chicken
- **1** tablespoon olive oil or cooking oil
- **1** teaspoon dried oregano, crushed
- **½** teaspoon ground cumin
- **1** lime, cut into 6 wedges
- **2** fresh cilantro sprigs
- **1** 15-ounce can black beans, rinsed and drained
- **1** small tomato, chopped
- **1** small cucumber, seeded and chopped
- **¼** cup chopped green onions
- **2** tablespoons snipped fresh cilantro or parsley
- **1** teaspoon finely shredded lime peel
- **2** tablespoons lime juice
- **1** tablespoon olive oil or cooking oil
- **1** clove garlic, minced
- **¼** teaspoon salt
  Fresh cilantro sprigs (optional)
  Lime wedges (optional)

# Roasted Chicken With Cherry Sauce

*No brandy on hand? Just add an additional 2 tablespoons apple juice or apple cider.*

**Prep:** 45 minutes  **Roast:** 1¾ hours  **Stand:** 10 minutes  **Makes:** 10 servings

1 5- to 6-pound whole roasting chicken
1 tablespoon olive oil or cooking oil
½ teaspoon garlic powder
½ teaspoon dried tarragon, crushed
¼ teaspoon salt
¼ teaspoon pepper
½ of a medium lemon, sliced
1 fresh parsley sprig
3 tablespoons brown sugar
4 teaspoons cornstarch
2 cups frozen tart red cherries
¾ cup apple juice or apple cider
1 tablespoon lemon juice
2 tablespoons brandy

*1.* Brush chicken with oil. In a small bowl combine garlic powder, tarragon, salt, and pepper; sprinkle on the outside of the chicken and rub in. Place lemon slices and parsley in chicken's body cavity. Skewer neck skin to back. Tie legs to tail. Twist wing tips under back. Place chicken, breast side up, on a rack in a shallow roasting pan.

*2.* Insert an oven-going meat thermometer into center of an inside thigh muscle, making sure bulb does not touch bone. Roast, uncovered, in a 325° oven for 1¾ to 2½ hours or until meat thermometer registers 180°. At this time, the drumsticks move easily in their sockets and chicken is no longer pink. When the bird is two-thirds done, cut string between the legs so thighs will cook evenly.

*3.* Remove chicken from oven. Cover and let stand 10 minutes before carving.

*4.* Meanwhile, for sauce, in a medium saucepan stir together the brown sugar and cornstarch. Stir in the cherries, apple juice, and lemon juice. Cook and stir until thickened and bubbly. Cook and stir for 2 minutes more. Stir in brandy. Heat through. Serve sauce with chicken.

Nutrition Facts per serving: 304 calories, 14 g total fat, 93 mg cholesterol, 212 mg sodium, 11 g carbohydrate, 32 g protein.

# Roasted Pesto Chicken

*Garnish the pesto-flavor chicken with additional fresh basil.*

**Prep:** 45 minutes  **Roast:** 1¾ hours  **Stand:** 10 minutes  **Makes:** 10 servings

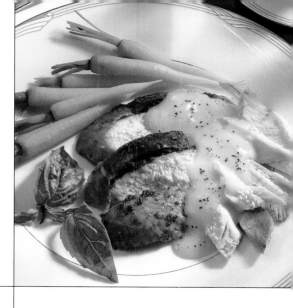

**1.** For pesto, in a food processor bowl or blender container combine the 1 cup basil, the walnuts, and the 2 cloves garlic. Cover and process or blend until mixed. With motor running, add olive oil in a slow, steady stream. Add Parmesan cheese and pepper to taste. Process or blend until smooth.

**2.** Starting at the neck opening, slip your fingers between the skin and breast meat and between the skin and leg meat of the bird, forming pockets. Spoon some of the pesto into pockets. Spoon some of the pesto loosely into the neck cavity. Skewer neck skin to back. Lightly spoon some of the pesto into the chicken's body cavity. Rub remaining pesto over skin of chicken. Tie legs to the tail. Twist wing tips under back. Place chicken, breast side up, on a rack in shallow roasting pan.

**3.** Insert an oven-going meat thermometer into center of an inside thigh muscle. Roast, uncovered, in a 325° oven for 1¾ to 2½ hours or until thermometer registers 180°, drumsticks move easily in their sockets, and chicken is no longer pink. When the bird is two-thirds done, cut the string between legs so the thighs will cook evenly. Remove chicken from oven. Cover and let stand 10 minutes before carving.

**4.** Meanwhile, for sauce, in a small saucepan cook the 1 clove garlic in hot margarine or butter. Stir in flour. Add broth and white wine. Cook and stir until thickened and bubbly. Cook and stir for 1 minute more. Serve sauce with sliced chicken.

1 cup lightly packed fresh basil
½ cup chopped walnuts
2 cloves garlic, minced
¼ cup olive oil
½ cup grated Parmesan cheese
    Coarsely ground black pepper
1 5- to 6-pound whole roasting
    chicken
1 clove garlic, minced
2 tablespoons margarine
    or butter
2 tablespoons all-purpose flour
1 cup chicken broth
2 tablespoons dry white wine

**Nutrition Facts per serving:** 391 calories, 26 g total fat, 97 mg cholesterol, 252 mg sodium, 3 g carbohydrate, 35 g protein.

# Apple-and-Wild-Rice-Stuffed Chicken

*Add vegetables and apples to a packaged rice mix and you've got an irresistible stuffing for this company-special chicken.*

**Prep:** 35 minutes  **Roast:** 1¾ hours  **Stand:** 10 minutes  **Makes:** 10 servings

1 6-ounce package long grain and wild rice mix

8 ounces sliced fresh mushrooms (3 cups)

2 medium cooking apples (such as Granny Smith or Jonathan), cored and chopped

1 cup shredded carrot

½ cup thinly sliced green onions

½ teaspoon pepper

1 5- to 6-pound whole roasting chicken

2 to 3 tablespoons apple jelly, melted

Apple wedges (optional)

**1.** For stuffing, cook rice according to package directions, except add mushrooms, chopped apples, shredded carrot, green onions, and pepper to rice before cooking.

**2.** Spoon some of the stuffing loosely into the chicken's neck cavity. Skewer neck skin to back. Lightly spoon the remaining stuffing into the body cavity. Tie legs to tail. Twist wing tips under back. Place chicken, breast side up, on a rack in a shallow roasting pan.

**3.** Insert an oven-going meat thermometer into the center of an inside thigh muscle, making sure bulb does not touch bone. Roast, uncovered, in a 325° oven for 1¾ to 2½ hours or until meat thermometer registers 180°. At this time, drumsticks move easily in their sockets and chicken is no longer pink. When the bird is two-thirds done, cut the string between the legs so thighs will cook evenly. Brush chicken with melted jelly once or twice during the last 10 minutes of roasting.

**4.** Remove the chicken from oven. Cover and let stand for 10 minutes before carving. Transfer chicken to a serving platter. Spoon some of the stuffing around the chicken. If desired, garnish with apple wedges. Pass the remaining stuffing.

Nutrition Facts per serving: 332 calories, 13 g total fat, 93 mg cholesterol, 365 mg sodium, 19 g carbohydrate, 34 g protein.

# Glazed Chicken and Vegetables

*The carrots, potatoes, and apples cook alongside the chicken during the last few minutes of roasting.*

**Prep:** 15 minutes **Roast:** 1¼ hours **Stand:** 10 minutes **Makes:** 6 servings

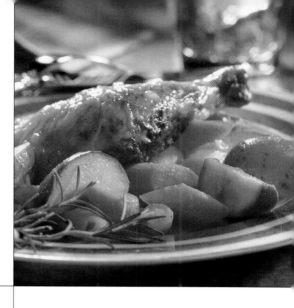

**1.** Skewer chicken's neck skin to back. Tie legs to tail. Twist wing tips under back. Place chicken, breast side up, on a rack in a shallow roasting pan; brush with cooking oil.

**2.** Insert an oven-going meat thermometer into center of an inside thigh muscle, making sure bulb does not touch bone. Roast, uncovered, in a 375° oven for 1 hour.

**3.** Meanwhile, in a medium saucepan cook potatoes and carrots in a large amount of boiling water for 20 to 25 minutes or until nearly tender; drain.

**4.** For glaze, in a small saucepan combine honey, mustard, margarine or butter, onion, curry powder, garlic salt, crushed red pepper, and ginger. Bring to boiling, stirring constantly. Remove from heat; set glaze aside.

**5.** Discard fat in roasting pan. Arrange potatoes, carrots, and apple wedges around chicken in pan. Spoon glaze over chicken, vegetables, and apples. Roast for 15 to 20 minutes more or until meat thermometer registers 180°. At this time, drumsticks move easily in their sockets and chicken is no longer pink. Remove chicken from oven; cover and let stand for 10 minutes before carving.

Nutrition Facts per serving: **422 calories, 17 g total fat, 66 mg cholesterol, 456 mg sodium, 46 g carbohydrate, 23 g protein.**

- 1 2½- to 3-pound whole broiler-fryer chicken
  Cooking oil
- 2 medium potatoes, peeled and quartered
- 6 carrots, bias-cut into ½-inch-thick slices
- ½ cup honey
- ¼ cup prepared mustard
- 2 tablespoons margarine or butter
- 2 tablespoons finely chopped onion
- 2 teaspoons curry powder
- ½ teaspoon garlic salt
- ¼ teaspoon crushed red pepper
- ¼ teaspoon ground ginger
- 2 medium apples, cored and cut into wedges

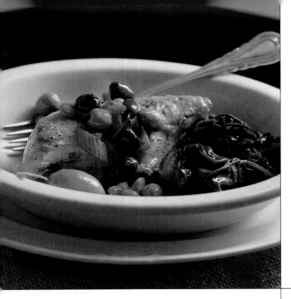

# Roast Chicken with Olive-Raisin Sauce

*The simple secret to seasoning these chicken breasts is putting fresh herbs under the skin before roasting.*

**Prep:** 15 minutes   **Roast:** 25 minutes   **Makes:** 4 servings

2 whole chicken breasts, halved

8 to 12 fresh sage leaves or 24 fresh marjoram sprigs

¼ teaspoon salt

¼ teaspoon ground black pepper

½ cup sliced celery

½ cup chopped onion

2 large cloves garlic, minced

2 tablespoons olive oil

½ cup chicken broth

½ cup dry red wine or additional ⅓ cup broth plus 2 tablespoons balsamic vinegar

½ cup pitted and halved mixed olives or kalamata olives

½ cup golden raisins

⅛ teaspoon ground red pepper (optional)

1 tablespoon snipped fresh marjoram

Cooked red Swiss chard (optional)

**1.** Loosen chicken skin and place 2 or 3 sage leaves or 6 marjoram sprigs under the skin of each piece of chicken. Sprinkle chicken with salt and black pepper.

**2.** Place chicken, skin side up, in a shallow roasting pan. Roast, uncovered, in a 425° oven for 25 to 30 minutes or until chicken is tender and no longer pink.

**3.** Meanwhile, in a large skillet cook celery, onion, and garlic in hot oil until tender. Add the ½ cup broth, the wine or ⅓ cup broth plus the balsamic vinegar, the olives, raisins, and, if desired, ground red pepper. Bring to boiling; reduce heat. Simmer, uncovered, about 7 minutes or until slightly thickened. Stir in the snipped marjoram; simmer 1 minute more.

**4.** Spoon the sauce over roasted chicken breast halves. If desired, serve with cooked Swiss chard.

Nutrition Facts per serving: **412 calories, 18 g total fat, 95 mg cholesterol, 555 mg sodium, 20 g carbohydrate, 35 g protein.**

# Cornish Hen with Root Vegetables

*Each person gets a whole Cornish hen in this wonderful oven-roasted dinner. If you prefer smaller portions, you can serve half a hen to each of four diners.*

**Prep:** 20 minutes  **Roast:** 1 hour  **Stand:** 10 minutes  **Makes:** 2 servings

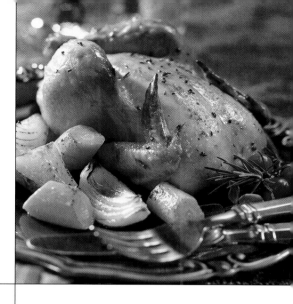

**1.** Rub the skins of the hens with garlic. Rub the balsamic vinegar, then 2 teaspoons of the olive oil onto the skins. If using snipped fresh rosemary, place half of it in the body cavities and rub the remainder on the skins. (Or rub the dried rosemary just on the skins.) Place hens, breast sides up, in a 13×9×2-inch baking pan.

**2.** Surround the hens with the vegetables. Drizzle the remaining olive oil over the vegetables, turning them to lightly coat. Sprinkle vegetables and hens with salt and pepper.

**3.** Roast hens and vegetables, uncovered, in a 375° oven for 1 to 1¼ hours or until hens are tender and no longer pink, basting the birds and vegetables once or twice.

**4.** Remove hens from oven. Cover and let stand for 10 minutes before serving. If desired, garnish with fresh rosemary or sage leaves and cherry tomatoes.

Nutrition Facts per serving: 964 calories, 54 g total fat, 240 mg cholesterol, 769 mg sodium, 45 g carbohydrate, 77 g protein.

- 2 1½-pound Cornish game hens
- 2 large cloves garlic, crushed
- 2 teaspoons balsamic vinegar
- 4 teaspoons olive oil
- 4 teaspoons snipped fresh rosemary or 1 teaspoon dried rosemary, crushed
- 2 small onions, peeled and quartered
- 2 medium carrots, peeled and cut up
- 2 medium russet potatoes, cut up
- 2 medium parsnips or 2 turnips, peeled and cut up
- Salt
- Coarsely ground black pepper
- Fresh rosemary or sage leaves (optional)
- Cherry tomatoes (optional)

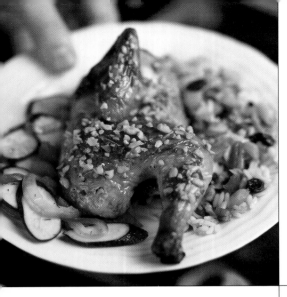

# A Honey of a Hen

*A simple two-ingredient glaze adds gloss and just the right touch of sweetness to these Cornish game hens.*

**Prep:** 15 minutes  **Roast:** 1 hour  **Makes:** 6 servings

3  1¼- to 1½-pound Cornish game hens, halved
2  tablespoons peanut oil or cooking oil
⅛  teaspoon salt
⅛  teaspoon pepper
2  tablespoons honey
2  tablespoons Grand Marnier or orange juice
½  cup finely chopped toasted walnuts
1  recipe Wild Rice Dressing
1  recipe Sautéed Vegetables
   Finely shredded orange peel (optional)

**1.** Twist wing tips of hens under backs. Place hen halves, cut sides down, in a shallow roasting pan. In a small bowl combine oil, salt, and pepper; brush mixture over hens. Cover and roast hens in a 375° oven for 35 minutes.

**2.** For glaze, in a small saucepan cook honey over medium heat until bubbly. Remove from heat. Stir in the Grand Marnier.

**3.** Uncover hens. Brush glaze evenly over the hens. Sprinkle with walnuts. Bake, uncovered, about 25 minutes more or until hens are tender and no longer pink (180°).

**4.** Meanwhile, prepare Wild Rice Dressing and Sautéed Vegetables. Remove hens from oven. Cover and let stand 10 minutes before serving. Serve hens with Wild Rice Dressing and Sautéed Vegetables. If desired, garnish with orange peel.

*Wild Rice Dressing:* Cook one 6-ounce package long grain and wild rice mix according to package directions. Cook 1 cup chopped celery and ⅔ cup chopped onion in 1 tablespoon hot butter until tender. Stir in ¾ cup pecans, ⅔ cup raisins, 4 crisp-cooked bacon slices, and ½ teaspoon paprika; fold into rice.

*Sautéed Vegetables:* Cut 2 medium yellow summer squash and 2 medium zucchini into ⅛-inch-thick diagonal slices. Cut 1 medium red onion into thin, bite-size strips. Cook and stir the vegetables in 2 tablespoons hot olive oil for 2 minutes. Stir in ¼ cup dry white wine and ½ teaspoon dried thyme, crushed. Cook and stir for 3 to 4 minutes or until onion is crisp-tender.

Nutrition Facts per serving: 833 calories, 52 g total fat, 182 mg cholesterol, 738 mg sodium, 52 g carbohydrate, 39 g protein.

# Spinach-Stuffed Turkey Breast

*The savory stuffing is tucked under the turkey's skin in this impressive poultry dish.*

**Prep:** 20 minutes   **Roast:** 2½ hours   **Stand:** 15 minutes   **Makes:** 8 servings

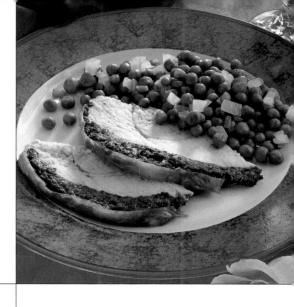

**1.** Thaw turkey, if frozen. Drain spinach thoroughly and squeeze out excess liquid. Place spinach in a food processor bowl with cream cheese, Parmesan cheese, water, basil, nutmeg, and pepper. Cover and process until well mixed.

**2.** With a small sharp knife, loosen turkey breast skin from meat and pull skin back, leaving skin attached along one side. Spread spinach mixture over exposed portion of meat; pull skin back over filling. Secure skin with wooden picks along sides of breast. Place turkey, skin side up, on a rack in a shallow roasting pan. Insert an oven-going meat thermometer into center of breast below stuffing, making sure bulb does not touch bone. Cover turkey loosely with foil.

**3.** Roast in a 325° oven for 2 hours. Remove foil. Roast for 30 minutes to 1 hour more or until meat thermometer registers 170° and juices run clear. Cover and let stand for 15 minutes before carving. To carve, start at outside of breast half; slice downward, keeping slices thin. Continue slicing slightly higher up on the breast.

Nutrition Facts per serving: **170 calories, 6 g total fat, 62 mg cholesterol, 176 mg sodium, 3 g carbohydrate, 25 g protein.**

- 1 2½- to 3-pound fresh or frozen bone-in turkey breast half
- 1 10-ounce package frozen chopped spinach, thawed
- ½ of an 8-ounce package reduced-fat cream cheese (Neufchâtel), softened
- 3 tablespoons grated Parmesan cheese
- 2 tablespoons water
- 1 teaspoon dried basil, crushed
- ¼ teaspoon ground nutmeg
- ¼ teaspoon pepper

# Turkey Breast with Roasted Asparagus

*Use some of spring's first tender shoots to make the roasted asparagus that accompanies this mustard-and-herb-glazed turkey.*

**Prep:** 30 minutes   **Roast:** 1½ hours   **Stand:** 15 minutes   **Makes:** 10 to 12 servings

- 2 fresh or frozen boneless turkey breast halves (with skin on) (2½ to 3 pounds total)
- ¼ cup margarine or butter, softened
- 2 teaspoons Dijon-style mustard
- ¾ teaspoon dried tarragon, crushed
- ¼ teaspoon salt
- ⅛ teaspoon ground black pepper
- 1 7-ounce jar roasted red sweet peppers, drained and coarsely chopped
- ½ cup snipped fresh parsley
- 1½ pounds fresh asparagus spears, trimmed
- 1 tablespoon olive oil
- ¼ teaspoon salt

**1.** Thaw turkey, if frozen. In a small bowl combine margarine, mustard, tarragon, ¼ teaspoon salt, and the black pepper.

**2.** Remove skin from turkey; set aside. Lay one turkey breast half, boned side up, on work surface. Make 4 or 5 shallow cuts in the thickest portion of breast (do not cut through). Place turkey breast between 2 pieces of plastic wrap. Using the flat side of a meat mallet, lightly pound turkey breast to an even thickness (about ¾ inch). Remove plastic wrap. Repeat with remaining turkey breast. Dot breast halves with half of the margarine mixture; set remaining mixture aside. Top turkey evenly with red peppers and parsley. Starting with a short side, roll up each turkey breast into a spiral. Wrap reserved skin around each roll. Tie with 100%-cotton string. Place on a rack in a shallow roasting pan.

**3.** In a small saucepan melt remaining margarine mixture; brush over surface of turkey. Insert an oven-going meat thermometer into the center of one of the turkey rolls. Roast in a 325° oven for 1½ to 1¾ hours or until meat thermometer registers 170° and juices run clear.

**4.** Meanwhile, in a large bowl toss together asparagus, oil, and ¼ teaspoon salt. Add asparagus to the roasting pan around the turkey for the last 15 to 20 minutes of roasting. Remove turkey from oven. Cover turkey and asparagus; let stand for 15 minutes before slicing. Serve turkey with asparagus.

Nutrition Facts per serving: **212 calories, 9 g total fat, 80 mg cholesterol, 220 mg sodium, 2 g carbohydrate, 28 g protein.**

# Chutney-Glazed Turkey Breast

*The glossy red glaze makes this a perfect choice for a holiday meal.*

**Prep:** 10 minutes  **Roast:** 1½ hours  **Stand:** 10 minutes  **Makes:** 6 servings

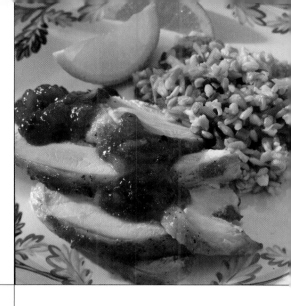

**1.** Thaw turkey, if frozen. Skin turkey breast, if desired. Place turkey, skin side up, on a rack in a shallow roasting pan. Brush with oil; sprinkle with salt and pepper. Insert an oven-going meat thermometer in the thickest part of the breast, making sure bulb does not touch bone. Roast in a 325° oven, uncovered, for 1¼ to 1½ hours or until meat thermometer registers 150°.

**2.** Meanwhile, for glaze, in a small saucepan stir together cranberry sauce, chutney, and orange peel; heat through. Spoon some of the glaze over turkey. Roast for 15 to 20 minutes more or until meat thermometer registers 170° and juices run clear.

**3.** Transfer turkey breast to a cutting board. Cover and let stand for 10 minutes before carving. Serve remaining glaze with sliced turkey.

Nutrition Facts per serving: **276 calories, 9 g total fat, 64 mg cholesterol, 154 mg sodium, 22 g carbohydrate, 24 g protein.**

- 1  1¾- to 2-pound fresh or frozen bone-in turkey breast portion
- 1  tablespoon olive oil or cooking oil
- ¼  teaspoon salt
- ⅛  teaspoon pepper
- ½  cup whole cranberry sauce
- ½  cup snipped chutney
- 1  teaspoon finely shredded orange peel

# Orange and Herb-Roasted Turkey

*When the turkey is done, the drumsticks should move easily in their sockets and the thickest parts of the drumsticks should be very soft when pressed.*

**Prep:** 25 minutes  **Roast:** 3¾ hours  **Stand:** 15 minutes  **Makes:** 10 to 12 servings

1  **14-pound fresh or frozen turkey**
   **Salt**
   **Freshly ground black pepper**
1  **medium onion, cut into wedges**
1  **medium orange, cut into wedges**
6  **fresh rosemary sprigs (each 4 to 5 inches long)**
4  **fresh thyme sprigs (each 4 to 5 inches long)**
1 to 2  **tablespoons cooking oil**
1  **6-ounce can frozen orange juice concentrate, thawed**
¾  **cup reduced-sodium chicken broth**
¼  **cup margarine or butter, melted**
   **Reduced-sodium chicken broth (optional)**
4  **teaspoons finely snipped fresh rosemary or 2 teaspoons dried rosemary, crushed**
¼  **cup reduced-sodium chicken broth**
3  **tablespoons cornstarch**
   **Candied fruit slices and/or fresh fruit slices (such as pears, oranges, and kumquats) (optional)**

**1.** Thaw turkey, if frozen. Season turkey's cavity generously with salt and pepper. Place onion, orange, and herb sprigs in large cavity. Skewer neck skin to back. Tie legs to tail. Twist wing tips under back. Place, breast up, on rack in a shallow roasting pan. Brush with oil. Insert an oven-going meat thermometer into center of an inside thigh muscle. Cover turkey loosely with foil.

**2.** Roast in 325° oven about 3¾ hours total. After 2½ hours, cut string between legs. Continue to roast, covered with foil, about 20 minutes more or until thermometer registers 160°. Combine juice concentrate, the ¾ cup broth, and the margarine. Brush some of the juice mixture over bird. Continue roasting, uncovered, until thermometer registers 180°, brushing with juice mixture every 15 minutes. Reserve any remaining mixture for gravy. Remove bird from oven; discard ingredients from cavity. Transfer bird to a platter. Cover; let stand 15 to 20 minutes before carving.

**3.** Meanwhile, for gravy, strain juices from roasting pan into a large glass measure; scrape browned bits from pan into cup. Skim off and discard fat. Add any remaining juice mixture to juices in measuring cup. Measure 3 cups of the liquid, adding additional chicken broth if necessary. Pour juices into a saucepan. Add snipped or crushed rosemary. Combine the ¼ cup broth and the cornstarch. Add to saucepan. Cook and stir until thickened and bubbly; cook and stir 2 minutes more. Season to taste. If desired, garnish turkey with fruit. Pass gravy with turkey.

Nutrition Facts per serving: 469 calories, 23 g total fat, 185 mg cholesterol, 261 mg sodium, 10 g carbohydrate, 52 g protein.

# Turkey with Herb Gravy

*Use fresh fruits, such as apples, pears, and champagne grapes, to garnish the turkey.*

**Prep:** 35 minutes  **Roast:** 4 hours  **Stand:** 15 minutes  **Makes:** 12 to 16 servings

**1.** Loosely fill neck and body cavities of turkey with Harvest Stuffing. Skewer neck skin to back. Tie legs to tail. Twist wing tips under back. Arrange next 5 ingredients in a shallow roasting pan; add wine. Place turkey, breast up, on vegetables. Brush with butter; sprinkle with salt and pepper. Insert an oven-going meat thermometer into center of an inside thigh muscle. Cover loosely with foil.

**2.** Roast in a 325° oven for 4 to 5 hours total. After 3 hours, cut string between legs. Continue to roast, covered with foil except for the last 30 minutes of roasting, 1 to 2 hours more or until thermometer registers 180° and stuffing registers 165°. Transfer to a serving platter. Cover; let stand 15 to 20 minutes before carving.

**3.** For gravy, scrape vegetables and drippings from pan into a large strainer set over a large glass measure. Press vegetables to extract liquid. Let stand 5 minutes. Skim off fat, reserving ¼ cup. Return reserved fat to roasting pan; heat until bubbly. Whisk in flour; cook until golden. Whisk in broth, brandy (if desired), and reserved drippings; cook for 2 to 3 minutes or until slightly thickened. Season to taste. Serve turkey with stuffing and gravy.

***Harvest Stuffing:*** Cook 1 cup shredded carrots, 1 cup chopped celery, and ½ cup chopped onion in ½ cup butter until tender. Stir in ¼ teaspoon salt, ¼ teaspoon ground nutmeg, and ¼ teaspoon pepper. Mix 8 cups dry bread cubes; 2 cups chopped, peeled apples; ½ cup chopped walnuts; and ¼ cup toasted wheat germ. Stir in carrot mixture. Drizzle with ½ to 1 cup chicken broth to moisten; toss.

**1** 14- to 18-pound fresh turkey
**1** recipe Harvest Stuffing
**2** medium onions, quartered
**4** shallots, quartered
**1** head garlic, peeled
**1** bunch fresh thyme
**1** bunch fresh sage
**1** cup dry white wine
**2** tablespoons melted butter
**2½** teaspoons salt
**½** teaspoon freshly ground black pepper
**¼** cup all-purpose flour
**1** cup chicken broth
**2** tablespoons apple brandy (optional)

**Nutrition Facts per serving:** 913 calories, 46 g total fat, 310 mg cholesterol, 1,181 mg sodium, 25 g carbohydrate, 91 g protein.

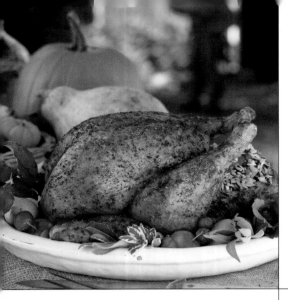

# Herb-Rubbed Turkey With Pear Stuffing

*Garnish the golden brown bird with a variety of fresh fruits and assorted fresh herbs.*

**Prep:** 45 minutes  **Roast:** 3¼ hours  **Stand:** 15 minutes  **Makes:** 10 to 12 servings

1 12- to 14-pound fresh or
    frozen turkey
3 tablespoons dried sage
    leaves
3 tablespoons dried savory
    leaves
1½ teaspoons whole white or
    black peppercorns
1 teaspoon celery salt
1 teaspoon paprika
1 recipe Pear Stuffing
    Cooking oil or olive oil

*1.* Thaw turkey, if frozen. In a blender container combine sage, and next 4 ingredients. Cover; blend until coarsely ground. Spoon Pear Stuffing into bird's neck and body cavities. Skewer neck skin to back. Tie legs to tail. Twist wing tips under back. Brush with oil; rub with herb mixture. Place bird, breast side up, on rack in shallow roasting pan. Insert oven-going meat thermometer into center of an inside thigh muscle. Cover bird loosely with foil.

*2.* Roast in 325° oven for 3¼ to 4½ hours total. After 2½ hours, cut string between legs. Continue to roast, covered with foil except for the last 30 minutes of roasting, 45 minutes to 2 hours more or until thermometer registers 180° and stuffing registers 165°. (When done, drumsticks move easily in sockets and thickest parts of drumsticks are very soft when pressed.) Transfer to serving platter. Cover; let stand 15 to 20 minutes before carving.

*Pear Stuffing:* Cook ½ cup wild rice in 2 tablespoons hot margarine for 2 minutes. Carefully add two 14-ounce cans chicken broth. Bring to boiling; reduce heat. Cover and simmer for 30 minutes. Add 1¼ cups dried orzo (rosamarina). Return to boiling; reduce heat. Cover; simmer 10 to 12 minutes more. Stir in 2 medium red pears, cored and cut into ½-inch cubes; ¾ cup toasted chopped hazelnuts; ½ cup sliced green onions; ½ cup golden raisins; and 1 tablespoon grated fresh ginger.

Nutrition Facts per serving: 940 calories, 45 g total fat, 290 mg cholesterol, 807 mg sodium, 33 g carbohydrate, 96 g protein.

# Turkey with Cranberry Sauce

*When cranberries are in season, buy extra and freeze them so you can make this ruby-sauced turkey breast throughout the year.*

**Prep:** 10 minutes **Roast:** 2½ hours **Stand:** 15 minutes **Makes:** 8 servings

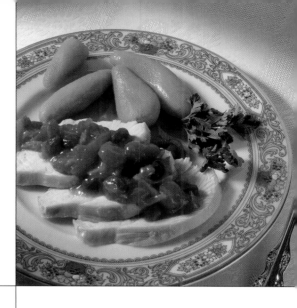

**1.** Thaw turkey, if frozen. Skin turkey breast. Place turkey breast, bone side down, on a rack in a shallow roasting pan. Insert an oven-going meat thermometer into the thickest part of turkey, making sure bulb does not touch bone. Cover turkey loosely with foil.

**2.** Roast in a 325° oven for 2½ to 3 hours or until meat thermometer registers 170° and juices run clear. Remove foil for the last 30 minutes of roasting. Cover; let stand for 15 minutes before slicing.

**3.** Meanwhile, for sauce, in a small saucepan combine cranberries, carrot, orange peel, orange juice, sugar, raisins, and cloves. Bring to boiling; reduce heat. Simmer, uncovered, for 3 to 4 minutes or until cranberry skins pop.

**4.** In a small bowl combine cold water and cornstarch; stir into cranberry mixture. Cook and stir until thickened and bubbly. Cook and stir for 2 minutes more. Serve turkey with sauce.

Nutrition Facts per serving: **154 calories, 2 g total fat, 50 mg cholesterol, 49 mg sodium, 11 g carbohydrate, 22 g protein.**

- 1  2½- to 3-pound fresh or frozen bone-in turkey breast half
- 1½ cups cranberries
- ½ cup coarsely shredded carrot
- ½ teaspoon finely shredded orange peel
- ½ cup orange juice
- 2 tablespoons sugar
- 2 tablespoons raisins
   Dash ground cloves
- 1 tablespoon cold water
- 2 teaspoons cornstarch

# oven specials

*Work wonders with your oven when you bake any of these chicken and turkey entrées. Select from casseroles, glazed pieces, rolled or stuffed bundles, savory pies, loaves, enchiladas, and more.*

Chicken and Barley Bake, page 159

# Chicken and Wild Rice Roll-Ups

*To end up with 1 cup cooked wild rice, start with ½ cup uncooked wild rice and 1 cup water. Simmer, covered, about 40 minutes or until most of the water is absorbed.*

**Prep:** 30 minutes  **Bake:** 30 minutes  **Makes:** 6 servings

1 cup hot cooked wild rice
1 cup ricotta cheese
⅓ cup finely shredded
    Parmesan cheese
⅓ cup bottled minced roasted
    garlic or 2 tablespoons
    minced garlic (about
    12 cloves)
1 teaspoon snipped fresh
    rosemary or ½ teaspoon
    dried rosemary, crushed
    Salt
    Pepper
6 medium skinless, boneless
    chicken breast halves
    (about 1½ pounds total)
2 tablespoons butter
1 recipe Red Pepper Sauce
    Fresh chives (optional)

**1.** For stuffing, in a medium bowl stir together the wild rice, cheeses, garlic, and rosemary. Season to taste with salt and pepper. Set aside.

**2.** Place each breast half between 2 pieces of plastic wrap. Pound lightly with the flat side of a meat mallet into a rectangle about ⅛ inch thick. Remove plastic wrap. Spoon about ⅓ cup of the stuffing into the center of each piece. Fold in bottom and sides of each piece; roll up. Secure with wooden toothpicks.

**3.** In a medium skillet cook chicken on all sides in hot butter until browned. Transfer to 2-quart rectangular baking dish. Set aside skillet to use for sauce. Bake chicken in 350° oven for 30 to 35 minutes or until no longer pink. Discard toothpicks.

**4.** To serve, cut each chicken roll into slices. Spoon the Red Pepper Sauce over chicken. If desired, garnish with chives.

***Red Pepper Sauce:*** In the reserved skillet combine ¼ cup chicken broth and 2 tablespoons dry white wine or chicken broth. Cook about 2 minutes or until reduced by half, stirring to loosen browned bits. Stir in 2 tablespoons chopped green onion, 1 tablespoon minced shallot or green onion, 1½ teaspoons snipped fresh parsley, and 1 clove garlic, minced. Cook 1 minute. Stir in 1 cup whipping cream. Bring to boiling; reduce heat to medium. Cook and stir 3 to 4 minutes or until slightly thickened. Stir in one 12-ounce jar roasted red sweet peppers, drained and cut into strips, and 4 teaspoons snipped fresh chives.

Nutrition Facts per serving: 444 calories, 29 g total fat, 150 mg cholesterol, 280 mg sodium, 14 g carbohydrate, 32 g protein.

# Bistro Chicken and Garlic

*The garlic mellows as it bakes to give the sauce its full flavor.*

**Prep:** 20 minutes  **Bake:** 12 minutes  **Makes:** 4 servings

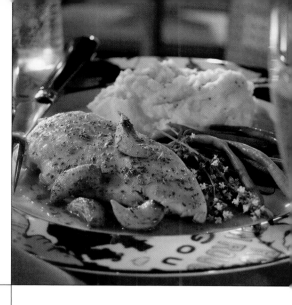

**1.** Peel papery outer leaves from head of garlic, leaving skin of cloves intact. (This will facilitate squeezing garlic from peel after it is cooked.) Separate the cloves.

**2.** In a large ovenproof skillet cook garlic cloves and chicken in hot oil over medium-high heat about 4 minutes or until chicken is lightly browned, turning chicken and stirring garlic cloves once. Sprinkle chicken with basil, thyme, rosemary, salt, and pepper. Cover skillet and transfer to a 400° oven. Bake, covered, for 12 to 15 minutes or until chicken is tender and no longer pink and garlic is tender.

**3.** Using a slotted spatula, transfer chicken to a serving platter, reserving juices in skillet; keep warm. Transfer garlic cloves to a small bowl; set aside for 1 to 2 minutes to cool slightly. Add vermouth or white wine to skillet. Squeeze softened garlic from skins into skillet; discard skins. Bring to boiling on range top; reduce heat. Boil gently, uncovered, about 6 minutes or until sauce thickens slightly, stirring frequently. Pour garlic sauce over chicken. If desired, garnish with herb sprigs.

Nutrition Facts per serving: **177 calories, 7 g total fat, 60 mg cholesterol, 189 mg sodium, 3 g carbohydrate, 22 g protein.**

- 1 **head garlic**
- 4 **medium skinless, boneless chicken breast halves (about 1 pound total)**
- 1 **tablespoon olive oil**
- ¼ **teaspoon dried basil, crushed**
- ¼ **teaspoon dried thyme, crushed**
- ¼ **teaspoon dried rosemary, crushed**
- ¼ **teaspoon salt**
- ⅛ **teaspoon freshly ground black pepper**
- ¼ **cup dry vermouth or dry white wine**
  **Fresh herb sprigs (optional)**

# Chicken Mole with Pumpkin Seeds

*A hint of chocolate—here in the form of cocoa powder—rounds out the flavor of savory mole sauce.*

**Prep:** 15 minutes **Bake:** 20 minutes **Makes:** 4 servings

**Nonstick cooking spray**

**4 small skinless, boneless chicken breast halves or large skinless, boneless chicken thighs (about 12 ounces total)**

**¼ cup finely chopped onion**

**2 cloves garlic, minced**

**1 teaspoon olive oil or cooking oil**

**1½ teaspoons chili powder**

**½ teaspoon ground cumin**

**1 8-ounce can reduced-sodium tomato sauce**

**2 tablespoons raisins**

**2 tablespoons snipped fresh cilantro or ½ teaspoon ground coriander**

**2 tablespoons toasted hulled pumpkin seeds, sunflower seeds, or sliced almonds**

**1 teaspoon unsweetened cocoa powder**

**½ teaspoon instant chicken bouillon granules**

**Hot cooked rice**

**Carrot strips (optional)**

**Fresh cilantro sprigs (optional)**

*1.* Coat a 2-quart rectangular baking dish with nonstick cooking spray. Arrange chicken breast halves in dish. Bake in a 400° oven for 15 minutes.

*2.* Meanwhile, for mole sauce, in a medium saucepan cook onion and garlic in hot oil for 2 minutes. Stir in chili powder and cumin; cook for 1 minute. Stir in tomato sauce, raisins, snipped cilantro or ground coriander, 1 tablespoon of the pumpkin seeds, the cocoa powder, and bouillon granules. Bring to boiling; reduce heat. Cover and simmer for 3 minutes.

*3.* Transfer sauce to a blender container or food processor bowl. Cover and blend or process until sauce is nearly smooth.

*4.* Spoon about 2 tablespoons of the mole sauce over each piece of chicken. Bake for 5 to 10 minutes more or until chicken is tender and no longer pink.

*5.* Serve chicken over hot cooked rice. Sprinkle chicken with remaining pumpkin seeds. If desired, garnish with carrot strips and cilantro sprigs. Pass remaining mole sauce.

Nutrition Facts per serving: **267 calories, 6 g total fat, 45 mg cholesterol, 180 mg sodium, 31 g carbohydrate, 21 g protein.**

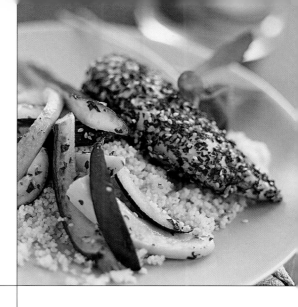

# Chicken with Herb Rub

*Brown the chicken in a skillet and then transfer it to the oven to ensure it's cooked through.*

**Prep:** 15 minutes **Bake:** 12 minutes **Cook:** 6 minutes **Makes:** 4 servings

**1.** In a small bowl combine fennel seeds, mint, sesame seeds, thyme, salt, and pepper. Rub herb mixture over both sides of each chicken breast half.

**2.** In a 12-inch nonstick ovenproof skillet cook chicken in hot oil over medium-high heat about 6 minutes or until browned, turning to brown evenly.

**3.** Cover skillet; transfer to a 400° oven. Bake, covered, for 12 to 15 minutes or until chicken is tender and no longer pink.

Nutrition Facts per serving: **195 calories, 7 g total fat, 66 mg cholesterol, 646 mg sodium, 2 g carbohydrate, 27 g protein.**

- 2 to 4 teaspoons fennel seeds, crushed
- ½ cup fresh mint leaves, snipped
- 2 tablespoons sesame seeds
- 2 teaspoons dried thyme, crushed
- 1 teaspoon salt
- ¼ teaspoon pepper
- 4 medium skinless, boneless chicken breast halves (about 1 pound total)
- 1 tablespoon olive oil or cooking oil

# Crispy Chicken Sticks

*Save cleanup time—and mess—by lining the baking sheet with foil before coating it with nonstick cooking spray.*

**Prep:** 15 minutes  **Bake:** 20 minutes  **Makes:** 4 servings

4 medium skinless, boneless
   chicken breast halves
   (about 1 pound total)
⅓ cup finely crushed
   cornflakes
¼ cup yellow cornmeal
1 tablespoon grated
   Parmesan cheese
⅛ teaspoon ground red pepper
   (optional)
⅓ cup all-purpose flour
   Water
   Nonstick cooking spray
½ cup plain fat-free yogurt
1 tablespoon prepared
   mustard or Dijon-style
   mustard
   Celery sticks and/or carrot
   slices (optional)
   Celery leaves (optional)

**1.** Cut chicken into pieces about 3½×1 inches.

**2.** In shallow bowl combine crushed cornflakes, cornmeal, Parmesan cheese, and, if desired, ground red pepper. Dip each chicken piece into flour, then into a little water. Roll in cornmeal mixture to coat.

**3.** Coat a large baking sheet with nonstick cooking spray. Arrange chicken pieces in a single layer on the baking sheet. Bake in a 375° oven for 20 to 25 minutes or until tender and no longer pink.

**4.** Meanwhile, for dipping sauce, stir together yogurt and mustard. Serve chicken with dipping sauce. If desired, serve with celery sticks and carrot slices. If desired, garnish with celery leaves.

Nutrition Facts per serving: **203 calories, 4 g total fat, 46 mg cholesterol, 169 mg sodium, 20 g carbohydrate, 21 g protein.**

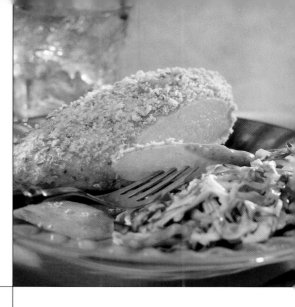

# German-Style Chicken

*Vary the flavor of the three-ingredient brush-on by using your choice of sweet or hot Hungarian paprika.*

**Prep:** 15 minutes  **Bake:** 45 minutes  **Makes:** 4 servings

**1.** In a small bowl combine mustard, sherry, and paprika. Brush 2 tablespoons of the mustard-sherry mixture evenly over tops of chicken breast halves. Place chicken, mustard sides up, in a 3-quart rectangular baking dish. Sprinkle with bread crumbs, patting lightly.

**2.** Bake in a 375° oven for 45 to 50 minutes or until chicken is tender and no longer pink. Serve chicken with the remaining mustard-sherry mixture.

Nutrition Facts per serving: **232 calories, 9 g total fat, 83 mg cholesterol, 306 mg sodium, 4 g carbohydrate, 31 g protein.**

¼ **cup Dusseldorf or horseradish mustard**
2 **tablespoons dry sherry**
½ **teaspoon sweet Hungarian paprika or ¼ teaspoon hot Hungarian paprika**
4 **medium skinless, boneless chicken breast halves (about 1 pound total)**
½ **cup soft rye bread crumbs**

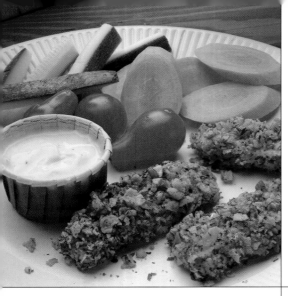

# Nutty Chicken Fingers

*Lunch is ready in a jiffy with these crunchy coated chicken strips.*

**Prep:** 12 minutes  **Bake:** 7 minutes  **Makes:** 3 servings

⅓ cup crushed cornflakes

½ cup finely chopped pecans

1 tablespoon dried parsley
   flakes

⅛ teaspoon salt

⅛ teaspoon garlic powder

12 ounces skinless, boneless
   chicken breasts, cut into
   3×1-inch strips

2 tablespoons fat-free milk
   Reduced-calorie ranch-style
   dressing (optional)

**1.** In a shallow dish combine crushed cornflakes, pecans, parsley, salt, and garlic powder. Dip chicken into milk, then roll in cornflake mixture. Place in a 15×10×1-inch baking pan.

**2.** Bake in a 400° oven for 7 to 9 minutes or until chicken is tender and no longer pink. If desired, serve chicken with ranch-style dressing.

Nutrition Facts per serving: **279 calories, 15 g total fat, 66 mg cholesterol, 219 mg sodium, 8 g carbohydrate, 29 g protein.**

# Pesto Chicken and Peppers

*The pesto recipe makes more than you need. Freeze the remaining pesto in ¼-cup portions so it will be at the ready next time you make this chicken dish.*

**Prep:** 40 minutes  **Bake:** 16 minutes  **Makes:** 4 servings

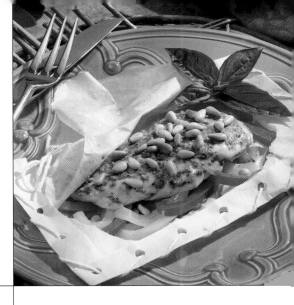

**1.** Place each breast half between 2 pieces of plastic wrap. Pound with flat side of meat mallet into rectangle about ½ inch thick. Set aside. Fold each sheet of parchment or foil in half crosswise. Open up to lie flat. Arrange pepper strips and onion rings in the center of one side of each sheet. Place chicken breast halves over vegetables. Spread Reduced-Fat Pesto evenly over chicken; sprinkle with pine nuts.

**2.** Fold the paper over the chicken. Fold each of the short sides toward the center of the package, making a 1-inch fold on each edge. Fold the bottom edge toward the center, making a 1-inch fold. Punch holes at 1-inch intervals through the three folded edges. Weave 100%-cotton kitchen string through holes, tying ends of each string with a bow. Place on baking sheet.

**3.** Bake in a 400° oven for 16 to 18 minutes or until chicken is tender and no longer pink.

***Reduced-Fat Pesto:*** In a blender container or food processor bowl combine 1 cup firmly packed fresh basil leaves; ½ cup torn fresh spinach leaves; ¼ cup grated Parmesan cheese; ¼ cup pine nuts or almonds; 2 cloves garlic, quartered; and ¼ teaspoon salt. Cover and blend or process with several on-off turns until a paste forms, stopping the machine several times and scraping side. With machine running slowly, gradually add 2 tablespoons olive oil or cooking oil and 2 tablespoons water. Blend or process until the consistency of soft butter. Makes ¾ cup.

4 medium skinless, boneless
   chicken breast halves
   (about 1 pound total)
4 13×10-inch sheets
   parchment paper or foil
1 red sweet pepper, cut into
   long, thin strips
1 yellow or green sweet
   pepper, cut into long,
   thin strips
1 small onion, thinly sliced
   and separated into rings
¼ cup Reduced-Fat Pesto
¼ cup pine nuts, toasted

Nutrition Facts per serving: 237 calories, 13 g total fat, 61 mg cholesterol, 144 mg sodium, 6 g carbohydrate, 26 g protein.

# Blackened Chicken

*An avocado, papaya, and sweet pepper salsa complements the well-seasoned chicken.*

**Prep:** 30 minutes **Bake:** 15 minutes **Makes:** 4 servings

2 tablespoons rice vinegar
2 tablespoons olive oil
¼ teaspoon ground cumin
⅛ teaspoon salt
  Dash ground black pepper
1 avocado, halved, seeded, peeled, and chopped
½ of a papaya, peeled, seeded, and chopped
⅓ cup finely chopped red sweet pepper
¼ cup snipped fresh cilantro
4 medium skinless, boneless chicken breast halves (about 1 pound total)
1 tablespoon blackened steak seasoning
1 tablespoon olive oil

**1.** For salsa, in a large bowl whisk together rice vinegar, the 2 tablespoons olive oil, the cumin, salt, and black pepper. Add avocado, papaya, sweet pepper, and cilantro; toss together. Set aside.

**2.** Lightly sprinkle both sides of each chicken breast half with blackened steak seasoning.

**3.** In a large ovenproof skillet cook chicken breast halves in the 1 tablespoon hot oil until browned, turning frequently to brown evenly. Bake in a 375° oven about 15 minutes or until the chicken is tender and no longer pink. Do not turn chicken breasts during baking.

**4.** To serve, spoon some of the salsa over the chicken. Pass the remaining salsa (or serve it with chips, if you like).

Nutrition Facts per serving: **305 calories, 21 g total fat, 59 mg cholesterol, 128 mg sodium, 7 g carbohydrate, 22 g protein.**

# Tomato-Stuffed Chicken Rolls

*Serve these tomato-and-cheese-stuffed chicken rolls with hot cooked pasta, spaghetti sauce, and a tossed salad.*

**Prep:** 35 minutes **Bake:** 20 minutes **Makes:** 8 servings

**1.** Place each chicken breast half between 2 pieces of plastic wrap. Pound lightly with the flat side of a meat mallet into a rectangle about ⅛ inch thick. Remove plastic wrap.

**2.** In a small bowl combine tomatoes, Parmesan cheese, the ½ teaspoon herb, and the pepper. Spread tomato mixture over chicken rectangles. Fold in long sides of each chicken rectangle. Starting from short side, roll up each chicken breast to enclose filling. Secure with wooden toothpicks.

**3.** In a shallow dish combine the egg white and water. In another shallow dish combine crushed cornflakes and the 1 teaspoon herb. Dip each chicken roll into the egg white mixture. Roll in the cornflake mixture to coat.

**4.** Coat a 3-quart rectangular baking dish with nonstick cooking spray. Place chicken rolls, seam sides down, in dish. Bake in a 400° oven for 20 to 25 minutes or until chicken is tender and no longer pink. Remove toothpicks. Slice chicken rolls. If desired, serve with warm spaghetti sauce and hot cooked pasta.

**Nutrition Facts per serving:** 129 calories, 4 g total fat, 47 mg cholesterol, 155 mg sodium, 5 g carbohydrate, 19 g protein.

- 8 small skinless, boneless chicken breast halves (about 1½ pounds total)
- 2 medium tomatoes, seeded and chopped
- ¼ cup grated Parmesan cheese
- ½ teaspoon dried Italian seasoning, oregano, or basil, crushed
- ¼ teaspoon pepper
- 1 beaten egg white
- 1 tablespoon water
- ⅔ cup finely crushed cornflakes
- 1 teaspoon dried Italian seasoning, oregano, or basil, crushed
  Nonstick cooking spray
  Bottled low-fat spaghetti sauce, warmed (optional)
  Hot cooked herb linguine or other pasta (optional)

# Chicken in Phyllo

*Steamed sugar snap peas are a delicious side dish for these poultry and cream cheese bundles.*

**Prep:** 25 minutes  **Bake:** 20 minutes  **Makes:** 4 servings

½ of an 8-ounce package
    reduced-fat cream cheese
    (Neufchâtel), softened
¼ cup sliced green onions
1 tablespoon fat-free milk
½ teaspoon dried basil,
    crushed
½ teaspoon dried rosemary,
    crushed
6 sheets frozen phyllo dough,
    thawed
    Nonstick cooking spray
4 medium skinless, boneless
    chicken breast halves
    (about 1 pound total)
2 teaspoons margarine or
    butter, melted
1 tablespoon grated Parmesan
    cheese

**1.** In a blender container or food processor bowl combine cream cheese, green onions, milk, basil, and rosemary. Cover and blend or process until well mixed; set aside.

**2.** Lay one sheet of the phyllo dough on a flat surface; coat with nonstick cooking spray. Top with a second sheet; coat again. Repeat with a third sheet of phyllo dough. Cut stack of phyllo in half crosswise. Repeat with remaining phyllo and nonstick cooking spray. On each half, lay a chicken breast diagonally across one corner of the dough.

**3.** Spoon one-quarter of the cheese mixture over each chicken breast half. Fold corner nearest chicken over filling; fold in sides and roll up. Coat a 13×9×2-inch baking pan with nonstick cooking spray. Place bundles, seam sides down, in pan. Brush bundles with melted margarine; sprinkle with Parmesan cheese.

**4.** Bake in a 400° oven for 20 to 30 minutes or until chicken is no longer pink and phyllo is a deep golden brown.

Nutrition Facts per serving: **309 calories, 15 g total fat, 83 mg cholesterol, 358 mg sodium, 16 g carbohydrate, 27 g protein.**

# Lemon-Tarragon Chicken in a Clay Pot

*If you don't have a clay pot, use the directions given for an ovenproof Dutch oven.*

**Prep:** 20 minutes   **Soak:** 30 minutes   **Bake:** 45 minutes   **Makes:** 4 servings

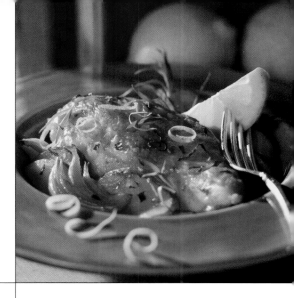

**1.** Do not preheat oven when using clay pot. Submerge the top and bottom portions of a 2- to 3-quart clay pot (unglazed) in a sink of cool water; allow to soak for 30 minutes. In a small bowl combine dried tarragon, finely shredded lemon peel, salt, paprika, and ground red pepper; set aside.

**2.** Drain the clay pot. Place potatoes and onion in pot. Sprinkle with about half of the tarragon mixture. Place chicken pieces on top of potatoes and onion. Sprinkle with remaining tarragon mixture. Put top on clay pot; place in cold oven.

**3.** Set oven temperature to 425°. Bake for 45 to 50 minutes or until potatoes are tender and chicken is tender and no longer pink. Drizzle lemon juice over all. If desired, sprinkle with lemon peel curls and fresh tarragon; serve with lemon wedges.

Nutrition Facts per serving: 382 calories, 13 g total fat, 104 mg cholesterol, 500 mg sodium, 29 g carbohydrate, 37 g protein.

*Dutch-Oven Directions:* Preheat oven to 375°. In a small bowl combine dried tarragon, finely shredded lemon peel, salt, paprika, and ground red pepper. Place potatoes and onion in a large ovenproof Dutch oven. Sprinkle with about half of the tarragon mixture. Place chicken pieces on top of potatoes and onion. Sprinkle with remaining tarragon mixture. Cover and bake for 45 to 50 minutes or until potatoes are tender and chicken is tender and no longer pink. Drizzle lemon juice over all. If desired, sprinkle with lemon peel curls and fresh tarragon; serve with lemon wedges.

1 teaspoon dried tarragon, crushed
1 teaspoon finely shredded lemon peel
¾ teaspoon salt
½ teaspoon paprika
⅛ teaspoon ground red pepper
4 small potatoes, sliced ¼ inch thick (about 1 pound)
1 large onion, cut into 8 wedges
2 pounds meaty chicken pieces (breasts, thighs, and drumsticks)
1 tablespoon lemon juice
Lemon peel curls (optional)
Fresh tarragon leaves (optional)
Lemon wedges (optional)

# French-Glazed Chicken

*The combination of sweet and savory in the four-ingredient glaze is a perfect complement for chicken pieces.*

**Prep:** 10 minutes  **Bake:** 50 minutes  **Makes:** 4 servings

2 pounds meaty chicken
   pieces (breasts, thighs,
   and drumsticks)
¼ cup bottled French salad
   dressing
2 tablespoons peach jam,
   large pieces cut up
1 tablespoon water
1 teaspoon dried minced onion
   or 2 tablespoons finely
   chopped onion

**1.** Skin chicken, if desired. Place chicken pieces in a 3-quart rectangular baking pan.

**2.** For glaze, stir together the salad dressing, peach jam, water, and dried onion; set aside half of the glaze. Brush the remaining glaze lightly over the chicken.

**3.** Bake in a 375° oven for 45 to 55 minutes or until chicken is tender and no longer pink. Brush with reserved glaze; bake for 5 minutes more.

Nutrition Facts per serving: **353 calories, 19 g total fat, 106 mg cholesterol, 306 mg sodium, 10 g carbohydrate, 34 g protein.**

# Old English Chicken

*Look for juniper berries in the spice section of your supermarket.*

**Prep:** 15 minutes  **Bake:** 1 hour  **Makes:** 4 servings

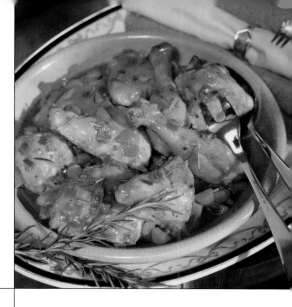

**1.** Place juniper berries and bay leaf in a small square of 100%-cotton cheesecloth; tie together to make a bundle. Set aside.

**2.** In a heavy, large 4- to 5-quart ovenproof Dutch oven cook bacon over medium heat until crisp; stir occasionally. Using a slotted spoon, transfer the bacon to paper towels to drain. In the same Dutch oven cook the chicken in the hot bacon drippings until browned, turning once. Remove chicken.

**3.** Reserve 1 tablespoon bacon drippings in the Dutch oven (if necessary, add cooking oil to make 1 tablespoon fat). Add the carrots, shallots or onion, and celery. Cook about 5 minutes or until vegetables are tender. Add the chicken broth, wine, and the cheesecloth bag; bring to boiling over high heat, scraping up browned bits from bottom and side of the Dutch oven. Add the thyme, rosemary, salt, and pepper. Return chicken and bacon to Dutch oven.

**4.** Bake, covered, in a 350° oven about 1 hour or until tender. Stir in the currant jelly. If desired, season to taste with salt and pepper. If desired, sprinkle with fresh rosemary leaves and garnish with rosemary sprigs.

Nutrition Facts per serving: 290 calories, 9 g total fat, 95 mg cholesterol, 406 mg sodium, 16 g carbohydrate, 32 g protein.

1 teaspoon whole juniper berries
1 large bay leaf
2 slices bacon, coarsely chopped
1 2½- to 3-pound broiler-fryer chicken, cut up and skinned
2 medium carrots, peeled and coarsely chopped
¼ cup finely chopped shallots or onion
¼ cup coarsely chopped celery
½ cup chicken broth
¼ cup dry red wine or port
½ teaspoon dried thyme, crushed
¼ teaspoon dried rosemary, crushed
¼ teaspoon salt
⅛ teaspoon pepper
2 tablespoons red currant jelly
Salt (optional)
Pepper (optional)
Fresh rosemary (optional)

# Chicken and Pasta Primavera

*For best color and flavor, use an assortment of cut-up vegetables.*

**Prep:** 25 minutes   **Bake:** 1 hour   **Makes:** 6 servings

2 to 2½ pounds meaty
   chicken pieces (breasts,
   thighs, and drumsticks)
4 cups assorted fresh
   vegetables, peeled,
   trimmed, and cut into
   1-inch pieces (such as
   carrots, celery, zucchini,
   and/or yellow summer
   squash)
1 medium onion, cut into
   wedges
1 tablespoon Dijon-style
   mustard
1 tablespoon olive oil
2 large cloves garlic, minced
1 teaspoon dried oregano,
   crushed
½ teaspoon dried thyme,
   crushed
½ teaspoon celery salt
¼ teaspoon pepper
⅛ teaspoon salt
6 ounces dried spaghetti
   Freshly shredded Parmesan
   cheese (optional)

**1.** Skin chicken, if desired. Set aside.

**2.** In a 13×9×2-inch baking pan combine vegetables and onion. In a small bowl stir together mustard and olive oil. Drizzle about 2 tablespoons of the mustard-oil mixture over vegetables. Sprinkle the garlic, oregano, thyme, celery salt, pepper, and salt over vegetables. Toss gently to coat.

**3.** Arrange the chicken pieces, bone sides down, on top of vegetables. Brush chicken with remaining mustard-oil mixture.

**4.** Bake in a 350° oven about 1 hour or until chicken is tender and no longer pink. Just before removing chicken from the oven, cook spaghetti according to package directions just until tender. Drain well. Remove chicken pieces to a serving platter. Cover and keep warm.

**5.** In a large serving bowl combine pasta with vegetables and juices from baking pan. Toss to combine. If desired, sprinkle with Parmesan cheese. Serve pasta and vegetables with the chicken pieces.

Nutrition Facts per serving: **329 calories, 12 g total fat, 69 mg cholesterol, 410 mg sodium, 27 g carbohydrate, 27 g protein.**

# Cranberry Chicken

*Looking for an easygoing main dish? This six-ingredient recipe fits the bill. It takes only 10 minutes to assemble.*

**Prep:** 10 minutes  **Bake:** 45 minutes  **Makes:** 4 servings

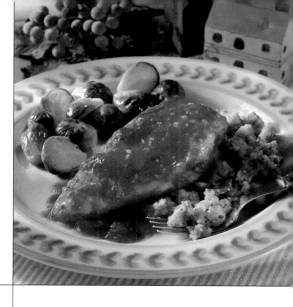

**1.** In a medium bowl stir together the cranberry sauce, salad dressing, dried onion, garlic salt, and pepper.

**2.** Skin chicken, if desired. Arrange chicken pieces in a 3-quart rectangular baking dish. Pour cranberry mixture over chicken.

**3.** Bake in a 350° oven for 45 to 50 minutes or until chicken is tender and no longer pink. Transfer chicken to a serving platter; skim fat from pan juices. Spoon juices over chicken.

Nutrition Facts per serving: 499 calories, 28 g total fat, 104 mg cholesterol, 630 mg sodium, 27 g carbohydrate, 34 g protein.

- 1 8-ounce can whole cranberry sauce
- ½ cup bottled Russian salad dressing
- 1 tablespoon dried minced onion
- ½ teaspoon garlic salt
- ¼ teaspoon pepper
- 2 pounds meaty chicken pieces (breasts, thighs, and drumsticks)

# Plum Wonderful Chicken

*A sweet-sour combo of plum sauce, lemonade concentrate, and chili sauce glazes the chicken.*

**Prep:** 35 minutes  **Bake:** 40 minutes  **Makes:** 6 servings

2½ to 3 pounds meaty chicken
  pieces (legs, breasts,
  thighs, and drumsticks),
  skinned
2 tablespoons olive oil or
  cooking oil
¼ cup chopped onion
1 clove garlic, minced
1 teaspoon grated fresh
  ginger
⅓ cup bottled plum sauce (half
  of an 8½-ounce jar)
¼ cup frozen lemonade
  concentrate
¼ cup bottled chili sauce
2 tablespoons soy sauce
1 tablespoon lemon juice
1 teaspoon dry mustard
  Sesame seeds (optional)
  Thinly sliced green onion
  (optional)
  Deep-fried rice sticks
  (optional)
  Steamed pea pods
  (optional)

**1.** In a skillet cook chicken in hot oil about 10 minutes or until browned, turning frequently to brown evenly. Remove chicken; place in a 3-quart rectangular baking dish. Drain drippings from skillet, reserving 1 tablespoon drippings in skillet. Add the onion, garlic, and ginger. Cook until onion is tender.

**2.** For sauce, in a small bowl stir together the plum sauce, lemonade concentrate, chili sauce, soy sauce, lemon juice, and dry mustard; carefully stir into onion mixture. Bring to boiling; reduce heat. Cover and simmer for 5 minutes; spoon sauce over chicken in dish.

**3.** Bake, uncovered, in a 350° oven for 40 to 45 minutes or until chicken is tender and no longer pink, spooning sauce over chicken occasionally. If desired, sprinkle with sesame seeds and green onion. If desired, serve chicken over rice sticks and pea pods.

Nutrition Facts per serving: 239 calories, 9 g total fat, 77 mg cholesterol, 556 mg sodium, 14 g carbohydrate, 26 g protein.

# Chicken and Barley Bake

*Look for pearl barley near the rices at your supermarket. Be sure to choose regular pearl barley rather than quick-cooking barley.*

**Prep:** 20 minutes **Bake:** 1 hour **Stand:** 10 minutes **Makes:** 4 servings

**1.** Coat an unheated large skillet with nonstick cooking spray. Preheat over medium heat. Add chicken and cook about 10 minutes or until browned, turning to brown evenly. Remove from skillet.

**2.** In same skillet combine the onion, carrot, water, pearl barley, bouillon granules, garlic, and poultry seasoning. Bring to boiling.

**3.** Pour hot barley mixture into a 1½-quart casserole. Arrange the chicken thighs on top of mixture.

**4.** Bake, covered, in a 350° oven about 1 hour or until barley and chicken are tender and chicken is no longer pink. Let stand, covered, for 10 minutes before serving. Sprinkle with parsley.

Nutrition Facts per serving: **219 calories, 7 g total fat, 49 mg cholesterol, 284 mg sodium, 23 g carbohydrate, 17 g protein.**

Nonstick cooking spray
4 chicken thighs, skinned
   (about 1½ pounds total)
1 cup chopped onion
¾ cup chopped carrot
¾ cup water
½ cup pearl barley
1 teaspoon instant chicken
   bouillon granules
1 clove garlic, minced
½ teaspoon poultry seasoning
2 tablespoons snipped fresh
   parsley

# Oven-Fried Herb Chicken

*Oven-frying gives chicken a crispy coating—without the mess of range-top frying in oil.*

**Prep:** 15 minutes  **Bake:** 40 minutes  **Makes:** 6 servings

2½ to 3 pounds meaty chicken
    pieces (breasts, thighs,
    and drumsticks)
⅔ cup finely crushed
    cornflakes
 1 teaspoon paprika
¾ teaspoon garlic salt or
    onion salt
½ teaspoon poultry seasoning
½ teaspoon dried basil,
    crushed
½ teaspoon dried oregano,
    crushed
¼ teaspoon pepper

**1.** Skin chicken, if desired. In a plastic bag or a bowl combine cornflakes, paprika, garlic salt or onion salt, poultry seasoning, basil, oregano, and pepper. Place chicken pieces, 1 or 2 at a time, in the cornflake mixture. Shake or turn to coat evenly. Place chicken pieces, skin sides up, on a rack in a shallow baking pan, making sure pieces do not touch.

**2.** Bake in a 375° oven for 40 to 50 minutes or until chicken is tender and no longer pink. Do not turn during baking.

Nutrition Facts per serving: 236 calories, 11 g total fat, 86 mg cholesterol, 395 mg sodium, 5 g carbohydrate, 28 g protein.

# Tangy Chicken

*Look for convenient tubes of already-cooked polenta in the produce section of your supermarket.*

**Prep:** 15 minutes  **Bake:** 45 minutes  **Makes:** 5 or 6 servings

**1.** In a small bowl combine salt and pepper. Sprinkle 1 teaspoon of the salt mixture over both sides of chicken.

**2.** Brush oil on the bottom of a broiler pan or shallow roasting pan. Add onions, shallots, the ¼ cup sage, and the remaining salt and pepper mixture to pan. Arrange chicken, skin sides up, on top of onions. Pour 3 tablespoons of the vinegar evenly over chicken. Sprinkle the 1 tablespoon sage over top.

**3.** Bake in a 400° oven about 45 minutes or until chicken is tender and no longer pink. Pour remaining vinegar over chicken. Transfer chicken and onions to a large serving plate. If desired, garnish with fresh sage sprigs. If desired, serve with polenta.

Nutrition Facts per serving: 575 calories, 39 g total fat, 208 mg cholesterol, 665 mg sodium, 10 g carbohydrate, 44 g protein.

1 teaspoon salt
½ teaspoon freshly ground pepper
3 pounds chicken thighs
1 teaspoon olive oil
1 large sweet onion (such as Vidalia or Walla Walla), cut into ½-inch-thick slices
1 large red onion, cut into ½-inch-thick slices
2 shallots, quartered
¼ cup snipped fresh sage
¼ cup sherry vinegar
1 tablespoon snipped fresh sage
Fresh sage sprigs (optional)
Purchased cooked polenta, baked according to package directions (optional)

# Spanish Chicken and Rice

*Just a hint of saffron adds a yellow tint and exotic flavor to this colorful one-dish meal.*

**Prep:** 35 minutes  **Bake:** 35 minutes  **Makes:** 6 servings

1 cup chopped onion

½ cup chopped green sweet pepper

2 cloves garlic, minced

2 teaspoons cooking oil

1¾ cups chicken broth

1 cup long grain rice

¼ cup dry white wine

1 bay leaf

⅛ teaspoon ground saffron or ground turmeric

1 cup frozen peas, thawed

½ cup sliced pimiento-stuffed olives

¼ cup snipped fresh parsley

2 to 2½ pounds meaty chicken pieces (breasts, thighs, and drumsticks)

1 tablespoon cooking oil

¼ teaspoon garlic salt

⅛ teaspoon paprika

Fresh parsley sprigs (optional)

**1.** In medium saucepan cook onion, green pepper, and garlic in the 2 teaspoons hot oil over medium-high heat until tender. Add chicken broth, uncooked rice, wine, bay leaf, and saffron or turmeric. Bring to boiling; reduce heat. Cover and simmer for 10 minutes. Discard bay leaf. Stir in peas, olives, and snipped parsley. Spoon into a 3-quart rectangular baking dish.

**2.** Skin chicken, if desired. In a large skillet cook chicken in the 1 tablespoon hot oil over medium-high heat about 10 minutes or until browned, turning to brown evenly. Arrange chicken over rice in baking dish. Sprinkle chicken with garlic salt and paprika. Cover baking dish with foil.

**3.** Bake in a 350° oven for 35 to 40 minutes or until chicken is tender and no longer pink. If desired, garnish with fresh parsley sprigs.

Nutrition Facts per serving: **386 calories, 15 g total fat, 69 mg cholesterol, 694 mg sodium, 33 g carbohydrate, 28 g protein.**

# Two-Bean Cassoulet

*Using canned beans shortcuts this classic French country supper.*

**Prep:** 25 minutes **Bake:** 25 minutes **Makes:** 6 servings

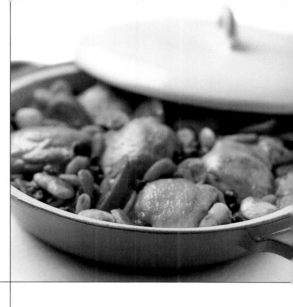

**1.** In a large ovenproof skillet cook chicken in hot oil over medium-low heat about 10 minutes or until browned, turning to brown evenly. Remove chicken from skillet, reserving drippings. Add carrots, onion, and garlic to drippings in skillet. Cover and cook about 10 minutes or until carrots are just tender, stirring occasionally.

**2.** Stir in the drained beans, tomato sauce, wine, thyme, and allspice. Stir in sausage. Arrange chicken thighs on top.

**3.** Bake in a 350° oven for 25 to 30 minutes or until chicken is tender and no longer pink.

Nutrition Facts per serving: 332 calories, 9 g total fat, 101 mg cholesterol, 1,022 mg sodium, 27 g carbohydrate, 34 g protein.

6 skinless, boneless chicken thighs (about 1¼ pounds total)

1 tablespoon olive oil or cooking oil

3 medium carrots, thinly sliced

½ cup chopped onion

2 cloves garlic, minced

1 15-ounce can butter beans, rinsed and drained

1 15-ounce can black beans, rinsed and drained

1 8-ounce can tomato sauce

¼ cup dry red wine

1 teaspoon dried thyme, crushed

¼ teaspoon ground allspice

8 ounces cooked smoked turkey sausage, cut into ½-inch-thick slices

# Chicken and Vegetable Pizza

*Starting with refrigerated pizza dough enables you to get freshly made pizza on the table in only 30 minutes.*

**Start to Finish:** 30 minutes  **Makes:** 4 servings

1 10-ounce package
   refrigerated pizza dough

1 large onion, sliced and
   separated into rings

1 medium red or green sweet
   pepper, chopped

1 cup sliced fresh mushrooms

1 teaspoon bottled minced
   garlic or 2 cloves garlic,
   minced

1 tablespoon cooking oil
   or olive oil

9 ounces skinless, boneless
   chicken breasts, cut into
   bite-size strips

1½ cups shredded mozzarella
   cheese (6 ounces)

1 tablespoon snipped fresh
   basil or ½ teaspoon dried
   basil, crushed

1 teaspoon sesame seeds
   (optional)

**1.** Unroll pizza dough; pat into a greased 12-inch pizza pan. Bake in a 425° oven for 8 minutes.

**2.** Meanwhile, in a large skillet cook onion, sweet pepper, mushrooms, and garlic in hot oil over high heat for 2 to 3 minutes or until crisp-tender. Remove from skillet.

**3.** Add chicken to hot skillet; cook for 2 to 3 minutes or until no longer pink. (Add more oil as necessary during cooking.) Return vegetables to skillet; toss to mix. Heat through.

**4.** Sprinkle half of the mozzarella cheese over pizza crust. Spoon chicken mixture evenly over cheese on crust. Top with remaining cheese. Sprinkle with basil and, if desired, sesame seeds. Bake in the 425° oven for 5 to 7 minutes more or until cheese melts.

Nutrition Facts per serving: **385 calories, 15 g total fat, 57 mg cholesterol, 457 mg sodium, 34 g carbohydrate, 28 g protein.**

# Chicken and Biscuit Pie

*If you prefer, use a 2-quart rectangular baking dish instead of the individual casseroles.*

**Prep:** 35 minutes  **Cook:** 20 minutes  **Bake:** 20 minutes  **Makes:** 4 servings

**1.** In a 4-quart Dutch oven combine chicken, water, and bay leaf. Bring to boiling; reduce heat. Cover and simmer for 20 to 25 minutes or until chicken is tender and no longer pink. Drain, reserving cooking liquid. Discard bay leaf. Cool chicken slightly; discard bones and cut chicken into bite-size pieces.

**2.** Meanwhile, in saucepan cook potatoes and onion in boiling water about 10 minutes or until tender. Drain; keep warm.

**3.** For sauce, in a small saucepan stir together dry milk powder, flour, basil, poultry seasoning, salt, and pepper. Add 2 cups of the reserved chicken cooking liquid, stirring until smooth. Cook and stir over medium heat until thickened and bubbly. Gently stir together the cut-up chicken, drained vegetables, peas, and sauce; keep warm while preparing Green Onion Biscuit Topper.

**4.** Spoon chicken mixture into four 14-ounce individual casserole dishes. Drop Green Onion Biscuit Topper onto warm mixture to form 2 biscuits on each casserole. Bake in a 400° oven for 20 to 25 minutes or until biscuits are golden and wooden toothpick inserted into biscuits comes out clean.

***Green Onion Biscuit Topper:*** In a medium bowl stir together ⅔ cup all-purpose flour; 1 tablespoon thinly sliced green onion; 1 teaspoon baking powder; 1 teaspoon sugar; ¼ teaspoon dried basil, crushed; and dash salt. In a small bowl stir together ⅓ cup fat-free milk and 4 teaspoons cooking oil. Stir milk mixture into flour mixture just until combined.

Nutrition Facts per serving: 462 calories, 14 g total fat, 61 mg cholesterol, 315 mg sodium, 52 g carbohydrate, 32 g protein.

1½ pounds chicken breasts, skinned
2¼ cups water
1 bay leaf
2 cups cubed peeled potatoes
1 cup chopped onion
½ cup nonfat dry milk powder
5 tablespoons all-purpose flour
1 teaspoon dried basil, crushed
¾ teaspoon poultry seasoning
¼ teaspoon salt
⅛ teaspoon pepper
1 cup loose-pack frozen peas
1 recipe Green Onion Biscuit Topper

# Chicken and Prosciutto Pasta

*Prosciutto and capers add a gourmet touch to this company-special dish that's based on two refrigerated pasta sauces.*

**Prep:** 30 minutes  **Bake:** 25 minutes  **Makes:** 6 servings

Nonstick cooking spray
6 ounces dried penne pasta
  (about 2 cups)
12 ounces skinless, boneless
  chicken breasts, cut into
  ½-inch-wide strips
2 cloves garlic, minced
1 tablespoon olive oil
4 ounces sliced prosciutto or
  ham, coarsely chopped
½ of a medium green sweet
  pepper, cut into bite-size
  strips
½ of a medium yellow sweet
  pepper, cut into bite-size
  strips
1 teaspoon dried basil,
  crushed
1 tablespoon drained capers
  (optional)
1 15-ounce container
  refrigerated marinara sauce
1 10-ounce container
  refrigerated Alfredo sauce
⅓ cup finely shredded
  Parmesan cheese
  Fresh basil sprigs (optional)

**1.** Coat a 2-quart casserole with nonstick cooking spray; set aside. Cook pasta according to package directions. Drain and return pasta to saucepan; set aside.

**2.** Meanwhile, in a large skillet cook and stir chicken and garlic in hot oil over medium-high heat for 2 minutes. Add prosciutto, green and yellow pepper strips, dried basil, and, if desired, capers. Cook and stir for 2 to 3 minutes more or until chicken is no longer pink and peppers are crisp-tender. Add to pasta in saucepan; mix well.

**3.** Layer half of the pasta mixture in the prepared casserole. Top with 1 cup of the marinara sauce. Top with the remaining pasta mixture; spoon Alfredo sauce over. Drizzle with remaining marinara sauce. Sprinkle with Parmesan cheese.

**4.** Bake in a 350° oven for 25 to 35 minutes or until heated through. If desired, garnish with fresh basil sprigs.

Nutrition Facts per serving: 465 calories, 26 g total fat, 62 mg cholesterol, 839 mg sodium, 30 g carbohydrate, 28 g protein.

# Apricot Chicken

*To bake acorn squash halves with the chicken, arrange them, cut sides down, in a baking dish. Bake in the 375° oven for 30 minutes. Turn over. Cover; bake for 20 to 25 minutes more or until tender.*

**Prep:** 10 minutes  **Bake:** 45 minutes  **Makes:** 4 servings

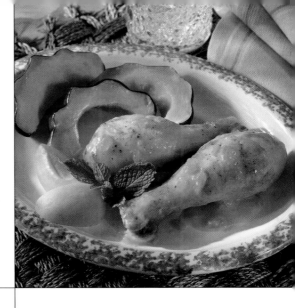

**1.** Skin chicken, if desired. Arrange chicken pieces in a 3-quart rectangular baking pan, skin sides up, making sure pieces do not touch. Sprinkle lightly with salt and pepper.

**2.** Bake in a 375° oven for 40 minutes. Drain off fat.

**3.** Meanwhile, in a small bowl stir together yogurt, apricot jam, and cumin. Spoon yogurt mixture over chicken. Bake for 5 to 10 minutes more or until chicken is tender and no longer pink. If desired, garnish with apricot wedges and herb sprigs.

Nutrition Facts per serving: **351 calories, 14 g total fat, 106 mg cholesterol, 176 mg sodium, 21 g carbohydrate, 35 g protein.**

2 **pounds meaty chicken pieces (breasts, thighs, and drumsticks)**
  **Salt**
  **Pepper**
⅓ **cup plain yogurt**
⅓ **cup apricot jam, large pieces cut up**
1½ **teaspoons ground cumin**
  **Fresh apricot wedges (optional)**
  **Fresh herb sprigs (optional)**

# Chicken Manicotti with Chive Cream Sauce

*These stuffed pasta shells are bursting with a tasty chicken filling studded with colorful roasted red sweet peppers and broccoli.*

**Prep:** 30 minutes  **Bake:** 25 minutes  **Makes:** 6 servings

12 dried manicotti shells

 1 8-ounce container soft-style cream cheese with chives and onion

⅔ cup milk

¼ cup grated Romano or Parmesan cheese (1 ounce)

 2 cups chopped cooked chicken (10 ounces)

 1 10-ounce package frozen chopped broccoli, thawed and drained

½ of a 7-ounce jar roasted red sweet peppers, drained and sliced, or one 4-ounce jar diced pimiento, drained

¼ teaspoon ground black pepper

Paprika

***1.*** Cook manicotti shells according to package directions. Drain shells; rinse with cold water. Drain again.

***2.*** Meanwhile, for sauce, in a heavy, small saucepan melt cream cheese over medium-low heat, stirring constantly. Slowly add milk, stirring until smooth. Stir in Romano or Parmesan cheese. Remove from heat.

***3.*** For filling, in a medium bowl stir together ¾ cup of the sauce, the chicken, broccoli, roasted red sweet peppers or pimiento, and black pepper. Using a small spoon, carefully fill each manicotti shell with about ⅓ cup of the filling.

***4.*** Arrange the filled shells in a 3-quart rectangular baking dish. Pour the remaining sauce over the shells. Sprinkle with paprika. Cover with foil. Bake in a 350° oven for 25 to 30 minutes or until heated through.

Nutrition Facts per serving: **396 calories, 18 g total fat, 92 mg cholesterol, 257 mg sodium, 31 g carbohydrate, 25 g protein.**

# Chicken-Artichoke Turnovers

*Sour cream and Monterey Jack cheese add a creamy richness to these plump turnovers.*

**Prep:** 30 minutes  **Bake:** 25 minutes  **Makes:** 6 turnovers

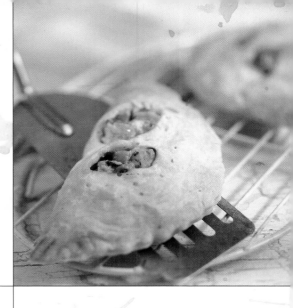

**1.** Thaw patty shells; set aside. For filling, in a medium bowl stir together sour cream, chili powder, garlic, and lemon juice. Stir in chicken, Monterey Jack cheese, artichoke hearts, chili peppers, green onions, and parsley.

**2.** On a lightly floured surface, roll each patty shell to a 7-inch circle. Place about ½ cup of the filling on half of each circle. For each turnover, moisten edge of circle with water; fold other half of circle over filling. Press with tines of a fork to seal.

**3.** Line a baking sheet with foil; place turnovers on baking sheet. Cut slits in the top of each turnover to allow steam to escape. Brush tops with milk. Bake in a 400° oven for 25 to 30 minutes or until golden brown.

Nutrition Facts per serving: **367 calories, 23 g total fat, 48 mg cholesterol, 378 mg sodium, 22 g carbohydrate, 18 g protein.**

- 1 **10-ounce package (6) frozen patty shells**
- ¼ **cup light dairy sour cream**
- 1 to 1½ **teaspoons chili powder**
- 2 **cloves garlic, minced**
- 1 **teaspoon lemon juice**
- 1½ **cups chopped cooked chicken (about 8 ounces)**
- ¾ **cup shredded Monterey Jack cheese (3 ounces)**
- ¾ **cup coarsely chopped, drained artichoke hearts (half of a 14-ounce can)**
- 1 **4-ounce can diced green chili peppers, drained**
- 2 **green onions, thinly sliced**
- 1 **tablespoon snipped fresh parsley**
  **Milk**

# Deep-Dish Chicken Pie

*If you don't have any leftover cooked chicken on hand, purchase a deli-roasted chicken and use its meat.*

**Prep:** 50 minutes  **Bake:** 30 minutes  **Cool:** 20 minutes  **Makes:** 6 servings

1 recipe Pastry Topper
3 medium leeks or 1 large
    onion, chopped
1 cup sliced fresh mushrooms
¾ cup sliced celery
½ cup chopped red sweet
    pepper
2 tablespoons margarine
    or butter
⅓ cup all-purpose flour
1 teaspoon poultry seasoning
¼ teaspoon salt
¼ teaspoon ground black
    pepper
1½ cups chicken broth
1 cup half-and-half, light
    cream, or milk
2½ cups chopped cooked
    chicken (about 12 ounces)
1 cup frozen peas
1 beaten egg

**1.** On a lightly floured surface roll Pastry Topper into a rectangle ⅛ inch thick and at least 13×9 inches. Trim to a 12×8-inch rectangle. Using a sharp knife, cut slits in pastry to allow steam to escape. (Or if desired, use a small cookie cutter to cut shapes from pastry; reserve shapes.) Set aside.

**2.** In a large saucepan cook leeks or onion, mushrooms, celery, and sweet pepper in hot margarine or butter for 4 to 5 minutes or until tender. Stir in the flour, poultry seasoning, salt, and black pepper. Add broth and half-and-half, light cream, or milk all at once. Cook and stir until thickened and bubbly. Stir in the chicken and peas. Pour into a 2-quart rectangular baking dish.

**3.** Place pastry over the hot chicken mixture in baking dish; turn edges of pastry under and flute to top edges of dish. Brush with beaten egg. If desired, place reserved pastry shapes on top of pastry. Brush again with egg.

**4.** Bake in a 400° oven for 30 to 35 minutes or until pastry is golden brown. Cool 20 minutes before serving.

***Pastry Topper:*** In a medium bowl stir together 1¼ cups all-purpose flour and ¼ teaspoon salt. Using a pastry blender, cut in ⅓ cup shortening until pieces are the size of small peas. Sprinkle 1 tablespoon cold water over part of the mixture; gently toss with fork. Push moistened dough to side of bowl. Repeat with an additional 3 to 4 tablespoons cold water, using 1 tablespoon at a time, until all of the dough is moistened. Form into a ball.

Nutrition Facts per serving: 484 calories, 26 g total fat, 107 mg cholesterol, 538 mg sodium, 35 g carbohydrate, 27 g protein.

# Chicken Enchiladas

*Using chicken and lower-fat dairy products in these enchiladas results in a healthier version of a Tex-Mex favorite.*

**Prep:** 45 minutes  **Bake:** 50 minutes  **Makes:** 8 enchiladas

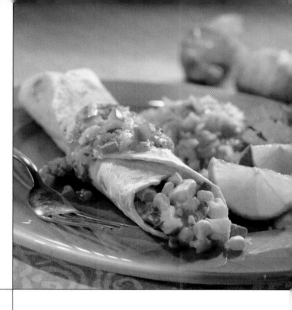

**1.** Stack tortillas; wrap tightly in foil. Heat in a 350° oven for 10 minutes to soften.

**2.** For filling, in a medium bowl stir together chicken or turkey, corn, cream cheese, sour cream, and green onions.

**3.** Coat a 3-quart rectangular baking dish with nonstick cooking spray; set aside. Spoon about ⅓ cup of the filling onto each tortilla near an edge; roll up. Arrange filled tortillas in prepared baking dish.

**4.** For sauce, in a blender container combine fresh or undrained canned tomatillos, chili peppers, onion, cilantro, sugar, and cumin. Add 1 cup broth if using fresh tomatillos or ½ cup broth if using canned tomatillos. Cover; blend until smooth. Transfer to a saucepan. Bring to boiling; reduce heat. Simmer, uncovered, for 10 minutes.

**5.** Pour sauce over enchiladas. Cover with foil. Bake in a 350° oven about 45 minutes or until heated through. Remove foil; sprinkle enchiladas with shredded cheese. Bake 5 minutes more or until cheese is melted. If desired, top enchiladas with chopped tomato.

Nutrition Facts per enchilada: 255 calories, 10 g total fat, 40 mg cholesterol, 470 mg sodium, 27 g carbohydrate, 17 g protein.

8 8-inch flour tortillas
1½ cups chopped cooked
    chicken or turkey
    (about 8 ounces)
1 11-ounce can whole kernel
    corn with sweet peppers,
    drained
⅓ cup tub light cream cheese
¼ cup fat-free or light dairy
    sour cream
¼ cup sliced green onions
    Nonstick cooking spray
2½ cups cut-up fresh tomatillos
    or one 18-ounce can
    tomatillos
1 4-ounce can diced green
    chili peppers, drained
¼ cup chopped onion
¼ cup fresh cilantro leaves
½ teaspoon sugar
¼ teaspoon ground cumin
½ to 1 cup reduced-sodium
    chicken broth
¾ cup shredded reduced-fat
    Monterey Jack cheese
    (3 ounces)
1 medium tomato, chopped
    (optional)

# Green and Red Chicken Enchiladas

*Tomatillos (sometimes called Mexican green tomatoes) contribute the green and tomato contributes the red to this hearty casserole.*

**Prep:** 40 minutes  **Bake:** 35 minutes  **Makes:** 6 servings

1 pound fresh tomatillos, husked and chopped, or one 18-ounce can tomatillos, rinsed, drained, and cut up

1½ cups chopped onion

¼ cup firmly packed fresh cilantro leaves or fresh parsley sprigs

1 4-ounce can diced green chili peppers, drained

¼ teaspoon ground cumin

¼ teaspoon ground black pepper

1 cup chopped tomato

3 cups shredded cooked chicken or turkey (about 1 pound)

Nonstick cooking spray

⅔ cup low-sodium tomato juice

12 6-inch corn tortillas

⅔ cup shredded reduced-fat Monterey Jack cheese

**1.** In a blender container or food processor bowl combine tomatillos, 1 cup of the onion, the cilantro or parsley, chili peppers, cumin, and black pepper. Cover and blend or process until smooth. Set aside.

**2.** In a nonstick skillet cook tomato and remaining onion for 3 minutes. Stir in chicken and 1 cup of the tomatillo mixture; heat through. Coat a 3-quart rectangular baking dish with nonstick cooking spray.

**3.** To assemble enchiladas, pour tomato juice into a shallow dish. Dip a tortilla into tomato juice, coating both sides. Place tortilla on a work surface. Spoon about 3 tablespoons of the chicken mixture down the center of tortilla; roll up. Place, seam side down, in prepared baking dish. Repeat with remaining tomato juice, tortillas, and chicken mixture. Spoon remaining tomatillo mixture over enchiladas.

**4.** Bake, covered, in a 350° oven about 30 minutes or until heated through. Sprinkle with cheese; bake about 5 minutes more or until cheese melts.

Nutrition Facts per serving: **375 calories, 13 g total fat, 67 mg cholesterol, 313 mg sodium, 35 g carbohydrate, 30 g protein.**

# Chicken with Fettuccine

*Round out the meal with sautéed sliced red onions and sweet pepper strips seasoned with a little snipped fresh rosemary and a splash of red wine vinegar.*

**Prep:** 30 minutes  **Bake:** 15 minutes  **Makes:** 4 servings

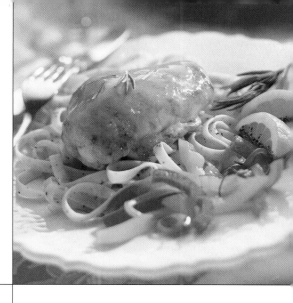

**1.** For chicken rolls, place each breast half between 2 pieces of plastic wrap. Pound lightly with flat side of meat mallet into rectangle about ⅛ inch thick. Remove plastic wrap. Stir together ground chicken and next 5 ingredients. Place a mound of the mixture in the center of each chicken piece. Fold in bottom and sides; roll up. Press edges to seal.

**2.** In a large skillet melt butter with 1 tablespoon olive oil. Add chicken rolls. Cook about 5 minutes or until golden, turning to brown evenly. Transfer to a 2-quart rectangular baking dish. Brush with maple syrup; sprinkle with the 1 teaspoon snipped rosemary. Bake in 400° oven for 15 to 18 minutes or until internal temperature registers 165° on instant-read thermometer.

**3.** Meanwhile, cook pasta according to package directions; drain. Toss in lemon juice and 1 tablespoon olive oil. Season to taste with salt and pepper. Serve Maple Sauce over chicken and pasta.

*Maple Sauce:* In large saucepan combine 1 cup chicken broth, 1 cup vegetable broth, ⅓ cup dry white wine, and ½ teaspoon snipped fresh rosemary. Bring to boiling; reduce heat. Boil gently until reduced to about ¾ cup. Cook 2 tablespoons minced onion in 1 teaspoon hot olive oil until tender. Stir in 3 tablespoons maple syrup. When mixture is light brown, stir in 2 tablespoons lemon juice; add to the reduced broth. Cut up 3 tablespoons butter. While continuing to cook, add butter, one piece at a time, whisking until sauce is thickened and smooth. Season to taste with pepper.

Nutrition Facts per serving: 759 calories, 34 g total fat, 192 mg cholesterol, 1,084 mg sodium, 66 g carbohydrate, 47 g protein.

4 medium skinless, boneless chicken breast halves (about 1 pound total)
6 ounces uncooked ground chicken
1 tablespoon whipping cream or milk
1 beaten egg yolk
½ teaspoon snipped fresh rosemary
⅛ teaspoon salt
⅛ teaspoon pepper
1 tablespoon butter
1 tablespoon olive oil
2 tablespoons maple syrup
1 teaspoon snipped fresh rosemary
1 recipe Maple Sauce
8 ounces dried lemon fettuccine, fettuccine, lemon linguine, or linguine
3 tablespoons lemon juice
1 tablespoon olive oil
Salt
Pepper

# Chipotle-Chicken Casserole

*Check larger supermarkets or visit a Hispanic food market for canned chipotle peppers in adobo sauce.*

**Prep:** 20 minutes  **Bake:** 20 minutes  **Makes:** 4 servings

Nonstick cooking spray
2 cups frozen whole kernel
   corn
3 cups frozen diced hash
   brown potatoes
1 14½-ounce can diced
   tomatoes with basil, garlic,
   and oregano
2 canned chipotle peppers
   in adobo sauce, chopped
½ teaspoon chili powder
½ teaspoon ground cumin
½ teaspoon dried oregano,
   crushed
1 tablespoon olive oil
4 medium skinless, boneless
   chicken breast halves
   (about 1 pound total)
¼ teaspoon salt
¼ teaspoon chili powder
¼ teaspoon ground cumin
¾ cup shredded colby and
   Monterey Jack cheese
   (3 ounces)

**1.** Coat a 2-quart casserole with nonstick cooking spray; set aside. Coat an unheated large nonstick skillet with nonstick cooking spray. Preheat skillet over medium-high heat. Add corn; cook about 5 minutes or until corn begins to lightly brown. Add potatoes; cook and stir for 5 to 8 minutes more or until potatoes begin to brown. Stir in tomatoes, chipotle peppers, the ½ teaspoon chili powder, the ½ teaspoon cumin, and the oregano. Remove from heat; spoon into prepared casserole.

**2.** Wipe skillet clean. Add oil to skillet and heat over medium-high heat. Sprinkle chicken evenly with the salt, the ¼ teaspoon chili powder, and the ¼ teaspoon cumin. Cook chicken in hot oil until browned, turning to brown evenly. Place chicken on top of potato mixture in casserole.

**3.** Bake, uncovered, in a 375° oven about 20 minutes or until bubbly and chicken is no longer pink. Sprinkle with cheese.

Nutrition Facts per serving: 460 calories, 15 g total fat, 79 mg cholesterol, 939 mg sodium, 50 g carbohydrate, 33 g protein.

# Southern Baked Chicken With Fruit Salsa

*Dipping the chicken into buttermilk gives it a Southern flair.*

**Prep:** 35 minutes  **Bake:** 10 minutes  **Makes:** 6 servings

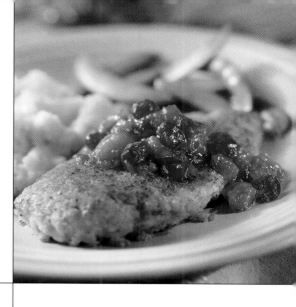

**1.** For salsa, in a saucepan combine rhubarb, sugar, cranberries, vinegar, and ginger. Bring to boiling, stirring occasionally; reduce heat. Simmer, uncovered, about 25 minutes or until rhubarb is tender. Remove from heat. Stir in strawberries; cool.

**2.** Meanwhile, place chicken in a large bowl. Pour buttermilk over; let stand for 15 minutes. In a shallow dish combine wheat germ, bread crumbs, flour, pepper, and salt. Drain chicken, discarding buttermilk. Dip chicken into the crumb mixture to coat evenly.

**3.** In a large skillet heat half of the oil. Add half of the chicken in a single layer. Cook chicken about 4 minutes or until browned, turning once. Carefully transfer to a 13×9×2-inch baking pan. Repeat with remaining chicken and remaining oil. Bake in a 400° oven about 10 minutes or until chicken is no longer pink. Serve with salsa.

Nutrition Facts per serving: **390 calories, 11 g total fat, 69 mg cholesterol, 440 mg sodium, 42 g carbohydrate, 32 g protein.**

- **2 cups fresh rhubarb cut into 1-inch pieces**
- **½ cup sugar**
- **½ cup dried cranberries**
- **¼ cup cider vinegar**
- **1 teaspoon grated fresh ginger**
- **1 cup coarsely chopped strawberries**
- **6 medium boneless, skinless chicken breast halves (about 1½ pounds total)**
- **1 cup buttermilk**
- **½ cup toasted wheat germ**
- **⅓ cup fine dry bread crumbs**
- **3 tablespoons all-purpose flour**
- **1½ teaspoons freshly ground black pepper**
- **¾ teaspoon salt**
- **3 tablespoons cooking oil**

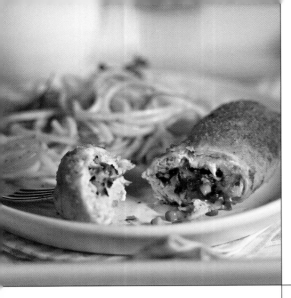

# Chicken Stuffed with Smoked Mozzarella

*If you can't find smoked mozzarella at your grocery store or cheese shop, use regular mozzarella instead.*

**Prep:** 40 minutes  **Bake:** 25 minutes  **Makes:** 6 servings

6 medium skinless, boneless
   chicken breast halves
   (about 1½ pounds total)
   Salt
   Pepper
¼ cup finely chopped shallots
   or onion
1 clove garlic, minced
2 teaspoons olive oil
½ of a 10-ounce package
   frozen chopped spinach,
   thawed and well drained
¾ cup shredded smoked
   mozzarella cheese
   (3 ounces)
3 tablespoons pine nuts or
   walnuts, toasted
¼ cup seasoned fine dry
   bread crumbs
¼ cup grated Parmesan
   cheese
1 tablespoon olive oil

**1.** Place each chicken breast half between 2 pieces of plastic wrap. Pound lightly with the flat side of a meat mallet into a rectangle about ⅛ inch thick. Remove plastic wrap. Season with salt and pepper.

**2.** For filling, in a medium skillet cook shallots and garlic in the 2 teaspoons hot oil until tender. Remove from heat; stir in spinach, smoked mozzarella, and nuts.

**3.** In a shallow bowl combine fine dry bread crumbs and Parmesan cheese.

**4.** Spoon 2 to 3 tablespoons of the filling into the center of each chicken piece. Fold in bottom and sides; roll up. Secure with wooden toothpicks.

**5.** Lightly brush chicken rolls with the 1 tablespoon olive oil; coat with bread crumb mixture. Place rolls, seam sides down, in a shallow baking pan. Bake in a 400° oven about 25 minutes or until chicken is tender and no longer pink. Discard toothpicks.

Nutrition Facts per serving: 274 calories, 11 g total fat, 77 mg cholesterol, 368 mg sodium, 6 g carbohydrate, 35 g protein.

# Creamy Chicken and Rice Bake

*Serve this hearty casserole with a crisp tossed salad and offer an assortment of fresh fruit for dessert.*

**Prep:** 25 minutes   **Bake:** 50 minutes   **Makes:** 4 servings

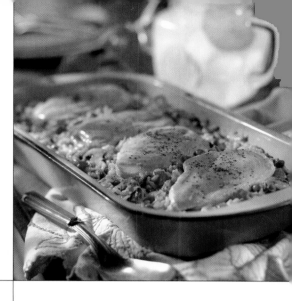

**1.** In a large skillet cook chicken in hot oil over medium-high heat until browned, turning to brown evenly. Remove chicken and set aside. Add mushrooms, onion, and sweet pepper to skillet; cook until vegetables are just tender. Stir in the condensed soup, milk, uncooked rice, carrot, marjoram, and black pepper. Bring to boiling. Stir in peas.

**2.** Coat a 2-quart rectangular baking dish with nonstick cooking spray. Spoon rice mixture into prepared dish. Arrange browned chicken breasts on top of rice mixture. Lightly sprinkle chicken with salt and pepper. Cover with foil.

**3.** Bake in a 375° oven about 50 minutes or until chicken is tender and no longer pink and rice is tender.

Nutrition Facts per serving: **364 calories, 7 g total fat, 62 mg cholesterol, 458 mg sodium, 44 g carbohydrate, 30 g protein.**

- 4 medium skinless, boneless chicken breast halves (about 1 pound total)
- 2 teaspoons cooking oil
- 1 cup sliced fresh mushrooms
- ½ cup chopped onion
- ¼ cup chopped red sweet pepper
- 1 10¾-ounce can reduced-fat and reduced-sodium condensed cream of celery soup
- 1 cup fat-free milk
- ⅔ cup long grain rice
- ½ cup shredded carrot
- ½ teaspoon dried marjoram, crushed
- ⅛ teaspoon ground black pepper
- 1 cup frozen peas
   Nonstick cooking spray
   Salt
   Pepper

# Turkey Lasagna Rolls

*With a ricotta-spinach filling and hearty ground turkey-tomato sauce, these pasta spirals have all the flavors of classic lasagna.*

**Prep:** 25 minutes  **Cook:** 25 minutes  **Bake:** 30 minutes  **Stand:** 5 minutes
**Makes:** 8 servings

8 ounces uncooked ground
   turkey
1 medium onion, chopped
2 cloves garlic, minced
1 cup sliced fresh mushrooms
1 cup water
1 7½-ounce can tomatoes,
   cut up
1 6-ounce can tomato paste
1½ teaspoons dried oregano,
   crushed
1 teaspoon dried basil,
   crushed
8 dried lasagna noodles
1 beaten egg
1 15-ounce carton ricotta
   cheese
1 10-ounce package frozen
   chopped spinach, thawed
   and well drained
1½ cups shredded mozzarella
   cheese (6 ounces)
1 cup grated Parmesan
   cheese (4 ounces)
   Fresh parsley sprigs
   (optional)

**1.** For sauce, in a large skillet cook turkey, onion, and garlic until turkey is browned. Drain off fat. Stir in mushrooms, water, undrained tomatoes, tomato paste, oregano, and basil. Bring to boiling; reduce heat. Cover and simmer for 25 minutes.

**2.** Meanwhile, cook the lasagna noodles according to package directions. Drain noodles; rinse with cold water. Drain again.

**3.** For filling, in a medium bowl stir together egg, ricotta cheese, spinach, 1 cup of the mozzarella cheese, and ¾ cup of the Parmesan cheese.

**4.** To assemble rolls, spread about ½ cup of the filling over each lasagna noodle. Roll up noodle, starting from a short end. Place lasagna rolls, seam sides down, in a 2-quart rectangular baking dish. Pour sauce over lasagna rolls. Cover with foil.

**5.** Bake in a 375° oven for 25 minutes. Remove foil. Sprinkle with remaining mozzarella cheese. Bake for 5 to 10 minutes more or until heated through. Let stand 5 minutes before serving. Sprinkle with remaining Parmesan cheese. If desired, garnish with parsley sprigs.

Nutrition Facts per serving: 345 calories, 15 g total fat, 75 mg cholesterol,
511 mg sodium, 28 g carbohydrate, 26 g protein.

# Turkey Loaf with Pesto

*To ensure that the loaf is fully cooked, be sure to use an instant-read thermometer to measure the temperature in the center of the loaf—it needs to be at least 165°.*

**Prep:** 15 minutes **Bake:** 45 minutes **Stand:** 5 minutes **Makes:** 4 servings

**1.** In a large bowl combine egg, bread crumbs, the ¾ cup cheese, desired liquid, pesto, nutmeg, and pepper. Add turkey; mix well. Form into a loaf and place in an 8×4×2-inch loaf pan.

**2.** Bake turkey loaf in a 350° oven for 45 to 50 minutes or until done (165°).*

**3.** Transfer loaf to a serving platter. If desired, top with additional cheese. Let stand for 5 minutes before slicing.

Nutrition Facts per serving: **315 calories, 21 g total fat, 111 mg cholesterol, 364 mg sodium, 6 g carbohydrate, 24 g protein.**

***Note:*** The internal color of a ground poultry loaf is not a reliable doneness indicator. A turkey or chicken loaf cooked to 165°, regardless of color, is safe. Use an instant-read thermometer to check the internal temperature. To measure the doneness of a loaf, insert an instant-read thermometer into the center of the loaf to a depth of 2 to 3 inches.

***Crockery Cooker Directions:*** Prepare Turkey Loaf with Pesto as directed. Form 3 long strips of folded foil and place them in a spoke design under center of the uncooked loaf. Lift the ends of the foil strips and transfer the loaf to a 3½-quart electric crockery cooker. Cover and cook on low-heat setting for 8 to 10 hours or on high-heat setting for 4 to 5 hours. Leave the foil strips under the loaf during cooking, then use strips to lift the loaf out of the cooker when the loaf is done.

1 beaten egg
¾ cup soft rye bread crumbs
   (1 slice)
¾ cup shredded provolone
   or mozzarella cheese
   (3 ounces)
3 tablespoons beer, milk,
   or water
2 tablespoons purchased pesto
¼ teaspoon ground nutmeg
¼ teaspoon pepper
1 pound uncooked ground
   turkey
   Shredded provolone or
   mozzarella (optional)

# Ginger Turkey Meat Loaf

*To keep this loaf extra-lean, purchase ground turkey breast.*

**Prep:** 20 minutes  **Bake:** 55 minutes  **Stand:** 5 minutes  **Makes:** 6 servings

Nonstick cooking spray
1 egg
1 beaten egg white
1 cup soft whole wheat bread
   crumbs (about 1⅓ slices)
½ cup finely chopped green
   onions
1 2-ounce jar diced pimiento,
   drained
2 tablespoons reduced-sodium
   soy sauce
1 tablespoon milk or water
¼ teaspoon pepper
1½ pounds uncooked ground
   turkey
2 tablespoons apricot
   preserves
¼ teaspoon ground ginger
   Fresh tomato wedges
   (optional)
   Fresh sage (optional)

*1.* Coat a 9×5×3-inch loaf pan with nonstick cooking spray. Set aside.

*2.* In a large bowl combine the egg, egg white, bread crumbs, green onions, pimiento, soy sauce, milk or water, and pepper. Add the ground turkey; mix well. Press mixture into the prepared pan, patting to smooth the top. Bake in a 350° oven for 45 minutes.

*3.* In a small bowl stir together the apricot preserves and ginger; brush over surface of loaf. Bake for 10 to 15 minutes more or until done (165°).* Remove from oven; pour off any drippings. Let stand for 5 minutes; invert onto a plate. Turn right side up for slicing. If desired, garnish with tomato wedges and fresh sage.

Nutrition Facts per serving: **200 calories, 10 g total fat, 78 mg cholesterol, 289 mg sodium, 10 g carbohydrate, 18 g protein.**

*Note:* The internal color of a ground poultry loaf is not a reliable doneness indicator. A turkey or chicken loaf cooked to 165°, regardless of color, is safe. Use an instant-read thermometer to check the internal temperature. To measure the doneness of a loaf, insert an instant-read thermometer into the center of the loaf to a depth of 2 to 3 inches.

# Turkey Meatballs in Wine Sauce

*Take your choice of snipped fresh or crushed dried thyme to subtly season these savory meatballs.*

**Prep:** 30 minutes  **Bake:** 30 minutes  **Makes:** 5 servings

**1.** In a medium bowl stir together egg white, soft bread crumbs, ¼ cup of the onion, the milk, thyme, salt, and pepper. Add turkey; mix well. Shape mixture into 1-inch meatballs.

**2.** Coat a 13×9×2-inch baking pan with nonstick cooking spray. Place meatballs in the baking pan. Bake in a 350° oven for 30 to 35 minutes or until meatballs are done (165°).* Drain off any juices.

**3.** Meanwhile, coat an unheated large skillet with nonstick cooking spray. Preheat over medium heat. Add mushrooms and remaining onion. Cook until onion is tender. In a small bowl combine water, cornstarch, and bouillon granules. Stir cornstarch mixture into mushroom mixture. Cook and stir until thickened and bubbly. Stir in meatballs and wine; heat through. Stir in parsley. Serve over hot cooked noodles. If desired, garnish with carrot curls.

Nutrition Facts per serving: **333 calories, 9 g total fat, 72 mg cholesterol, 389 mg sodium, 39 g carbohydrate, 20 g protein.**

***Note:*** The internal color of ground poultry meatballs is not a reliable doneness indicator. Turkey or chicken meatballs cooked to 165°, regardless of color, are safe. Use an instant-read thermometer to check the internal temperature. To measure the doneness of meatballs, insert an instant-read thermometer into the center of a meatball.

- 1 egg white
- 1 cup soft bread crumbs
- ½ cup finely chopped onion
- 2 tablespoons fat-free milk
- ¾ teaspoon snipped fresh thyme or ¼ teaspoon dried thyme, crushed
- ¼ teaspoon salt
   Dash pepper
- 1 pound uncooked ground turkey
   Nonstick cooking spray
- 2 cups sliced fresh mushrooms
- 1 cup cold water
- 2 tablespoons cornstarch
- 1 teaspoon instant chicken bouillon granules
- ⅓ cup dry white wine
- 2 tablespoons snipped fresh parsley
   Hot cooked noodles
   Carrot curls (optional)

# Turkey Piccata with Artichokes

*This adaptation of an Italian classic uses turkey instead of the traditional veal and adds artichokes for a heartier dish.*

**Prep:** 20 minutes  **Bake:** 12 minutes  **Makes:** 6 servings

Nonstick cooking spray
1 pound turkey breast
    tenderloin steaks*
¼ cup fat-free milk
1½ cups soft whole wheat
    bread crumbs
1 teaspoon dried Italian
    seasoning, crushed
1 9-ounce package frozen
    artichoke hearts, thawed
1¼ cups reduced-sodium
    chicken broth
2 shallots, sliced, or
    2 tablespoons finely
    chopped onion
2 tablespoons lemon juice
1 tablespoon cornstarch
1 tablespoon Dijon-style
    mustard
½ teaspoon dried Italian
    seasoning, crushed
⅛ teaspoon pepper
    Lemon slice twists
    (optional)

**1.** Coat a 15×10×1-inch baking pan with nonstick cooking spray. Cut turkey steaks into 6 serving-size pieces. Pour milk into a shallow bowl. In another shallow bowl stir together bread crumbs and the 1 teaspoon Italian seasoning. Dip turkey pieces into milk, then into the bread crumb mixture to coat.

**2.** Arrange turkey in a single layer in the prepared pan. Bake in a 450° oven about 12 minutes or until turkey is tender and no longer pink and crumb coating is crisp.

**3.** Meanwhile, for sauce, cut any large artichoke hearts in half. In a medium saucepan combine artichoke hearts, broth, and shallots or onion. Bring to boiling; reduce heat. Cover and simmer for 5 minutes. In a small bowl combine lemon juice, cornstarch, mustard, the ½ teaspoon Italian seasoning, and the pepper; add to saucepan. Cook and stir until thickened and bubbly; cook and stir for 2 minutes more. Serve sauce over turkey. If desired, garnish with lemon slice twists.

Nutrition Facts per serving: **142 calories, 3 g total fat, 33 mg cholesterol, 333 mg sodium, 12 g carbohydrate, 18 g protein.**

***Note:*** If you can't find turkey breast tenderloin steaks, buy two turkey breast tenderloins and split them in half lengthwise.

# Creamy Turkey Pie

*If bulk turkey sausage isn't available, purchase uncooked ground turkey and season it yourself.*

**Prep:** 25 minutes  **Bake:** 30 minutes  **Stand:** 5 minutes  **Makes:** 6 servings

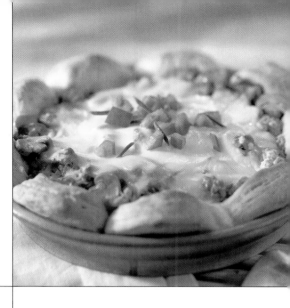

**1.** In a large skillet cook turkey sausage or ground turkey and onion until meat is browned. Drain off fat. Stir in cream cheese until melted; stir in mushrooms. Cover and keep warm.

**2.** For crust, lightly grease a 9-inch deep-dish pie plate. Arrange biscuits in pie plate, pressing together onto the bottom and up side to form an even crust. Spoon turkey mixture into crust, spreading evenly.

**3.** In a blender container or food processor bowl combine egg, cottage cheese, and flour. Cover and blend or process until smooth. Spread evenly over turkey mixture. Bake in a 350° oven about 30 minutes or until edge is browned and top is set. Let stand for 5 to 10 minutes before serving. If desired, garnish with chopped tomato and snipped chives.

Nutrition Facts per serving: **420 calories, 24 g total fat, 85 mg cholesterol, 1,406 mg sodium, 26 g carbohydrate, 26 g protein.**

***Note:*** If using ground turkey, add ¼ teaspoon salt; ¼ teaspoon dried sage, crushed; and ¼ teaspoon pepper to meat mixture.

1 pound bulk turkey sausage
  or uncooked ground turkey*
1 medium onion, chopped
1 3-ounce package cream
  cheese, cubed
1 4½-ounce jar sliced
  mushrooms, drained
1 7½-ounce package
  (10) refrigerated biscuits
1 egg
1 cup cream-style cottage
  cheese
1 tablespoon all-purpose flour
  Chopped tomato (optional)
  Snipped fresh chives
  (optional)

# Biscuit-Topped Turkey Casserole

*This low-fat version of home-style pot pie uses reduced-fat biscuit mix, lean turkey breast, and fat-free milk.*

**Prep:** 25 minutes   **Bake:** 20 minutes   **Makes:** 6 servings

1 cup reduced-sodium chicken broth

½ cup finely chopped onion

½ cup finely chopped celery

1½ cups frozen loose-pack peas and carrots

⅓ cup reduced-sodium chicken broth

3 tablespoons all-purpose flour

2 cups cubed cooked turkey breast (10 ounces)

1 cup evaporated fat-free milk

1½ teaspoons snipped fresh sage or ½ teaspoon dried sage, crushed

⅛ teaspoon pepper

1¼ cups reduced-fat packaged biscuit mix

½ cup fat-free milk

2 tablespoons snipped fresh parsley

**1.** In a medium saucepan combine the 1 cup broth, the onion, and celery; cook, covered, for 5 minutes. Add peas and carrots; bring to boiling.

**2.** In a small bowl stir the ⅓ cup broth into the flour until well mixed; stir into vegetable mixture in saucepan. Cook and stir until thickened and bubbly. Stir in turkey, evaporated milk, sage, and pepper. Pour into a 2-quart casserole.

**3.** In a small bowl stir together the biscuit mix, fat-free milk, and parsley. Stir with a fork just until moistened. Drop into 6 mounds on top of the hot turkey mixture. Bake, uncovered, in a 425° oven for 20 to 25 minutes or until biscuits are golden.

Nutrition Facts per serving: **246 calories, 4 g total fat, 34 mg cholesterol, 548 mg sodium, 30 g carbohydrate, 22 g protein.**

# Turkey with Tomato Relish

*A simple tomato relish seasoned with cilantro and diced green chile peppers complements the crumb-coated turkey steaks.*

**Prep:** 20 minutes **Bake:** 30 minutes **Makes:** 4 servings

**1.** Coat a 2-quart rectangular baking dish with nonstick cooking spray. Set aside. In a shallow dish combine crushed crackers, cumin, and celery seeds. Coat turkey with cracker mixture. Place in the prepared dish. Drizzle with the melted butter or margarine. Bake, uncovered, in a 375° oven about 30 minutes or until turkey is tender and no longer pink.

**2.** Meanwhile, for relish, in a medium bowl combine the drained tomatoes, chile peppers, onion, and snipped cilantro. Stir in the vinegar, sugar, and salt. Cover and chill in the refrigerator until serving time. Serve turkey with the relish. If desired, garnish with cilantro sprigs.

Nutrition Facts per serving: **164 calories, 6 g total fat, 45 mg cholesterol, 490 mg sodium, 11 g carbohydrate, 18 g protein.**

***Note:*** If you can't find turkey breast tenderloin steaks, buy two turkey breast tenderloins and split them in half lengthwise.

Nonstick cooking spray
½ cup finely crushed reduced-fat salsa-flavored or reduced-fat cheese-flavored crackers
¼ teaspoon ground cumin
¼ teaspoon celery seeds
4 turkey breast tenderloin steaks* (about 12 ounces total)
1 tablespoon butter or margarine, melted
1 14½-ounce can diced tomatoes, drained
1 4-ounce can diced green chile peppers, drained
½ cup finely chopped onion
2 to 4 tablespoons snipped fresh cilantro
1 tablespoon vinegar
1 teaspoon sugar
⅛ teaspoon salt
Fresh cilantro sprigs (optional)

# Sweet-and-Sour Stuffed Cabbage Leaves

*Tender cabbage leaves are filled with a savory mixture of lean ground turkey breast, rice, golden raisins, and seasonings.*

**Prep:** 35 minutes **Bake:** 20 minutes **Makes:** 4 servings

8 whole large outer leaves from a large head savoy or green cabbage

12 ounces uncooked ground turkey breast

1 medium onion, chopped

2 cloves garlic, minced

⅓ cup golden raisins

¼ teaspoon salt

⅛ teaspoon ground red pepper

1 cup cooked white rice

1 egg white

1 tablespoon snipped fresh chives

2 8-ounce cans low-sodium tomato sauce

½ cup water

3 tablespoons brown sugar

3 tablespoons lemon juice

**1.** Cook cabbage leaves in a large pot of gently boiling water for 4 to 5 minutes or until tender. Transfer to a colander; rinse with cold water. Cut out a 1-inch section of tough stem from each cabbage leaf by making a "V" cut with a sharp knife. Set cabbage leaves aside.

**2.** In a large nonstick skillet cook ground turkey, onion, and garlic until turkey is browned. Stir in raisins, salt, and red pepper; cook 1 minute. Transfer to a large bowl; cool slightly. Stir in rice, egg white, and chives.

**3.** Meanwhile, in a medium saucepan combine tomato sauce, water, brown sugar, and lemon juice. Bring to boiling; reduce heat. Boil gently, uncovered, for 5 to 7 minutes or until slightly thickened, stirring occasionally.

**4.** Spoon a scant ½ cup of the turkey mixture onto center of each cabbage leaf. Tuck sides over filling; roll up. Spoon about ½ cup of the tomato sauce mixture into bottom of a 2-quart rectangular baking dish. Place cabbage rolls, seam sides down, in dish. Spoon remaining tomato sauce mixture evenly over cabbage rolls. Bake in a 350° oven about 20 minutes or until sauce is bubbly.

Nutrition Facts per serving: **275 calories, 2 g total fat, 37 mg cholesterol, 225 mg sodium, 44 g carbohydrate, 21 g protein.**

# Turkey Enchiladas

*Round out the meal with a tossed green salad, fresh fruit, and tall glasses of Mexican beer or iced tea.*

**Prep:** 40 minutes  **Bake:** 44 minutes  **Makes:** 12 enchiladas

**1.** In a covered small saucepan cook onion in a small amount of boiling water over medium heat until tender; drain. In a medium bowl stir together cream cheese, the 1 tablespoon water, the cumin, black pepper, and salt. Stir in cooked onion, turkey, and toasted pecans.

**2.** Stack tortillas; wrap in foil. Heat in a 350° oven for 10 to 15 minutes to soften.

**3.** Meanwhile, coat a 3-quart rectangular baking dish with nonstick cooking spray. For each enchilada, spoon about ¼ cup of the turkey mixture onto a tortilla; roll up. Place tortillas, seam sides down, in the prepared dish.

**4.** For sauce, in a medium bowl stir together soup, sour cream, milk, and the 2 to 4 tablespoons jalapeño peppers; pour mixture over enchiladas. Cover with foil and bake in a 350° oven about 40 minutes or until heated through. Sprinkle enchiladas with the shredded cheddar cheese. Bake enchiladas, uncovered, for 4 to 5 minutes more or until cheese melts. If desired, top with snipped cilantro or parsley, chopped tomato, and additional jalapeño peppers.

**Nutrition Facts per enchilada:** 256 calories, 10 g total fat, 44 mg cholesterol, 271 mg sodium, 21 g carbohydrate, 21 g protein.

½ cup chopped onion
½ of an 8-ounce package reduced-fat cream cheese (Neufchâtel), softened
1 tablespoon water
1 teaspoon ground cumin
¼ teaspoon ground black pepper
⅛ teaspoon salt
4 cups chopped cooked turkey or chicken breast (20 ounces)
¼ cup chopped pecans, toasted
12 7- to 8-inch flour tortillas
Nonstick cooking spray
1 10¾-ounce can reduced-fat and reduced-sodium condensed cream of chicken soup
1 8-ounce carton light dairy sour cream
1 cup fat-free milk
2 to 4 tablespoons finely chopped pickled jalapeño peppers
½ cup shredded reduced-fat sharp cheddar cheese (2 ounces)
Snipped fresh cilantro or parsley (optional)
Chopped tomato (optional)
Chopped pickled jalapeño peppers (optional)

# White Bean and Sausage Rigatoni

*Turkey kielbasa stars in this Italian-style one-dish meal.*

**Prep:** 25 minutes   **Bake:** 25 minutes   **Makes:** 4 servings

8 ounces dried rigatoni
   (about 3¼ cups)
2 14½-ounce cans low-sodium
   stewed tomatoes
1 15-ounce can Great
   Northern beans, rinsed
   and drained
8 ounces cooked turkey
   kielbasa, bias-sliced
½ of a 10-ounce package
   frozen chopped spinach,
   thawed and well drained
½ of a 6-ounce can tomato
   paste
¼ cup dry red wine or reduced-
   sodium chicken broth
1½ teaspoons Italian seasoning,
   crushed
¼ cup shredded or grated
   Parmesan cheese
   (1 ounce)

*1.* In a large saucepan cook pasta according to package directions; drain and return to saucepan.

*2.* Add undrained tomatoes, drained beans, kielbasa, spinach, tomato paste, wine or chicken broth, and Italian seasoning to the cooked pasta. Stir to mix. Spoon into a 2-quart casserole or baking dish. Sprinkle with Parmesan cheese.

*3.* Bake, uncovered, in a 375° oven for 25 to 30 minutes or until bubbly and heated through.

Nutrition Facts per serving: 498 calories, 7 g total fat, 41 mg cholesterol, 920 mg sodium, 79 g carbohydrate, 29 g protein.

# Spicy Pasta Pie

*A saucy turkey sausage and mushroom mixture fills the vermicelli crust in this hearty main dish.*

**Prep:** 25 minutes  **Bake:** 25 minutes  **Stand:** 10 minutes  **Makes:** 6 servings

**1.** Cook vermicelli according to package directions, except omit any oil and salt. Drain well. Toss with the egg white. Coat a 9-inch quiche dish or pie plate with nonstick cooking spray. Press vermicelli mixture into bottom of prepared dish. Sprinkle with mozzarella cheese. Set aside.

**2.** Meanwhile, in a large skillet cook the turkey sausage, mushrooms, onion, and garlic until sausage is browned and onion is tender. Drain off fat. Stir in the undrained tomatoes, tomato paste, Italian seasoning, and crushed red pepper. Pour sausage mixture over cheese layer.

**3.** Cover dish loosely with foil. Bake in a 350° oven for 25 to 30 minutes or until heated through. Sprinkle with the Parmesan or Romano cheese. Let stand for 10 minutes before serving. If desired, garnish with celery leaves. To serve, cut into wedges.

Nutrition Facts per serving: 316 calories, 14 g total fat, 41 mg cholesterol, 732 mg sodium, 22 g carbohydrate, 26 g protein.

- **4 ounces dried vermicelli,** broken
- **1 beaten egg white** Nonstick cooking spray
- **1 cup shredded mozzarella cheese (4 ounces)**
- **1 pound bulk turkey sausage**
- **1 cup sliced fresh mushrooms**
- **½ cup chopped onion**
- **1 clove garlic, minced**
- **1 7½-ounce can low-sodium tomatoes, cut up**
- **½ of a 6-ounce can tomato paste**
- **1 teaspoon dried Italian seasoning, crushed**
- **⅛ teaspoon crushed red pepper**
- **2 tablespoons grated Parmesan or Romano cheese** Celery leaves (optional)

# grilled or broiled dishes

No matter whether you prefer grilling outdoors or broiling in
the kitchen, here's a family-pleasing assortment
of no-fuss recipes for whole birds, poultry pieces, and kabobs.

Spice-Grilled Chicken, page 193

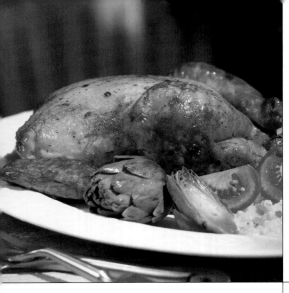

# Honey-Soy Grilled Chicken

*Check in the spice section of your supermarket or at an Asian food store for five-spice powder.*

**Prep:** 15 minutes  **Marinate:** 6 to 24 hours  **Grill:** 1¼ hours  **Stand:** 10 minutes
**Makes:** 6 to 8 servings

1 3- to 4-pound whole broiler-
    fryer chicken
¼ cup water
¼ cup soy sauce
¼ cup dry sherry
1 green onion, sliced
2 cloves garlic, minced
½ teaspoon five-spice powder
1 tablespoon cooking oil
1 tablespoon honey

**1.** Remove the neck and giblets from chicken. Skewer neck skin to back. Tie legs to tail. Twist wing tips under back. Place chicken in a heavy, large self-sealing plastic bag set in deep bowl.

**2.** For marinade, in a small bowl combine water, soy sauce, sherry, green onion, garlic, and five-spice powder. Pour over chicken. Seal bag; turn to coat chicken. Marinate in the refrigerator for at least 6 hours or up to 24 hours, turning bag occasionally. Drain chicken, discarding marinade. Brush chicken with oil.

**3.** In a grill with a cover arrange medium-hot coals around a drip pan. Test for medium heat above the pan. Place chicken, breast side up, on grill rack over drip pan. Cover and grill for 1¼ to 1¾ hours or until an instant-read thermometer inserted in an inside thigh muscle registers 180°, brushing occasionally with the honey during the last 10 minutes of grilling. When done, drumsticks move easily in their sockets and chicken is no longer pink.

**4.** Remove chicken from grill. Cover and let stand for 10 minutes before carving.

Nutrition Facts per serving: **251 calories, 14 g total fat, 79 mg cholesterol, 245 mg sodium, 3 g carbohydrate, 25 g protein.**

# Spice-Grilled Chicken

*To broil the apricots for the garnish, brush fresh apricot halves with melted margarine or butter and broil 3 inches from the heat for 3 to 6 minutes or until lightly browned.*

**Prep:** 20 minutes  **Grill:** 1 hour  **Stand:** 5 minutes  **Makes:** 4 to 6 servings

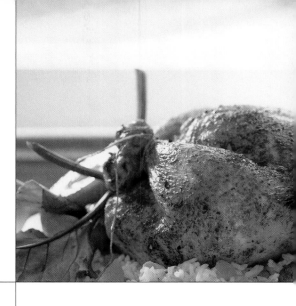

**1.** In a small bowl combine the brown sugar, cinnamon, paprika, salt, pepper, and allspice. Set aside 1½ teaspoons of the cinnamon mixture. Remove the neck and giblets from the whole chicken. Pat chicken dry with paper towels. Brush with the cooking oil; gently rub remaining cinnamon mixture onto chicken. Skewer neck skin to back. Tie legs to tail. Twist wing tips under the back.

**2.** In a grill with a cover arrange medium-hot coals around a drip pan. Test for medium heat above pan. Place whole chicken, breast side up, on the grill rack over drip pan. Cover and grill 1 to 1¼ hours or until an instant-read thermometer inserted in an inside thigh muscle registers 180°. At this time, the drumsticks move easily in their sockets and chicken is no longer pink. (Or grill drumsticks on grill rack for 50 to 60 minutes or until tender and no longer pink. An instant-read thermometer inserted in thickest part of drumstick should register 180°.)

**3.** Meanwhile, in a medium saucepan combine the broth, rice, and the reserved cinnamon mixture. Bring to boiling; reduce heat. Cover and simmer for 15 minutes. Remove from heat. Stir in dried apricots and raisins. Cover and let stand for 5 minutes before serving.

**4.** Serve rice with chicken; sprinkle with chopped peanuts. If desired, garnish with Swiss chard and broiled apricots.

**Nutrition Facts per serving:** 646 calories, 23 g total fat, 207 mg cholesterol, 1,012 mg sodium, 54 g carbohydrate, 58 g protein.

- **2 teaspoons** brown sugar
- **1½ teaspoons** ground cinnamon
- **1 teaspoon** smoked paprika or paprika
- **½ teaspoon** salt
- **½ teaspoon** pepper
- **½ teaspoon** ground allspice
- **1 3-pound** whole broiler-fryer chicken or 12 chicken drumsticks
- **4 teaspoons** cooking oil
- **2 cups** chicken broth
- **1 cup** jasmine or long grain rice
- **¼ cup** snipped dried apricots
- **¼ cup** golden raisins
- **2 tablespoons** chopped peanuts
  Swiss chard (optional)
  Halved fresh apricots, broiled (optional)

# All-American Barbecued Chicken

*Round out your All-American cookout with grilled corn on the cob, pasta salad, and lemonade.*

**Prep:** 25 minutes   **Grill:** 40 minutes   **Makes:** 4 to 6 servings

1 medium onion, finely
   chopped
1 tablespoon cooking oil
1 cup catsup
½ cup water
¼ cup vinegar
2 to 3 tablespoons
   brown sugar
2 tablespoons Worcestershire
   sauce
2 dashes bottled hot
   pepper sauce
1 2½- to 3-pound broiler-fryer
   chicken, quartered

**1.** For sauce, in a medium saucepan cook onion in hot oil until tender. Stir in catsup, water, vinegar, brown sugar, Worcestershire sauce, and bottled hot pepper sauce. Bring to boiling; reduce heat. Simmer sauce, uncovered, about 15 minutes or until of desired consistency.

**2.** Break chicken's wing, hip, and drumstick joints so pieces lie flat. Twist wing tips under back. Grill chicken, skin sides down, on the rack of an uncovered grill directly over medium coals for 40 to 50 minutes or until tender and no longer pink (180°), turning once. [Or place chicken on the unheated rack of a broiler pan. Broil 4 to 5 inches from the heat for 28 to 32 minutes or until tender and no longer pink (180°), turning once.] Brush with sauce during the last 10 minutes of grilling or broiling. Heat any remaining sauce until boiling. Serve warmed sauce with chicken.

Nutrition Facts per serving: 407 calories, 19 g total fat, 98 mg cholesterol, 996 mg sodium, 29 g carbohydrate, 32 g protein.

# Five-Spice Grilled Chicken

*The Asian spice blend five-spice powder typically contains star anise, cinnamon, fennel, black or Szechwan pepper, and cloves.*

**Prep:** 10 minutes   **Marinate:** 6 to 24 hours   **Grill:** 50 minutes   **Makes:** 4 servings

**1.** For marinade, in a small bowl combine soy sauce, orange juice, five-spice powder, and garlic. Place chicken in a heavy, large self-sealing plastic bag set into a deep bowl. Pour the marinade over chicken. Seal bag; turn chicken to coat well. Marinate in the refrigerator for at least 6 hours or up to 24 hours, turning chicken occasionally. Remove chicken from bag. Discard marinade.

**2.** In a grill with a cover arrange medium-hot coals around a drip pan. Test for medium heat above pan. Place chicken, bone sides down, on grill rack over drip pan. Cover and grill for 50 to 60 minutes or until chicken is tender and no longer pink (180°), turning once and brushing occasionally with the honey during the last 5 minutes of grilling. If desired, serve chicken over pasta tossed with carrot strips. If desired, garnish with cucumber slices.

Nutrition Facts per serving: 294 calories, 15 g total fat, 99 mg cholesterol, 607 mg sodium, 6 g carbohydrate, 31 g protein.

¼ **cup soy sauce**
2 **tablespoons orange juice**
1 **teaspoon five-spice powder**
1 **clove garlic, minced**
1 **2½- to 3-pound broiler-fryer chicken, quartered**
2 **tablespoons honey**
   **Hot cooked pasta (optional)**
   **Carrot strips (optional)**
   **Cucumber slices (optional)**

# Sweet-and-Spicy Barbecued Chicken

*The glossy red sauce gets its sweet from orange marmalade and its spicy from chili powder and bottled hot pepper sauce.*

**Prep:** 10 minutes  **Grill:** 50 minutes  **Makes:** 4 servings

½ **cup catsup**

¼ **cup orange marmalade**

1 **tablespoon vinegar**

½ **teaspoon celery seeds**

½ **teaspoon chili powder**

¼ **to ½ teaspoon bottled hot pepper sauce**

1 **2½- to 3-pound broiler-fryer chicken, cut up**

**1.** For sauce, stir together catsup, marmalade, vinegar, celery seeds, chili powder, and hot pepper sauce.

**2.** In a grill with a cover arrange medium-hot coals around a drip pan. Test for medium heat above the pan. Place chicken pieces, bone sides down, on grill rack over pan. Cover and grill for 50 to 60 minutes or until chicken is tender and no longer pink, turning once and brushing occasionally with sauce during the last 10 minutes of grilling. Heat any remaining sauce until boiling. Serve warmed sauce with chicken.

Nutrition Facts per serving: 358 calories, 16 g total fat, 99 mg cholesterol, 504 mg sodium, 24 g carbohydrate, 31 g protein.

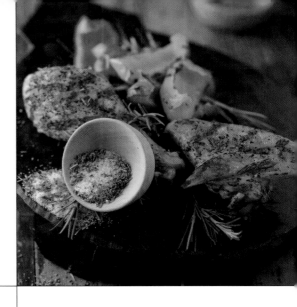

# Herb-Rubbed Grilled Chicken

*This five-ingredient rub is also delicious on pork chops.*

**Prep:** 10 minutes  **Grill:** 35 minutes  **Makes:** 6 servings

**1.** In a small bowl combine salt, thyme, rosemary, savory, and pepper. Sprinkle mixture evenly over chicken pieces; rub in with your fingers.

**2.** Lightly grease the rack of an uncovered grill. Place chicken, bone sides up, on rack. Grill directly over medium coals for 35 to 45 minutes or until chicken is tender and no longer pink, turning once.

Nutrition Facts per serving: 113 calories, 2 g total fat, 50 mg cholesterol, 312 mg sodium, 0 g carbohydrate, 21 g protein.

½ **teaspoon salt**
½ **teaspoon dried thyme, crushed**
½ **teaspoon dried rosemary, crushed**
½ **teaspoon dried savory, crushed**
¼ **teaspoon pepper**
2½ **to 3 pounds chicken pieces (breasts, thighs, drumsticks, and wings)**

# Texas-Style Barbecued Chicken Legs

*Vinegar, lemon juice, and Worcestershire sauce add tang to the catsup-based sauce.*

**Prep:** 20 minutes  **Grill:** 35 minutes  **Makes:** 6 servings

1 medium onion, finely
    chopped
2 cloves garlic, minced
1 teaspoon chili powder
¼ teaspoon ground sage
1 tablespoon margarine or
    butter, melted
½ cup catsup
2 tablespoons water
2 tablespoons vinegar
1 tablespoon sugar
1 tablespoon lemon juice
1 tablespoon Worcestershire
    sauce
½ teaspoon salt
½ teaspoon bottled hot
    pepper sauce
¼ teaspoon cracked
    black pepper
6 chicken legs (thigh-
    drumstick pieces)
    (about 2½ pounds total)

**1.** For sauce, in a saucepan cook onion, garlic, chili powder, and sage in margarine or butter until onion is tender. Stir in catsup, water, vinegar, sugar, lemon juice, Worcestershire sauce, salt, bottled hot pepper sauce, and black pepper. Bring to boiling; reduce heat. Simmer, uncovered, about 5 minutes or to desired consistency, stirring occasionally.

**2.** Grill chicken, skin sides down, on the rack of an uncovered grill directly over medium coals for 35 to 45 minutes or until chicken is tender and no longer pink, turning once. (Or place chicken on the unheated rack of a broiler pan. Broil 4 to 5 inches from the heat for 25 to 35 minutes, turning once.) Brush with sauce during the last 10 minutes of grilling or broiling. Heat any remaining sauce until boiling. Serve warmed sauce with chicken.

Nutrition Facts per serving: **276 calories, 15 g total fat, 86 mg cholesterol, 596 mg sodium, 11 g carbohydrate, 25 g protein.**

# Asian Chicken Kabobs

*To trim prep time—and mess—thread the chicken on wooden skewers before marinating.*

**Prep:** 25 minutes  **Marinate:** 2 to 24 hours  **Grill:** 12 minutes  **Makes:** 4 servings

**1.** For marinade, in a small bowl combine orange juice, soy sauce, sherry, ginger, and crushed red pepper. Thread chicken, accordion-style, onto bamboo skewers. Place kabobs in a heavy, large self-sealing plastic bag set in a shallow rectangular dish. Add marinade. Seal bag; turn bag to coat kabobs well. Marinate in the refrigerator for at least 2 hours or up to 24 hours, turning bag occasionally. Remove kabobs from bag, reserving marinade.

**2.** Grill kabobs on the rack of an uncovered grill directly over medium coals for 5 minutes. Brush chicken with reserved marinade; sprinkle with half of the sesame seeds. Turn chicken and brush with marinade. Discard any remaining marinade. Sprinkle with remaining sesame seeds. Grill for 7 to 10 minutes more or until chicken is tender and no longer pink. If desired, serve with orange wedges.

Nutrition Facts per serving: **176 calories, 8 g total fat, 68 mg cholesterol, 584 mg sodium, 3 g carbohydrate, 21 g protein.**

¼ **cup orange juice**
2 **tablespoons soy sauce**
2 **tablespoons dry sherry**
1 **teaspoon grated fresh ginger**
   **or** ¼ **teaspoon ground ginger**
⅛ **teaspoon crushed red pepper**
8 **skinless, boneless chicken thighs, cut into thin strips (about 1¼ pounds total)**
1 **teaspoon sesame seeds**
   **Orange wedges (optional)**

# Orange-Dijon Chicken

*Another time, serve the citrus-mustard glaze on grilled pork chops or roasted chicken.*

**Prep:** 15 minutes **Marinate:** 4 to 8 hours **Broil:** 12 minutes **Makes:** 4 servings

4 medium skinless, boneless
    chicken breast halves
    (about 1 pound total)
½ cup olive oil
3 cloves garlic, minced
½ teaspoon salt
⅛ teaspoon pepper
1 recipe Orange-Dijon Glaze
    Coarsely ground black
    pepper
    Shredded orange peel
    (optional)
    Fresh herb sprigs (optional)

*1.* Place chicken in a heavy, large self-sealing plastic bag set in a shallow dish.

*2.* In a small bowl stir together olive oil, garlic, salt, and the ⅛ teaspoon pepper. Pour over the chicken. Seal bag; turn to coat well. Marinate in the refrigerator for at least 4 hours or up to 8 hours, turning the bag occasionally.

*3.* Prepare Orange-Dijon Glaze. Cover and refrigerate.

*4.* Drain chicken, discarding marinade. Place chicken on unheated rack of a broiler pan. Broil the chicken 4 to 5 inches from the heat for 12 to 15 minutes or until no longer pink, turning once.

*5.* Meanwhile, in a small saucepan heat the Orange-Dijon Glaze until heated through.

*6.* Slice chicken breasts. Spoon Orange-Dijon Glaze over chicken; sprinkle with coarsely ground pepper. If desired, garnish with orange peel and herb sprigs.

***Orange-Dijon Glaze:*** In a small bowl stir together ¼ cup frozen orange juice concentrate, thawed; 2 to 4 tablespoons Dijon-style mustard; 2 tablespoons water; 1 tablespoon balsamic vinegar (optional); 1 tablespoon olive oil; 1 teaspoon snipped fresh basil; 1 teaspoon snipped fresh mint; and ½ teaspoon snipped fresh rosemary. Makes about ¾ cup glaze.

**Nutrition Facts per serving: 272 calories, 14 g total fat, 66 mg cholesterol, 199 mg sodium, 8 g carbohydrate, 27 g protein.**

# Hot 'n' Sweet Barbecued Chicken

*Use your favorite salsa as the base for this finger-licking sauce.*

**Prep:** 10 minutes  **Grill:** 50 minutes  **Makes:** 4 servings

**1.** For sauce, in a small bowl stir together salsa, catsup, marmalade, vinegar, chili powder, and Worcestershire sauce.

**2.** In a grill with a cover arrange medium-hot coals around a drip pan. Place chicken on grill rack directly over drip pan. Cover and grill for 50 to 60 minutes or until tender and no longer pink. Brush chicken generously with the sauce during the last 10 minutes of grilling. (Or arrange chicken in a 2-quart rectangular baking pan. Bake in a 375° oven for 30 minutes. Brush chicken generously with the sauce; bake for 10 to 15 minutes more or until tender and no longer pink.)

Nutrition Facts per serving: 261 calories, 7 g total fat, 92 mg cholesterol, 317 mg sodium, 18 g carbohydrate, 30 g protein.

¼ **cup bottled salsa**
¼ **cup catsup**
¼ **cup orange marmalade**
 1 **tablespoon vinegar**
½ **teaspoon chili powder**
½ **teaspoon Worcestershire sauce**
 2 **to 2½ pounds meaty chicken pieces (breasts, thighs, and drumsticks), skinned**

# Lemongrass Chicken And Rice Noodles

*Visit the nearest Asian market to get lemongrass, rice sticks, and fish sauce for this irresistible dish.*

**Prep:** 25 minutes   **Grill:** 12 minutes   **Makes:** 4 servings

¼ cup finely chopped green onions

¼ cup finely chopped lemongrass*

1 tablespoon grated fresh ginger

6 cloves garlic, minced

4 medium skinless, boneless chicken breast halves (about 1 pound total)

8 ounces dried rice sticks

¼ cup fish sauce

3 to 4 tablespoons lime juice

2 tablespoons brown sugar

1 to 2 cloves garlic, minced

1 cup shredded carrots

¼ cup coarsely snipped fresh cilantro

¼ cup coarsely chopped peanuts

**1.** For rub, in a food processor bowl or blender container combine green onions, lemongrass, ginger, and the 6 cloves garlic. Cover and process or blend with a few on-off turns until mixture forms a paste. Use your fingers to rub lemongrass-ginger paste evenly onto both sides of each chicken breast half.

**2.** Grill chicken on the rack of an uncovered grill directly over medium coals for 12 to 15 minutes or until chicken is tender and no longer pink, turning once. Cut chicken into thin, diagonal slices.

**3.** Meanwhile, in a large saucepan cook rice sticks in a large amount of boiling water for 3 to 4 minutes or just until tender; drain well. In a medium bowl combine fish sauce, lime juice, brown sugar, and the 1 to 2 cloves garlic; stir until brown sugar dissolves. Add hot cooked rice sticks, carrots, cilantro, and peanuts; toss lightly to coat.

**4.** Arrange sliced chicken over hot rice stick mixture. Serve chicken immediately.

Nutrition Facts per serving: **431 calories, 6 g total fat, 66 mg cholesterol, 471 mg sodium, 63 g carbohydrate, 30 g protein.**

***Note:*** Lemongrass, a highly aromatic, lemon-flavored herb, has layers similar to a leek. Trim off the fibrous ends and slice what remains into 3- to 4-inch sections. Cut each section in half lengthwise, exposing the layers. Rinse the pieces under cold water to remove any grit; finely chop the lemongrass.

# Southwestern Chicken Breasts

*A refreshing avocado-tomato topper complements these tender grilled chicken breasts.*

**Prep:** 20 minutes **Marinate:** 2 to 24 hours **Grill:** 12 minutes **Makes:** 6 servings

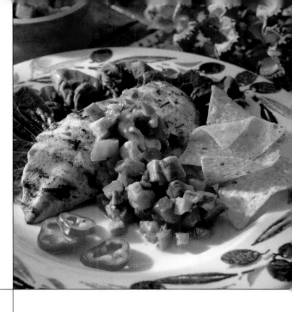

**1.** Place chicken in a heavy, large self-sealing plastic bag set in a shallow dish.

**2.** For marinade, in a small bowl combine the white wine, oil, tarragon, and salt. Pour over chicken. Seal bag; turn to coat chicken. Marinate in the refrigerator for at least 2 hours or up to 24 hours, turning bag occasionally.

**3.** In a medium bowl combine avocados, tomato, green onions, chili peppers, cilantro, honey, lemon juice, and garlic. Toss gently to mix. Cover and chill up to 2 hours.

**4.** Drain chicken, reserving marinade. Grill chicken on the rack of an uncovered grill directly over medium coals for 12 to 15 minutes or until tender and no longer pink, turning and brushing once with marinade halfway through grilling.

**5.** Serve the grilled chicken with avocado mixture and, if desired, lettuce leaves.

Nutrition Facts per serving: 239 calories, 16 g total fat, 50 mg cholesterol, 130 mg sodium, 5 g carbohydrate, 20 g protein.

***Note:*** Because chile peppers contain volatile oils that can burn your skin and eyes, avoid direct contact with them as much as possible. When working with chile peppers, wear plastic or rubber gloves. If your bare hands do touch the chile peppers, wash your hands and nails well with soap and warm water.

- **6 medium skinless, boneless chicken breast halves (about 1½ pounds total)**
- **¼ cup dry white wine**
- **2 tablespoons olive oil or cooking oil**
- **2 teaspoons snipped fresh tarragon or ¼ teaspoon dried tarragon, crushed**
- **¼ teaspoon salt**
- **2 avocados, seeded, peeled, and chopped**
- **1 tomato, chopped**
- **2 green onions, finely chopped**
- **2 tablespoons finely chopped, seeded fresh green chili peppers (such as jalapeño, serrano, or Anaheim)***
- **1 tablespoon snipped fresh cilantro**
- **1 tablespoon honey**
- **1 tablespoon lemon juice**
- **1 clove garlic, minced**
  **Lettuce leaves (optional)**

# Chicken Teriyaki With Summer Fruit

*For maximum color and flavor, combine two or three fresh fruits.*

**Prep:** 20 minutes   **Grill:** 12 minutes   **Makes:** 4 servings

2 cups finely chopped
   nectarines, finely chopped
   plums, and/or blueberries
2 tablespoons orange
   marmalade, melted
1 tablespoon lemon juice or
   lime juice
½ teaspoon grated fresh
   ginger
¼ teaspoon toasted
   sesame oil
   Few dashes bottled hot
   pepper sauce
1 tablespoon orange
   marmalade
1 tablespoon bottled reduced-
   sodium teriyaki sauce
4 medium skinless, boneless
   chicken breast halves
   (about 1 pound total)
   Fresh strawberries (optional)
   Flowering kale (optional)

**1.** In a small bowl stir together fruit, the 2 tablespoons melted orange marmalade, the lemon or lime juice, ginger, sesame oil, and hot pepper sauce. Set aside.

**2.** In another small bowl stir together the 1 tablespoon orange marmalade and the teriyaki sauce; brush over chicken breasts. Grill chicken on the rack of an uncovered grill directly over medium coals for 12 to 15 minutes or until tender and no longer pink, turning once. (Or place chicken on the unheated rack of a broiler pan. Broil 4 to 5 inches from the heat for 12 to 15 minutes or until tender and no longer pink, turning once.) Serve with the fruit mixture. If desired, garnish with fresh strawberries and kale.

Nutrition Facts per serving: **200 calories, 4 g total fat, 59 mg cholesterol, 136 mg sodium, 20 g carbohydrate, 22 g protein.**

# Four-Season Grilled Chicken

*With timings for both grilling and broiling, this onion-and-spice seasoned chicken is suited to any season.*

**Prep:** 10 minutes  **Grill:** 12 minutes  **Makes:** 6 servings

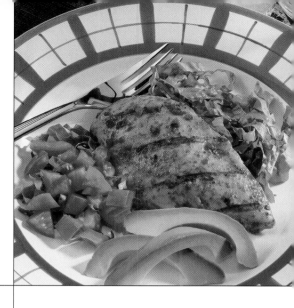

**1.** In a small saucepan cook onion and garlic in hot margarine or butter until tender. Stir in the chili powder, cumin, and ground red pepper. Cook for 1 minute. Brush half of the onion mixture over chicken.

**2.** Grill chicken on the rack of an uncovered grill directly over medium coals for 12 to 15 minutes or until chicken is tender and no longer pink, turning and brushing once with remaining onion mixture halfway through grilling. Discard any remaining onion mixture. (Or place chicken on the unheated rack of a broiler pan. Broil 4 to 5 inches from the heat for 12 to 15 minutes, turning and brushing once with remaining onion mixture halfway through broiling.) If desired, serve with shredded lettuce, chopped tomato, and avocado slices.

Nutrition Facts per serving: **171 calories, 6 g total fat, 66 mg cholesterol, 111 mg sodium, 2 g carbohydrate, 27 g protein.**

- 1 **medium onion, finely chopped**
- 1 **clove garlic, minced**
- 2 **tablespoons margarine or butter**
- 1 **teaspoon chili powder**
- ¼ **teaspoon ground cumin**
- ¼ **teaspoon ground red pepper**
- 6 **medium skinless, boneless chicken breast halves (about 1½ pounds total)**
  **Shredded lettuce (optional)**
  **Chopped tomato (optional)**
  **Avocado slices (optional)**

# Grilled Chicken with Black Bean Salsa

*A tantalizing honey-lime brush-on helps keep the chicken moist.*

**Prep:** 10 minutes  **Chill:** 30 minutes  **Grill:** 12 minutes  **Makes:** 4 servings

3 tablespoons lime juice
1 tablespoon honey
1 teaspoon paprika
½ teaspoon ground turmeric
⅛ teaspoon garlic powder
Dash salt
Dash ground red pepper
4 small skinless, boneless
  chicken breast halves
  (about 12 ounces total)
1 15-ounce can black beans,
  rinsed and drained
½ cup frozen whole kernel
  corn, cooked and drained
1 small tomato, chopped
2 tablespoons snipped fresh
  cilantro
1 fresh jalapeño pepper,
  seeded and finely chopped*
Tomato wedges (optional)

**1.** In a small bowl combine 1 tablespoon of the lime juice, the honey, paprika, turmeric, garlic powder, salt, and red pepper. Brush over both sides of chicken breasts. Cover and chill in refrigerator for 30 minutes.

**2.** Grill chicken on the rack of an uncovered grill directly over medium coals for 12 to 15 minutes or until tender and no longer pink, turning once.

**3.** Meanwhile, in a medium bowl combine the beans, corn, chopped tomato, cilantro, jalapeño pepper, and the remaining lime juice. Serve with the chicken. If desired, garnish with tomato wedges.

Nutrition Facts per serving: 202 calories, 3 g total fat, 45 mg cholesterol, 340 mg sodium, 25 g carbohydrate, 24 g protein.

***Note:*** Because chile peppers, such as jalapeños, contain volatile oils that can burn your skin and eyes, avoid direct contact with them as much as possible. When working with chile peppers, wear plastic or rubber gloves. If your bare hands do touch the chile peppers, wash your hands and nails well with soap and warm water.

# Grilled Jerk Chicken

*Taking this dish from mild to spicy is as easy as adjusting the amount of jalapeño pepper you add.*

**Prep:** 15 minutes  **Marinate:** 4 to 24 hours  **Grill:** 12 minutes  **Makes:** 4 servings

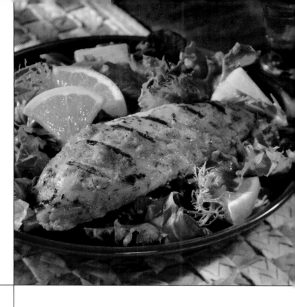

**1.** Place chicken in a heavy, large self-sealing plastic bag set in a shallow dish.

**2.** In a food processor bowl or blender container combine onion, jalapeño peppers, thyme, allspice, salt, nutmeg, and cloves. Cover and process or blend until almost smooth. With food processor or blender running, add the ¼ cup orange juice. Process or blend until almost smooth. Pour over chicken. Seal bag; turn to coat chicken. Marinate in the refrigerator for at least 4 hours or up to 24 hours, turning occasionally.

**3.** Drain chicken, discarding marinade. Grill chicken on the rack of an uncovered grill directly over medium coals for 12 to 15 minutes or until tender and no longer pink, turning once. If desired, place greens on plates with pineapple and oranges. Top with chicken. If desired, drizzle with additional orange juice.

Nutrition Facts per serving: **144 calories, 3 g total fat, 59 mg cholesterol, 189 mg sodium, 5 g carbohydrate, 22 g protein.**

***Note:*** Because chile peppers, such as jalapeños, contain volatile oils that can burn your skin and eyes, avoid direct contact with them as much as possible. When working with chile peppers, wear plastic or rubber gloves. If your bare hands do touch the chile peppers, wash your hands and nails well with soap and warm water.

- 4 **medium skinless, boneless chicken breast halves (about 1 pound total)**
- 1 **large onion, quartered**
- 1 to 2 **fresh jalapeño peppers, seeded and cut up***
- 1 **tablespoon snipped fresh thyme or 1 teaspoon dried thyme, crushed**
- ½ **teaspoon ground allspice**
- ¼ **teaspoon salt**
- ¼ **teaspoon ground nutmeg**
  **Dash ground cloves**
- ¼ **cup orange juice**
  **Torn mixed greens (optional)**
  **Pineapple wedges (optional)**
  **Orange slices, quartered (optional)**
  **Orange juice (optional)**

# Grilled Lime Chicken With Pineapple Salsa

*Get a head start on dinner by making the fruit-and-vegetable salsa up to 24 hours ahead.*

**Prep:** 20 minutes  **Grill:** 12 minutes  **Makes:** 6 servings

½ teaspoon finely shredded
  lime peel
¼ cup lime juice
1 tablespoon cooking oil
¼ teaspoon salt
¼ teaspoon coarsely ground
  black pepper
6 medium skinless, boneless
  chicken breast halves
  (about 1½ pounds total)
1 pound fresh pineapple
  chunks (3 cups)
1 large tomato, seeded
  and chopped
½ cup chopped red onion
½ cup chopped green or
  red sweet pepper
1 4-ounce can diced green
  chili peppers, drained
2 tablespoons snipped
  fresh cilantro
½ teaspoon finely shredded
  lime peel
2 tablespoons lime juice
1 clove garlic, minced

**1.** In a small bowl stir together ½ teaspoon lime peel, the ¼ cup lime juice, the oil, salt, and black pepper. Brush chicken with lime mixture.

**2.** Grill chicken on the rack of an uncovered grill directly over medium coals for 12 to 15 minutes or until chicken is tender and no longer pink, turning and brushing once with lime mixture halfway through grilling. (Or place chicken on the unheated rack of a broiler pan. Broil 4 to 5 inches from the heat for 12 to 15 minutes, turning and brushing once with lime mixture halfway through broiling.) Discard any remaining lime mixture.

**3.** Meanwhile, for salsa, place pineapple chunks in a food processor bowl or blender container. Cover and process or blend until chopped, but not pureed. Pour into a large bowl. Stir in tomato, red onion, green or red sweet pepper, green chili peppers, cilantro, ½ teaspoon lime peel, the 2 tablespoons lime juice, and the garlic. Cover and chill in the refrigerator until serving time. Serve with chicken.

Nutrition Facts per serving: **209 calories, 5 g total fat, 66 mg cholesterol, 216 mg sodium, 15 g carbohydrate, 28 g protein.**

# Polynesian Chicken Kabobs

*Sweet pineapple adds a touch of the tropics to these kabobs.*

**Prep:** 25 minutes  **Marinate:** 2 to 24 hours  **Grill:** 12 minutes  **Makes:** 6 servings

**1.** For marinade, in a small bowl combine soy sauce, lemon juice, garlic, ginger, and mustard. Place chicken in a heavy, large self-sealing plastic bag set into a shallow dish. Pour marinade over. Seal bag; turn to coat chicken. Marinate in the refrigerator for at least 2 hours or up to 24 hours, turning occasionally.

**2.** Remove chicken from bag, reserving marinade. On metal skewers, alternately thread chicken, pineapple, green pepper, and red pepper. Grill kabobs on the rack of an uncovered grill directly over medium coals for 12 to 15 minutes or until chicken is tender and no longer pink, turning and brushing once with reserved marinade halfway through grilling. Discard any remaining marinade. If desired, serve over hot cooked rice and garnish with green onion brushes.

Nutrition Facts per serving: 110 calories, 2 g total fat, 40 mg cholesterol, 723 mg sodium, 7 g carbohydrate, 15 g protein.

¼ cup soy sauce

2 tablespoons lemon juice

2 cloves garlic, minced

1 teaspoon grated fresh ginger or ⅛ teaspoon ground ginger

⅛ teaspoon dry mustard

1 pound skinless, boneless chicken breasts or thighs, cut into 1-inch pieces

1 cup fresh pineapple chunks or one 8-ounce can pineapple chunks, drained

1 medium green sweet pepper, cut into 1-inch pieces

1 medium red sweet pepper, cut into 1-inch pieces

Hot cooked rice (optional)

Green onion brushes (optional)

# Szechwan Chicken Strips

*In this recipe, "Szechwan" indicates the spicy hotness that comes from the Szechwan chili sauce or crushed red pepper.*

**Prep:** 15 minutes  **Marinate:** 15 minutes to 2 hours  **Grill:** 12 minutes
**Makes:** 4 servings

1 pound skinless, boneless chicken breasts, cut into bite-size strips
⅓ cup rice vinegar
¼ cup hoisin sauce
1 to 2 teaspoons Szechwan chili sauce or ¼ to ½ teaspoon crushed red pepper
1 clove garlic, minced
12 red and/or yellow cherry tomatoes
2 cups packaged shredded broccoli (broccoli slaw mix)
1 tablespoon chopped peanuts

*1.* Place chicken in a large, heavy self-sealing plastic bag set in a shallow dish.

*2.* For marinade, in a small bowl combine rice vinegar, hoisin sauce, Szechwan chili sauce or crushed red pepper, and garlic. Set aside half of the marinade to use as dressing. Pour remaining marinade over chicken. Seal bag; turn to coat chicken. Marinate in the refrigerator for at least 15 minutes or up to 2 hours, turning once.

*3.* Drain chicken, reserving marinade. On 4 metal or bamboo skewers,* thread chicken accordion style. Grill kabobs on the rack of an uncovered grill directly over medium coals for 12 to 15 minutes or until chicken is tender and no longer pink, turning once and brushing twice with marinade up to the last 5 minutes of grilling. Add tomatoes to ends of skewers for the last 2 to 3 minutes of grilling.

*4.* Serve chicken with shredded broccoli. Drizzle with the dressing and sprinkle with peanuts.

Nutrition Facts per serving: 202 calories, 4 g total fat, 59 mg cholesterol, 400 mg sodium, 15 g carbohydrate, 23 g protein.

*\*Note:* If using bamboo skewers, soak four 12-inch skewers in warm water for 30 minutes; drain.

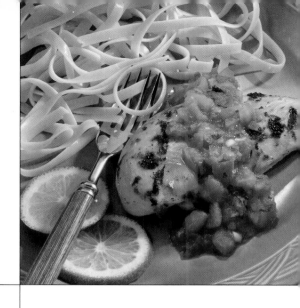

# Tequila and Lime Chicken

*For a less spicy topper, use mild or medium salsa instead of hot.*

**Prep:** 20 minutes  **Marinate:** 1 hour  **Grill:** 12 minutes  **Makes:** 6 servings

**1.** For marinade, in a shallow nonmetallic dish combine lime peel, lime juice, tequila, oil, orange liqueur or orange peel, garlic, salt, and pepper. Add chicken to marinade, turning to coat. Cover and marinate in the refrigerator for 1 hour.

**2.** Meanwhile, for tomato salsa, in a small bowl combine salsa, tomato, green onions, and cilantro. Set aside.

**3.** Drain chicken, reserving marinade. Stir honey into reserved marinade. Grill chicken on the rack of an uncovered grill directly over medium coals for 12 to 15 minutes or until chicken is tender and no longer pink, turning and brushing once with honey mixture halfway through grilling. (Or place chicken on the unheated rack of a broiler pan. Broil 4 to 5 inches from the heat for 12 to 15 minutes, turning and brushing once with honey mixture halfway through broiling.) Discard any remaining honey mixture. Serve with tomato salsa.

Nutrition Facts per serving: 217 calories, 4 g total fat, 66 mg cholesterol, 255 mg sodium, 11 g carbohydrate, 27 g protein.

- 2 teaspoons finely shredded lime peel
- ¼ cup lime juice
- ¼ cup tequila
- 1 tablespoon cooking oil
- 1 tablespoon orange liqueur or 1 teaspoon finely shredded orange peel
- 2 cloves garlic, minced
- ¼ teaspoon salt
- ¼ teaspoon pepper
- 6 medium skinless, boneless chicken breast halves (about 1½ pounds total)
- 1 cup hot chunky salsa
- 1 medium tomato, chopped
- 2 green onions, finely chopped
- 1 tablespoon snipped fresh cilantro
- 2 tablespoons honey

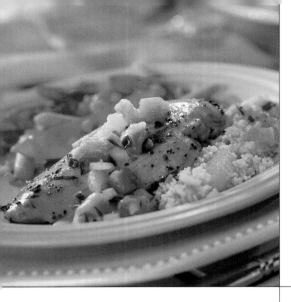

# Bahama-Marinated Grilled Chicken

*A savory blend of quinoa and couscous complements the grilled chicken breasts. Look for both quinoa—a grain long popular in South America—and couscous near the rice in large supermarkets.*

**Prep:** 25 minutes  **Marinate:** 2 to 12 hours  **Broil:** 12 minutes  **Makes:** 2 servings

2 medium skinless, boneless
    chicken breast halves
    (about 8 ounces total)
1 recipe Bahama Marinade
1 cup chicken broth
¼ cup quinoa
¼ cup quick-cooking couscous
1 orange, peeled, halved,
    and sliced
1 green onion, chopped
⅛ teaspoon pepper
1 recipe Melon-Sweet Onion
    Salsa (optional)

**1.** Place chicken in a shallow glass dish. Pour Bahama Marinade over. Cover; marinate in the refrigerator for at least 2 hours or up to 12 hours.

**2.** Bring broth to boiling. Add quinoa; reduce heat to low. Cover; cook 10 minutes. Stir in couscous; remove from heat. Cover; let stand 5 minutes. Stir in orange, onion, and pepper.

**3.** Drain chicken, discarding marinade. Place chicken on unheated rack of a broiler pan. Broil 4 to 5 inches from the heat 12 to 15 minutes or until no longer pink; turn once. Serve with couscous mixture. If desired, top with Melon-Sweet Onion Salsa.

***Bahama Marinade:*** In a small skillet heat ½ teaspoon cumin seeds over medium heat until lightly toasted. Remove from heat. Crush cumin seeds. In a small bowl combine crushed cumin seeds; ¼ cup rice vinegar; 3 tablespoons orange juice; 1 clove garlic, minced; ½ teaspoon dried oregano, crushed; ½ teaspoon paprika; ¼ teaspoon ground allspice; ¼ teaspoon coarsely ground black pepper; and dash ground red pepper.

Nutrition Facts per serving: **347 calories, 5 g total fat, 60 mg cholesterol, 450 mg sodium, 44 g carbohydrate, 31 g protein.**

***Melon-Sweet Onion Salsa:*** Combine 2 tablespoons orange marmalade; 2 tablespoons snipped fresh cilantro; 1 fresh jalapeño pepper, seeded and finely chopped (see note on page 207); 1 tablespoon rice vinegar; 1 clove garlic, minced; and ⅛ teaspoon salt. Stir in 1 cup chopped seeded watermelon; 1 small orange, peeled and chopped; and ¼ cup finely chopped sweet onion.

# Chicken and Prosciutto Roll-Ups

*For each serving, nestle the sliced chicken spirals on a bed of hot cooked spinach fettuccine.*

**Prep:** 25 minutes  **Grill:** 12 minutes  **Makes:** 4 servings

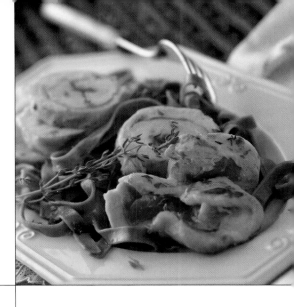

**1.** For sauce, in a small bowl combine wine and the snipped or dried thyme. Set aside.

**2.** Place each chicken piece between 2 pieces of plastic wrap. Pound lightly with the flat side of a meat mallet into a rectangle about ⅛ inch thick. Remove plastic wrap.

**3.** Place a slice of prosciutto and one-quarter of the cheese on each chicken piece. Arrange one-quarter of the roasted peppers on cheese near bottom edge of each chicken piece. Starting from bottom edge, roll up into a spiral; secure rolls with wooden toothpicks.

**4.** Grill chicken on the rack of an uncovered grill directly over medium coals for 12 to 15 minutes or until chicken is tender and no longer pink, turning to cook evenly and brushing with sauce twice during the last 5 minutes of grilling. If desired, serve over spinach fettuccine. If desired, garnish with thyme sprigs.

Nutrition Facts per serving: 214 calories, 9 g total fat, 76 mg cholesterol, 294 mg sodium, 2 g carbohydrate, 27 g protein.

¼ cup dry white wine

2 teaspoons snipped fresh thyme or ½ teaspoon dried thyme, crushed

4 medium skinless, boneless chicken breast halves (about 1 pound total)

4 thin slices prosciutto (about 1 ounce total), trimmed of fat

2 ounces fontina cheese, thinly sliced

½ of a 7-ounce jar roasted red sweet peppers, cut into thin strips (about ½ cup)

Hot cooked spinach fettuccine (optional)

Fresh thyme sprigs (optional)

# Grilled Chicken Burgers With Red Onions

*Check the internal temperature of the burgers with an instant-read thermometer to make sure they are thoroughly cooked.*

**Prep:** 20 minutes   **Grill:** 14 minutes   **Makes:** 4 servings

1 slightly beaten egg
½ cup fine dry seasoned
   bread crumbs
1 tablespoon coarse-grain
   brown mustard
1 pound uncooked ground
   chicken or turkey
4 ½-inch-thick slices red
   or yellow onion
1 tablespoon olive oil or
   cooking oil
½ teaspoon dried basil,
   crushed
   Lettuce leaves
8 thin slices tomato
4 kaiser or onion rolls, split
   Coarse-grain brown mustard
   (optional)

**1.** In a medium bowl combine egg, bread crumbs, and the 1 tablespoon mustard. Add ground chicken or turkey; mix well. With hands, shape mixture into four ¾-inch-thick patties. Set aside.

**2.** Thread 2 skewers horizontally through each onion slice. In a small bowl combine olive oil and basil; brush over onions.

**3.** Grill chicken patties on the grill rack of an uncovered grill directly over medium coals for 7 minutes. Turn patties; add onions on skewers and grill 7 to 11 minutes more or until onions are crisp-tender and patties are done (165°).* Place lettuce and 2 tomato slices on each roll bottom; top each with a chicken burger. Serve each burger with a grilled onion slice. Top with bun tops. If desired, pass additional mustard.

Nutrition Facts per serving: 378 calories, 13 g total fat, 108 mg cholesterol, 803 mg sodium, 40 g carbohydrate, 25 g protein.

***Note:*** The internal color of a ground poultry patty is not a reliable doneness indicator. A chicken or turkey patty cooked to 165°, regardless of color, is safe. Use an instant-read thermometer to check the internal temperature. To measure the doneness of a patty, insert an instant-read thermometer through the side of the patty to a depth of 2 to 3 inches.

# Chipotle-Rubbed Smoked Turkey

*The smoky flavor of chipotle peppers reinforces the wood-smoked flavor of the turkey.*

**Prep:** 1 hour  **Grill:** 1½ hours  **Stand:** 15 minutes  **Makes:** 8 to 10 servings

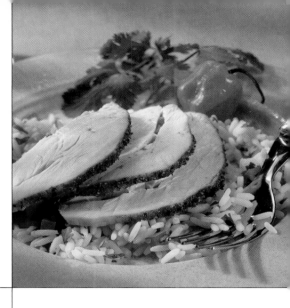

**1.** Thaw turkey, if frozen. At least 1 hour before grilling, soak wood chips in enough water to cover. Meanwhile, in a small bowl combine coriander, paprika, black pepper, and chipotle pepper or ground red pepper.

**2.** Remove skin and excess fat from turkey breast. Brush skinned surface of turkey with the oil. Rub with the spice mixture. Insert an oven-going meat thermometer into the thickest part of the turkey breast, making sure the bulb does not touch the bone.

**3.** Drain wood chips. In a covered grill arrange medium-hot coals around the outside edges of grill. Sprinkle half of the wood chips over coals; test for medium heat above the center of the grill (not over coals). Place turkey breast, bone side down, in a roasting pan on the center of grill rack (not over coals). Cover and grill for 45 minutes.

**4.** Sprinkle coals with remaining wood chips. Cover and grill for 45 minutes to 1¼ hours more or until meat thermometer registers 170°. Add more coals as needed. Remove turkey breast from grill. Loosely cover with foil; let stand for 15 minutes before slicing. If desired, serve with rice and garnish with cilantro and fresh chili peppers.

Nutrition Facts per serving: **105 calories, 3 g total fat, 41 mg cholesterol, 38 mg sodium, 0 g carbohydrate, 18 g protein.**

***Note:*** Dress up the rice by stirring in some chopped red sweet pepper and snipped fresh cilantro.

1  2- to 2½-pound fresh or frozen bone-in turkey breast half
3  cups hickory or mesquite wood chips
1  teaspoon ground coriander
½  teaspoon paprika
¼ to ½ teaspoon ground black pepper
1  small dried chipotle pepper, seeded and crushed, or ⅛ to ¼ teaspoon ground red pepper
2  teaspoons cooking oil
   Hot cooked rice* (optional)
   Fresh cilantro sprigs (optional)
   Fresh chili peppers (optional)

# Turkey Breast with Raspberry Salsa

*If you want a sauce with a little more kick, use your favorite medium or hot salsa.*

**Prep:** 10 minutes  **Grill:** 1 hour  **Stand:** 15 minutes  **Makes:** 8 servings

1 2- to 2½-pound fresh or
frozen bone-in turkey
breast half
⅓ cup seedless raspberry jam
1 tablespoon Dijon-style
mustard
1 teaspoon finely shredded
orange peel
½ cup mild salsa
Orange peel strips (optional)

*1.* Thaw turkey, if frozen. In a small bowl stir together raspberry jam, mustard, and the 1 teaspoon orange peel. Stir 3 tablespoons of the jam mixture into salsa. Cover and chill remaining jam mixture and the salsa mixture. If desired, skin turkey breast. Insert an oven-going meat thermometer into the thickest part of the turkey breast, making sure the bulb does not touch the bone.

*2.* In a covered grill arrange medium-hot coals around a drip pan. Test for medium heat above the pan. Place turkey, bone side down, on grill rack over drip pan. Cover and grill for 1 to 1¼ hours or until meat thermometer registers 170°, brushing occasionally with jam mixture during the last 30 minutes of grilling. Discard any remaining jam mixture.

*3.* Remove turkey from grill and cover with foil. Let stand for 15 minutes before slicing. Serve turkey with salsa mixture. If desired, garnish with orange peel strips.

Nutrition Facts per serving: **149 calories, 3 g total fat, 46 mg cholesterol, 147 mg sodium, 11 g carbohydrate, 20 g protein.**

# Turkey Steaks and Sweet Pepper-Citrus Salsa

*Keep mess to a minimum by using a self-sealing plastic bag to hold the turkey and the marinade.*

**Prep:** 15 minutes **Marinate:** 2 to 4 hours **Grill:** 12 minutes **Makes:** 6 servings

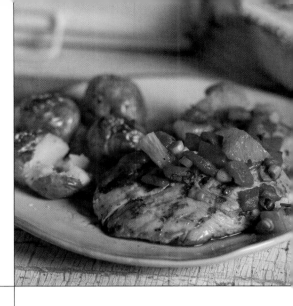

**1.** Place turkey in a heavy, large self-sealing plastic bag set in a shallow bowl.

**2.** For marinade, in a small bowl combine oil, lemon juice, orange peel, orange juice, garlic, salt, and pepper. Pour over turkey. Seal bag; turn to coat turkey. Marinate in refrigerator for at least 2 hours or up to 4 hours, turning occasionally.

**3.** Drain turkey, reserving marinade. Grill turkey on the rack of an uncovered grill directly over medium coals for 12 to 15 minutes or until turkey is tender and no longer pink, turning once halfway through grilling and brushing with reserved marinade during the first 6 minutes of grilling. Serve with Sweet Pepper-Citrus Salsa.

***Sweet Pepper-Citrus Salsa:*** In a small bowl combine one 7-ounce jar roasted red sweet peppers, drained and chopped; 1 orange, peeled, seeded, and cut up; 2 green onions, sliced; 2 tablespoons balsamic vinegar; and 1 tablespoon snipped fresh basil or 1 teaspoon dried basil, crushed. Cover and refrigerate salsa until serving time.

Nutrition Facts per serving: 222 calories, 10 g total fat, 50 mg cholesterol, 108 mg sodium, 10 g carbohydrate, 22 g protein.

***Note:*** Look for precut turkey breast steaks. If you find only the large whole turkey tenderloins, slice them crosswise into ½-inch-thick steaks.

- **6 turkey breast steaks (about 1½ pounds total)\***
- **⅓ cup olive oil**
- **¼ cup lemon juice**
- **1 teaspoon finely shredded orange peel**
- **¼ cup orange juice**
- **4 cloves garlic, minced**
- **¼ teaspoon salt**
- **¼ teaspoon pepper**
- **1 recipe Sweet Pepper-Citrus Salsa**

# Apricot-Stuffed Grilled Turkey Breast

*Grill this tender turkey breast filled with a fruit-and-nut dressing to juicy perfection over indirect heat.*

**Prep:** 25 minutes  **Grill:** 1 hour  **Stand:** 15 minutes  **Makes:** 8 servings

- 1 2- to 2½-pound fresh of frozen bone-in turkey breast half
- 1½ cups soft bread crumbs (2 slices)
- ½ cup snipped dried apricots
- ¼ cup chopped pecans, toasted
- 2 tablespoons apple juice or water
- 1 tablespoon cooking oil
- ¼ teaspoon dried rosemary, crushed
- ¼ teaspoon garlic salt
- 1 tablespoon Dijon-style mustard
- 1 tablespoon water

**1.** Thaw turkey breast half, if frozen. In a small bowl soak 4 to 6 wooden toothpicks in water for 10 minutes. Meanwhile, remove bone from turkey breast half. Cut a horizontal slit into thickest part of turkey breast half to form a 5×4-inch pocket. Set aside.

**2.** For stuffing, in a medium bowl combine bread crumbs, apricots, pecans, apple juice or water, oil, rosemary, and garlic salt. Spoon stuffing into pocket. Securely fasten the opening with water-soaked wooden toothpicks. Stir together mustard and the water; set aside.

**3.** In a grill with a cover arrange medium-hot coals around a drip pan. Test for medium heat above the drip pan. Place turkey on grill rack over pan. Cover and grill about 1 hour or until turkey is tender and no longer pink (an instant-read thermometer inserted in stuffing should register 165°), brushing with mustard mixture during the last 15 minutes of grilling. Discard any remaining mustard mixture.

**4.** Remove turkey from grill. Cover with foil. Let stand for 15 minutes before slicing.

Nutrition Facts per serving: **237 calories, 11 g total fat, 59 mg cholesterol, 205 mg sodium, 10 g carbohydrate, 24 g protein.**

# Grilled Turkey with Pepper Sauce

*Use the food processor for double duty in this recipe—first to quickly chop the sweet peppers and onions and then to puree the cooked vegetable mixture.*

**Prep:** 20 minutes  **Grill:** 25 minutes  **Makes:** 4 servings

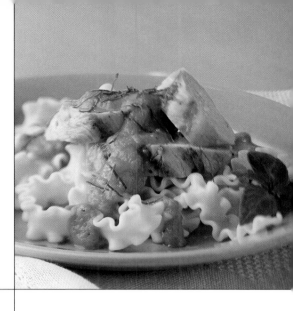

**1.** For sauce, in a large skillet cook sweet peppers and onion in 1 tablespoon of the hot oil over medium heat about 10 minutes or until vegetables are very tender, stirring occasionally. Transfer vegetables to a food processor bowl or blender container; add broth, salt, and black pepper. Cover and process or blend until mixture is smooth. Return to skillet; set aside.

**2.** In a small bowl combine the remaining oil and the garlic. Brush over turkey.

**3.** In a grill with a cover arrange medium-hot coals around a drip pan. Test for medium heat above the pan. Place turkey on the grill rack over the drip pan. Cover and grill for 25 to 30 minutes or until turkey is tender and no longer pink.

**4.** Cut the turkey into slices. Reheat the sauce until bubbly. Serve the turkey and sauce over pasta. Sprinkle with shredded basil. If desired, garnish with basil sprigs.

Nutrition Facts per serving: 380 calories, 9 g total fat, 68 mg cholesterol, 348 mg sodium, 38 g carbohydrate, 34 g protein.

- 2 medium red or yellow sweet peppers, chopped
- ½ cup finely chopped onion
- 2 tablespoons olive oil or cooking oil
- ¾ cup chicken broth
- ¼ teaspoon salt
- ¼ teaspoon ground black pepper
- 2 cloves garlic, minced
- 2 turkey breast tenderloins (about 1 pound total)
  Hot cooked mafalda or fettuccine
- 2 tablespoons finely shredded fresh basil
  Fresh basil sprigs (optional)

# Grilled Turkey Tenderloins With Onion-Cilantro Relish

*You can store cilantro and other fresh herbs for a few days in the refrigerator. Just immerse the freshly cut stems in about 2 inches of water. Cover the herbs loosely with plastic wrap and refrigerate.*

**Prep:** 15 minutes   **Grill:** 15 minutes   **Makes:** 4 servings

½ cup chopped onion

¼ cup fresh cilantro sprigs

⅛ teaspoon salt

⅛ teaspoon pepper

4 turkey breast tenderloin steaks* (about 1 pound total)

3 tablespoons lime juice or lemon juice

Lime and/or lemon wedges (optional)

Fresh cilantro sprigs (optional)

**1.** In a blender container or food processor bowl combine onion, the ¼ cup cilantro, the salt, and pepper. Cover and process until mixture is very finely chopped. Set aside.

**2.** Dip turkey breast tenderloin steaks into lime or lemon juice. Grill turkey on rack of an uncovered grill directly over medium coals for 7 minutes. Turn; brush with lime or lemon juice. Spread the onion mixture over turkey. Grill 8 to 11 minutes more or until turkey is tender and no longer pink.

**3.** If desired, serve with lime and/or lemon wedges and garnish with additional cilantro sprigs.

Nutrition Facts per serving: **124 calories, 2 g total fat, 50 mg cholesterol, 113 mg sodium, 3 g carbohydrate, 22 g protein.**

***Note:*** If you can't find turkey breast tenderloin steaks, buy two turkey breast tenderloins and split them in half lengthwise.

# Spicy Grilled Turkey Tenderloins

*Two types of pepper—ground black and crushed red—provide the just-right, spicy flavor.*

**Prep:** 10 minutes  **Marinate:** 30 minutes  **Grill:** 12 minutes  **Makes:** 4 servings

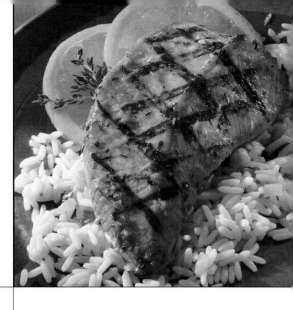

**1.** For marinade, in a shallow nonmetallic dish combine orange peel, orange juice, oil, cumin, thyme, salt, black pepper, and crushed red pepper. Add turkey to marinade, turning to coat. Cover and marinate in the refrigerator for 30 minutes.

**2.** Drain turkey, reserving marinade. Grill turkey on the rack of an uncovered grill directly over medium coals for 12 to 15 minutes or until tender and no longer pink, turning and basting once with reserved marinade halfway through grilling. Discard any remaining marinade. If desired, serve with hot cooked rice.

Nutrition Facts per serving: 182 calories, 9 g total fat, 50 mg cholesterol, 315 mg sodium, 2 g carbohydrate, 22 g protein.

***Note:*** If you can't find turkey breast tenderloin steaks, buy two turkey breast tenderloins and split them in half lengthwise.

****Note:*** Dress up the rice by stirring in some chopped red and/or yellow sweet pepper.

- 1 teaspoon finely shredded orange peel
- ¼ cup orange juice
- 2 tablespoons olive oil or cooking oil
- 1 teaspoon ground cumin
- 1 teaspoon dried thyme, crushed
- ½ teaspoon salt
- ¼ teaspoon ground black pepper
- ¼ teaspoon crushed red pepper
- 4 turkey breast tenderloin steaks* (about 1 pound total)
- Hot cooked rice** (optional)

# Broiled Chicken Thighs With Honey-Apricot Glaze

*If apricot doesn't suit your fancy, make this two-ingredient glaze with plum jam, raspberry preserves, or orange marmalade instead of the apricot preserves.*

**Prep:** 10 minutes  **Broil:** 12 minutes  **Makes:** 4 servings

1 pound skinless, boneless chicken thighs
1 tablespoon olive oil or cooking oil
¼ teaspoon garlic salt
⅛ teaspoon pepper
¼ cup apricot preserves
1 tablespoon honey
2 tablespoons vinegar

**1.** Place chicken pieces on unheated rack of a broiler pan. Brush with oil and sprinkle with garlic salt and pepper. Broil 4 to 5 inches from the heat for 5 minutes.

**2.** Meanwhile, in a small saucepan stir apricot preserves and honey over medium heat until melted. Remove from heat; stir in vinegar. Brush apricot mixture over chicken pieces; turn and brush with remaining apricot mixture. Broil for 7 to 10 minutes more or until chicken is tender and no longer pink.

Nutrition Facts per serving: **243 calories, 8 g total fat, 91 mg cholesterol, 144 mg sodium, 19 g carbohydrate, 23 g protein.**

# Broiled Chicken with Feta Cheese

*This flavorful dish is as easy as 1-2-3. Just brush chicken breasts with your favorite Italian dressing, broil, and sprinkle with crumbled feta cheese.*

**Prep:** 10 minutes  **Broil:** 12 minutes  **Makes:** 4 servings

**1.** Place chicken on the unheated rack of broiler pan. Brush with half of the Italian dressing. Broil 4 to 5 inches from the heat for 12 to 15 minutes or until chicken is tender and no longer pink, turning and brushing on all of the remaining Italian dressing halfway through broiling.

**2.** Sprinkle cheese evenly over chicken; broil just until cheese melts. Line 4 of the bread slices or the bun bottoms with lettuce; top with chicken. Sprinkle parsley over. Cover with remaining bread slices or bun tops.

Nutrition Facts per serving: 380 calories, 15 g total fat, 88 mg cholesterol, 773 mg sodium, 29 g carbohydrate, 31 g protein.

- **4 medium skinless, boneless chicken breast halves (about 1 pound total)**
- **2 tablespoons bottled clear Italian salad dressing**
- **½ cup crumbled feta cheese or blue cheese (2 ounces)**
- **8 slices sourdough bread or 4 hamburger buns (toasted, if desired)**
- **Lettuce leaves**
- **1 tablespoon snipped fresh parsley or 1 teaspoon dried parsley flakes, crushed**

# Broiled Chicken with Garlic Sauce

*Chives and dry mustard enhance the flavor of the mayonnaise-based garlic sauce.*

**Prep:** 10 minutes   **Broil:** 12 minutes   **Makes:** 4 servings

4 medium skinless, boneless chicken breast halves (about 1 pound total)

2 tablespoons olive oil or cooking oil

½ cup mayonnaise or salad dressing

2 tablespoons milk

1 tablespoon snipped fresh chives or 1 teaspoon dried chives

1½ teaspoons bottled minced garlic

1 teaspoon lemon juice

¼ teaspoon pepper

¼ teaspoon dry mustard

Lemon wedges (optional)

Fresh chives (optional)

**1.** Place chicken pieces on the unheated rack of a broiler pan. Brush with 1 tablespoon of the oil. Broil 4 to 5 inches from the heat for 12 to 15 minutes or until tender and no longer pink, turning and brushing with all of the remaining oil halfway through broiling.

**2.** Meanwhile, for garlic sauce, stir together mayonnaise or salad dressing, milk, snipped or dried chives, garlic, lemon juice, pepper, and mustard.

**3.** Transfer chicken to a heated serving platter. Spoon some of the garlic sauce over chicken; serve immediately. Pass remaining sauce. If desired, garnish with lemon wedges and fresh chives.

Nutrition Facts per serving: **387 calories, 32 g total fat, 76 mg cholesterol, 215 mg sodium, 2 g carbohydrate, 22 g protein.**

# Broiled Chili-Glazed Chicken and Peppers

*A combo of chili sauce and barbecue sauce makes a zesty brush-on for broiled chicken.*

**Prep:** 10 minutes  **Broil:** 12 minutes  **Makes:** 4 servings

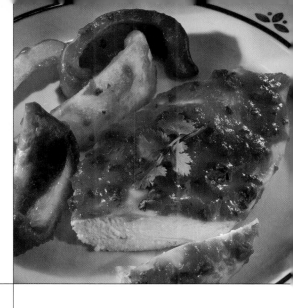

**1.** Place chicken on the unheated rack of a broiler pan. Halve peppers from stem to tip; remove center core. Cut each half into 4 wedges. Place peppers, cut sides down, on broiler pan.

**2.** In a small bowl stir together chili sauce, barbecue sauce, and the snipped cilantro or parsley. Brush chicken and pepper pieces lightly with chili sauce mixture. Broil 4 to 5 inches from heat for 12 to 15 minutes or until chicken is tender and no longer pink, turning and generously brushing once with chili sauce mixture halfway through broiling. Heat any remaining chili sauce mixture to boiling; serve with the chicken. Serve each chicken piece with 4 pepper wedges. If desired, garnish with cilantro or parsley sprigs.

Nutrition Facts per serving: **153 calories, 3 g total fat, 59 mg cholesterol, 319 mg sodium, 7 g carbohydrate, 23 g protein.**

- 4 **medium skinless, boneless chicken breast halves (about 1 pound total)**
- 2 **medium red, yellow, and/or green sweet peppers**
- ¼ **cup bottled chili sauce**
- 2 **tablespoons bottled barbecue sauce**
- 1 **tablespoon snipped fresh cilantro or parsley**
  **Fresh cilantro or parsley sprigs (optional)**

# Crispy Chicken Scaloppine

*Broiling, rather than frying, the scaloppine results in a crispy coating with less fat.*

**Prep:** 15 minutes  **Broil:** 6 minutes  **Makes:** 4 servings

4 medium skinless, boneless
   chicken breast halves
   (about 1 pound total)

1 large egg white

2 tablespoons water

1 cup soft bread crumbs

2 tablespoons snipped
   fresh parsley

1 teaspoon bottled minced
   garlic

¼ teaspoon freshly ground
   black pepper

   Salt

4 thin slices prosciutto
   (about 1½ ounces total)

2 tablespoons olive oil

   Lemon slices

   Fresh parsley sprigs
   (optional)

*1.* Place each chicken breast half between 2 pieces of plastic wrap. Pound lightly with the flat side of a meat mallet until about ⅛ inch thick. In a shallow dish whisk together the egg white and water. In another shallow dish combine the bread crumbs, parsley, garlic, and pepper.

*2.* Season chicken lightly with salt. Press 1 slice prosciutto onto each piece of chicken. Dip in egg white mixture, then in crumb mixture. Place on unheated rack of a broiler pan; sprinkle with 1 tablespoon of the oil.

*3.* Broil 5 to 6 inches from the heat for 3 minutes; turn and sprinkle with remaining oil. Broil about 3 minutes more or until no longer pink and coating is crisp. Top with lemon slices. If desired, garnish with parsley sprigs.

Nutrition Facts per serving: **245 calories, 10 g total fat, 75 mg cholesterol, 340 mg sodium, 6 g carbohydrate, 31 g protein.**

# Chicken Shish Kabobs

*Think ahead and make tabbouleh—the traditional serve-along for shish kabobs. Or serve the kabobs with hot cooked rice.*

**Prep:** 20 minutes **Marinate:** 1 hour **Broil:** 10 minutes **Makes:** 6 to 8 servings

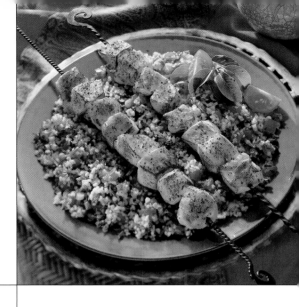

**1.** Place chicken in a heavy, large self-sealing plastic bag set in a shallow dish. Set aside.

**2.** In a small bowl stir together the lemon juice, oil, garlic, salt, and pepper. Pour over chicken. Seal bag; turn to coat chicken. Cover and marinate chicken in the refrigerator for 1 hour. (Don't marinate longer or the flavor will be too strong.)

**3.** Drain chicken, discarding marinade. Thread chicken chunks onto skewers. Place skewers on the unheated rack of a broiler pan. Broil 4 to 5 inches from the heat about 5 minutes. Turn the chicken and broil about 5 minutes more or until the chicken is tender and no longer pink. If desired, serve over Tabbouleh.

Nutrition Facts per serving: **274 calories, 16 g total fat, 79 mg cholesterol, 250 mg sodium, 2 g carbohydrate, 31 g protein.**

*Tabbouleh:* Place ½ cup uncooked bulgur (steamed cracked wheat) in a sieve; rinse with cold water and drain. In a large bowl combine bulgur, ¼ cup lemon juice, ¼ cup olive oil, 2 tablespoons water, ¼ teaspoon salt, and dash pepper. Stir in 2 cups finely snipped fresh parsley, 2 finely chopped tomatoes, 1 cup chopped green onions, and ⅓ cup finely snipped fresh mint leaves. Cover and chill in the refrigerator for at least 4 hours or up to 24 hours. Serve mixture on lettuce or cabbage leaves. Makes 6 side-dish servings.

- **2 pounds skinless, boneless chicken breasts, cut into 1-inch cubes**
- **½ cup lemon juice**
- **⅓ cup cooking oil or olive oil**
- **3 or 4 cloves garlic, minced**
- **½ teaspoon salt**
- **½ teaspoon ground white or black pepper**
- **1 recipe Tabbouleh (optional)**

# Chicken with Braised Spinach and Leek

*Choose an all-purpose apple such as Granny Smith or Golden Delicious for this flavorful entrée.*

**Prep:** 20 minutes  **Broil:** 12 minutes  **Makes:** 4 servings

½ cup apple jelly

2 tablespoons soy sauce

1 tablespoon snipped fresh thyme or 1 teaspoon dried thyme, crushed

1 teaspoon grated fresh ginger

1 teaspoon finely shredded lemon peel

4 small skinless, boneless chicken breast halves (about 12 ounces total)
Nonstick cooking spray

2 medium apples, coarsely chopped

1 medium leek (white part only), sliced, or ⅓ cup chopped onion

2 cloves garlic, minced

2 tablespoons apple juice or chicken broth

1 10-ounce package torn fresh spinach
Salt
Pepper

**1.** For glaze, in a small saucepan heat and stir apple jelly, soy sauce, thyme, ginger, and lemon peel just until jelly is melted. Remove from heat. Set aside ¼ cup of the glaze for dressing.

**2.** Place chicken on the unheated rack of a broiler pan. Broil 4 to 5 inches from the heat for 12 to 15 minutes or until chicken is tender and no longer pink, turning and brushing once with the remaining glaze halfway through broiling. (Or grill on the rack of an uncovered grill directly over medium coals for 12 to 15 minutes, turning and brushing once with the remaining glaze halfway through grilling.)

**3.** Meanwhile, coat a large saucepan or Dutch oven with nonstick cooking spray. Preheat over medium heat. Add apples, leek or onion, and garlic; cook for 3 minutes. Stir in the reserved glaze and the apple juice or chicken broth. Bring to boiling. Add spinach; toss just until wilted. Season spinach mixture to taste with salt and pepper.

**4.** To serve, cut each chicken piece crosswise into 6 to 8 slices. Divide the spinach mixture among 4 dinner plates. Top with sliced chicken.

Nutrition Facts per serving: 263 calories, 3 g total fat, 45 mg cholesterol, 654 mg sodium, 42 g carbohydrate, 19 g protein.

# Broiled Chicken with Tomato-Pepper Puree

*Since it starts with purchased cooked chicken breasts, this flavorful entrée is ready to serve in only 15 minutes.*

**Prep:** 10 minutes  **Broil:** 5 minutes  **Makes:** 4 servings

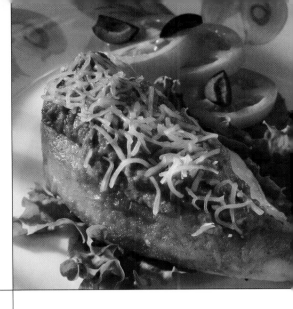

**1.** Place cooked chicken breast halves, skin sides up, on the unheated rack of a broiler pan.

**2.** For puree, drain tomatoes, reserving 1 tablespoon of the oil. Halve tomatoes; combine in a blender container with the reserved oil, red pepper, the 2 tablespoons olives, Italian seasoning, and garlic. Cover and blend until almost smooth. Spread over chicken.

**3.** Broil 4 to 5 inches from heat for 4 to 5 minutes or until heated through. Sprinkle with cheese; broil 1 to 2 minutes more or until cheese is melted. If desired, serve on lettuce leaves and garnish with tomatoes and additional olives.

Nutrition Facts per serving: 231 calories, 11 g total fat, 84 mg cholesterol, 209 mg sodium, 3 g carbohydrate, 29 g protein.

- **4 purchased broiled or roasted chicken breast halves**
- **¼ cup oil-packed dried tomatoes**
- **¼ cup purchased roasted red sweet pepper**
- **2 tablespoons sliced pitted ripe olives (half of a 2¼-ounce can)**
- **½ teaspoon dried Italian seasoning, crushed**
- **½ teaspoon bottled minced garlic**
- **½ cup finely shredded mozzarella cheese (2 ounces)**
- **Lettuce leaves (optional)**
- **Sliced tomatoes (optional)**
- **Sliced pitted ripe olives (optional)**

# Mustard-Puff Chicken

*To trim calories and fat, make this golden puff with fat-free mayonnaise dressing in place of the regular mayonnaise.*

**Start to Finish:** 15 minutes  **Makes:** 4 servings

4 medium skinless, boneless chicken breasts halves (about 1 pound total)
⅓ cup mayonnaise or salad dressing
1 tablespoon Dijon-style mustard
1 tablespoon sliced green onion
Dash ground red pepper

**1.** Place chicken on the unheated rack of a broiler pan. Broil 4 to 5 inches from the heat for 7 minutes.

**2.** Meanwhile, in a small bowl stir together mayonnaise or salad dressing, mustard, green onion, and ground red pepper. Turn chicken; brush liberally with mayonnaise mixture. Broil for 5 to 8 minutes more or until chicken is tender and no longer pink. Discard any remaining mayonnaise mixture.

Nutrition Facts per serving: **256 calories, 18 g total fat, 70 mg cholesterol, 252 mg sodium, 1 g carbohydrate, 22 g protein.**

# Broiled Turkey with Tropical Fruit Salsa

*Start with purchased fruit salad, add lime juice, green onion, and jalapeño pepper, and you've got a wonderful salsa. Look in your supermarket's produce section for cans or jars of the fruit medley.*

**Prep:** 10 minutes  **Broil:** 8 minutes  **Makes:** 4 servings

**1.** Place turkey or chicken on the unheated rack of a broiler pan. Brush with oil. Broil 4 to 5 inches from the heat for 5 minutes. Turn and brush with oil; season with salt and pepper. Broil for 3 to 5 minutes more for turkey (7 to 10 minutes more for chicken) or until tender and no longer pink.

**2.** Meanwhile, for salsa, in a medium bowl stir together chopped fruit, lime juice, green onion, and jalapeño pepper. Serve turkey topped with salsa. If desired, garnish with kiwi fruit and carambola and serve with hot cooked rice sprinkled with snipped parsley.

Nutrition Facts per serving: **227 calories, 6 g total fat, 50 mg cholesterol, 181 mg sodium, 22 g carbohydrate, 22 g protein.**

***Note:*** If you can't find turkey breast tenderloin steaks, buy two turkey breast tenderloins and split them in half lengthwise.

****Note:*** Because chile peppers, such as jalapeños, contain volatile oils that can burn your skin and eyes, avoid direct contact with them as much as possible. When working with chile peppers, wear plastic or rubber gloves. If your bare hands do touch the chile peppers, wash your hands and nails well with soap and warm water.

4 turkey breast tenderloin
  steaks* or 4 medium
  skinless, boneless chicken
  breast halves (about
  1 pound total)
  Olive oil or cooking oil
  Salt
  Pepper
1 16-ounce can tropical fruit
  salad, drained and chopped
2 tablespoons lime juice
1 green onion, sliced
1 teaspoon finely chopped
  fresh jalapeño or mild green
  chili pepper**
  Kiwi fruit slices (optional)
  Carambola (star fruit) slices
  (optional)
  Hot cooked rice (optional)
  Snipped fresh parsley
  (optional)

# salads and sandwiches

*If all you want for dinner is a salad or a sandwich, opt for one of these imaginative recipes. From grilled chicken salad to turkey burgers to a cooked chicken fix-up, you'll find the best ideas here.*

Muffuletta, page 268

# Chicken and Basil Pasta Salad

*If you prefer, use small pasta shells instead of corkscrew macaroni.*

**Prep:** 25 minutes  **Chill:** 2 to 6 hours  **Makes:** 6 servings

4 ounces dried corkscrew
   macaroni (about 1 cup)
¼ teaspoon salt
   Nonstick cooking spray
8 ounces skinless, boneless
   chicken breasts, cut into
   1-inch pieces
⅛ teaspoon salt
⅛ teaspoon pepper
4 plum tomatoes, halved
   lengthwise and sliced
1 small zucchini and/or yellow
   summer squash, halved
   lengthwise and sliced
¼ cup sliced green onions
⅔ cup bottled reduced-calorie
   or fat-free clear Italian
   salad dressing
¼ cup snipped fresh basil

**1.** Cook macaroni according to package directions, except omit any oil and use the ¼ teaspoon salt. Drain pasta. Rinse with cold water. Drain again.

**2.** Coat an unheated large skillet with nonstick cooking spray. Preheat over medium-high heat. Add the chicken; stir-fry for 3 to 4 minutes or until no longer pink. Sprinkle with the ⅛ teaspoon salt and the pepper. Remove chicken from heat.

**3.** In a large bowl toss together cooked macaroni, chicken, tomatoes, zucchini or summer squash, and green onions. Drizzle with salad dressing. Sprinkle with basil. Toss to coat. Cover and chill in the refrigerator for at least 2 hours or up to 6 hours. Toss salad before serving.

Nutrition Facts per serving: **153 calories, 4 g total fat, 22 mg cholesterol, 277 mg sodium, 18 g carbohydrate, 10 g protein.**

# Chicken Fiesta Salad

*Shortcut preparation by using purchased taco salad shells or bowl-shaped tostada shells instead of molding and baking the tortillas.*

**Prep:** 20 minutes  **Bake:** 20 minutes  **Cook:** 8 minutes  **Makes:** 4 servings

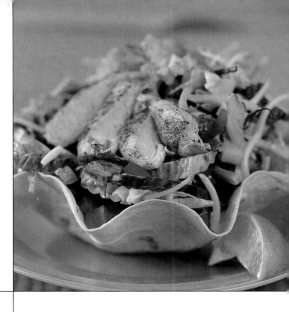

**1.** Lightly coat 2 tortilla/taco shell molds* or medium ovenproof bowls with nonstick cooking spray. Carefully press a tortilla into each mold or bowl, making sure the tortilla follows the shape of the mold or bowl. Bake in a 375° oven for 10 to 12 minutes or until golden brown. Let cool in molds or bowls for 5 minutes. Carefully remove tortilla shells; cool on a wire rack. Repeat with remaining 2 tortillas.

**2.** Meanwhile, sprinkle both sides of each chicken breast half with Cajun seasoning. In a large skillet cook chicken in hot oil over medium-high heat for 8 to 10 minutes or until tender and no longer pink. Cool chicken breasts slightly; slice.

**3.** In a large bowl toss together iceberg lettuce, romaine, carrots, and red cabbage. In another bowl toss together cheeses. Fill each tortilla shell with 3 cups of the lettuce mixture; top each with 2 tablespoons of the dressing, ¼ cup of the cheese mixture, ½ cup of the tomatoes, and 1 of the sliced chicken breasts. If desired, pass additional salad dressing.

Nutrition Facts per serving: **608 calories, 34 g total fat, 94 mg cholesterol, 976 mg sodium, 37 g carbohydrate, 40 g protein.**

***Note:*** Look for these molds at kitchenware shops or Spanish or Latino specialty stores.

---

Nonstick cooking spray
4 **burrito-size (12-inch) tortillas**
4 **medium skinless, boneless chicken breast halves (about 1 pound total)**
4 **teaspoons Cajun seasoning**
1 **tablespoon cooking oil**
1 **pound iceberg lettuce, cut into 1-inch-thick slices (8 packed cups)**
6 **ounces romaine, cut into 1-inch-thick slices (4 packed cups)**
1 **cup coarsely shredded carrots**
¼ **cup sliced red cabbage**
½ **cup shredded Monterey Jack cheese (2 ounces)**
½ **cup shredded cheddar cheese (2 ounces)**
½ **cup bottled ranch salad dressing**
2 **cups diced tomatoes**
   **Bottled ranch salad dressing (optional)**

# Fruited Chicken-Pasta Salad

*Water chestnuts and celery add a delightful crunch to this salad.*

**Prep:** 25 minutes  **Chill:** 4 to 24 hours  **Makes:** 4 or 5 servings

1 cup medium shell macaroni
    or elbow macaroni
1½ cups chopped cooked
    chicken or turkey (about
    8 ounces)
1 11-ounce can mandarin
    orange sections, drained
1 cup seedless red or green
    grapes, halved
1 8-ounce can sliced water
    chestnuts, drained
½ cup sliced celery
½ cup buttermilk ranch
    salad dressing
⅛ teaspoon pepper
    Milk
    Lettuce leaves

*1.* Cook pasta according to package directions. Drain pasta. Rinse with cold water. Drain again.

*2.* In a large bowl combine combine pasta, chicken or turkey, mandarin orange sections, grapes, water chestnuts, and celery.

*3.* For dressing, in a small bowl combine buttermilk ranch dressing and pepper. Pour dressing over chicken mixture. Toss lightly to coat. Cover and chill in the refrigerator for at least 4 hours or up to 24 hours.

*4.* Before serving, if necessary, stir in a little milk (1 to 2 tablespoons) to moisten. Serve on lettuce-lined dinner plates.

Nutrition Facts per serving: 387 calories, 22 g total fat, 37 mg cholesterol, 301 mg sodium, 31 g carbohydrate, 16 g protein.

# Jerk Chicken Salad

*Jamaican jerk seasoning—a blend of chile peppers, thyme, onion, garlic, and spices—is a Caribbean favorite for pepping up chicken. Look for the seasoning blend in your supermarket's spice section.*

**Prep:** 30 minutes  **Grill:** 20 minutes  **Makes:** 4 servings

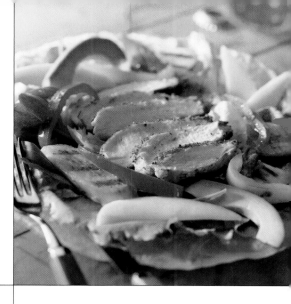

**1.** In a screw-top jar combine oil, lime juice, thyme, and honey; cover and shake well. Remove 1 tablespoon of the dressing. Set remaining dressing aside. Brush chicken and plantain or red bananas with the 1 tablespoon dressing (if using yellow banana, do not brush with dressing).

**2.** Rub jerk seasoning onto chicken. Grill chicken on the rack of an uncovered grill directly over medium coals for 12 to 15 minutes or until tender and no longer pink, turning once. Remove chicken from grill; cut into strips and set aside. Grill plantain or red banana slices (if using yellow banana, do not grill) and pepper strips on the rack of an uncovered grill over medium coals about 8 minutes or until tender.

**3.** In a large bowl gently toss together greens and reserved dressing. Divide among 4 dinner plates. Top each serving with one-fourth of the chicken, pepper strips, plantain or banana, avocado, and mango.

Nutrition Facts per serving: 492 calories, 29 g total fat, 59 mg cholesterol, 364 mg sodium, 38 g carbohydrate, 26 g protein.

*\*Note:* To cut mango into wedges, peel, if desired; cut in half by sliding a sharp knife next to the seed along each side of the mango. Cut each half into wedges.

⅓ cup olive oil

2 tablespoons lime juice

2 teaspoons snipped fresh thyme or ½ teaspoon dried thyme, crushed

1 teaspoon honey

1 pound skinless, boneless chicken breasts

1 plantain, 2 red bananas, or 1 large yellow banana, sliced

2 tablespoons Jamaican jerk seasoning

½ of a medium red sweet pepper, cut into strips

½ of a medium yellow sweet pepper, cut into strips

6 cups torn mixed salad greens

1 medium avocado, halved, seeded, peeled, and cut into thin wedges

1 medium mango, peeled and cut into thin wedges*

# Season's Finest Salad

*Fresh strawberries, plums or nectarines, and grilled chicken star in this taste-of-summer salad.*

**Prep:** 35 minutes  **Grill:** 12 minutes  **Stand:** 10 minutes  **Makes:** 4 servings

**4 medium skinless, boneless chicken breast halves (about 1 pound total)**

**3 cups lightly packed, torn fresh spinach leaves**

**1 cup lightly packed, torn fresh sorrel leaves or arugula leaves**

**1 small red onion, thinly sliced and separated into rings**

**2 tablespoons snipped fresh basil**

**3 cups pitted golden plums and/or nectarines cut into wedges**

**2 cups sliced fresh strawberries**

**1 recipe Strawberry Dressing or ¾ cup bottled berry vinaigrette salad dressing**

**Strawberry blossoms (optional)**

**1.** Lightly grease the rack of an uncovered grill. Place chicken on rack. Grill directly over medium coals for 12 to 15 minutes or until tender and no longer pink, turning once. Let chicken stand about 10 minutes or until cool enough to handle. Cut chicken into irregular pieces, each about 2×1 inches.

**2.** Meanwhile, in a large bowl combine spinach, sorrel or arugula, red onion rings, and basil. To serve, divide spinach mixture among 4 dinner-size shallow wooden bowls or dinner plates. Arrange fruit and chicken on greens. Drizzle with Strawberry Dressing or berry vinaigrette salad dressing. If desired, garnish with strawberry blossoms.

***Strawberry Dressing:*** In a food processor bowl or blender container combine ¾ cup cut-up fresh strawberries, 2 tablespoons bottled strawberry pourable fruit, 2 tablespoons olive oil, 4 teaspoons sherry vinegar or white wine vinegar, ½ teaspoon grated fresh ginger, ¼ teaspoon salt, and ⅛ teaspoon pepper. Cover and process or blend until smooth.

Nutrition Facts per serving: 357 calories, 12 g total fat, 59 mg cholesterol, 233 mg sodium, 41 g carbohydrate, 26 g protein.

# Sesame Chicken Kabob Salad

*Cooking the kabobs in the microwave oven is the secret to making this delicious salad quick to fix.*

**Start to Finish:** 30 minutes  **Makes:** 4 servings

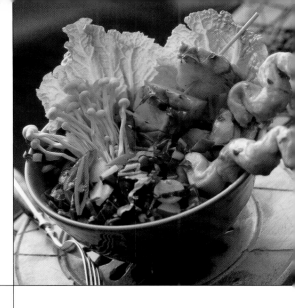

**1.** Cut each chicken breast half lengthwise into 4 strips. Thread 2 of the chicken strips on each of eight 6-inch wooden skewers. Place in a microwave-safe 2-quart rectangular baking dish.

**2.** In a small bowl stir together 2 tablespoons of the Sesame Dressing and the plum sauce or chili sauce; brush over kabobs. Cover dish with waxed paper. Microwave on 100% (high) power for 2 minutes. Turn kabobs over; rearrange in dish. Brush again with the dressing mixture. Microwave for 2 to 4 minutes more or until chicken is no longer pink. Discard any remaining dressing mixture.

**3.** Meanwhile, in a large bowl combine red cabbage and bok choy or iceberg lettuce. If desired, line 4 salad bowls or dinner plates with lettuce leaves. Divide red cabbage mixture among bowls or plates. Top with kabobs, pineapple, sugar snap peas, enoki mushrooms, and radishes. Drizzle remaining Sesame Dressing over salads. If desired, sprinkle with sesame seeds.

**Sesame Dressing:** In a screw-top jar combine 3 tablespoons salad oil, 3 tablespoons rice vinegar or white wine vinegar, 1 tablespoon toasted sesame oil, 1 tablespoon soy sauce, ½ teaspoon dry mustard, and ¼ teaspoon crushed red pepper. Cover and shake well.

Nutrition Facts per serving: 323 calories, 17 g total fat, 59 mg cholesterol, 324 mg sodium, 19 g carbohydrate, 24 g protein.

- 4 medium skinless, boneless chicken breast halves (about 1 pound total)
- 1 recipe Sesame Dressing
- 1 tablespoon bottled plum sauce or chili sauce
- 2 cups chopped red cabbage
- 2 cups sliced bok choy or iceberg lettuce
  Lettuce leaves (optional)
- 16 fresh pineapple wedges
- 16 sugar snap peas, sliced lengthwise
- ½ cup enoki mushrooms
- ½ cup cut-up radishes
  Toasted sesame seeds (optional)

# Chicken and Rice Salad

*To tote this hearty chicken, rice, and vegetable salad to a potluck or picnic, pack it with ice in an insulated cooler.*

**Prep:** 30 minutes   **Cook:** 15 minutes   **Chill:** 4 to 24 hours   **Makes:** 6 servings

---

 2 cups water
 1 cup long grain rice
 ½ cup roasted red sweet
    peppers, drained and
    chopped (½ of a
    7-ounce jar)
 ½ cup cooked or canned
    chickpeas (garbanzo
    beans), drained
 1 2¼-ounce can sliced
    ripe olives, drained
 ¼ cup thinly sliced green
    onions
 1 6- or 6½-ounce jar
    marinated artichoke hearts
12 ounces skinless, boneless
    chicken breasts, cut into
    bite-size strips
 2 teaspoons chili powder
 ½ teaspoon dried rosemary,
    crushed
 ½ cup crumbled feta cheese
    with basil and tomato or
    plain crumbled feta (half
    of a 4-ounce package)

**1.** In a medium saucepan combine water and rice. Bring to boiling; reduce heat. Cover and simmer about 15 minutes or until water is absorbed. Place in colander; rinse with cold water. Set aside to drain.

**2.** In a large bowl combine roasted sweet peppers, chickpeas, ripe olives, and green onions. Drain artichokes, reserving marinade. Chop artichokes; add to chickpea mixture along with cooked rice.

**3.** Meanwhile, sprinkle chicken with chili powder and rosemary. In a large nonstick skillet cook chicken in 1 tablespoon of the reserved artichoke marinade over medium heat for 3 to 4 minutes or until no longer pink.

**4.** Add chicken to rice mixture along with remaining artichoke marinade. Add feta cheese. Toss gently to combine. Cover and chill in the refrigerator for at least 4 hours or up to 24 hours.

Nutrition Facts per serving: **264 calories, 8 g total fat, 38 mg cholesterol, 376 mg sodium, 33 g carbohydrate, 16 g protein.**

# Strawberry Chicken Salad With Warm Citrus Dressing

*Bright-red fresh strawberries are featured in both the salad and the spicy-fruity dressing.*

**Start to Finish:** 30 minutes  **Makes:** 4 servings

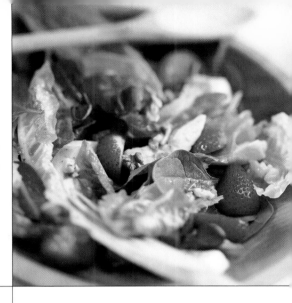

**1.** Sprinkle the chicken breast halves lightly with salt and pepper. In a large saucepan or skillet combine chicken and broth. Bring to boiling; reduce heat. Cover and simmer for 15 to 20 minutes or until tender and no longer pink. Use a slotted spoon to remove chicken from broth; cool chicken slightly. (Save broth and use later for chicken soup.)

**2.** Meanwhile, prepare Warm Citrus Dressing; keep warm.

**3.** Thinly slice chicken breasts. In a large bowl toss together the spinach, strawberries, and chicken. Drizzle Warm Citrus Dressing over salad. Sprinkle with nuts. Serve immediately.

***Warm Citrus Dressing:*** In a blender container or food processor bowl combine ½ cup cut-up fresh strawberries, ⅓ cup orange juice, 2 tablespoons salad oil, 2 teaspoons finely shredded lemon peel, 1 tablespoon lemon juice, 1 teaspoon sugar, ½ teaspoon chili powder, ¼ teaspoon salt, and ¼ teaspoon freshly ground black pepper. Cover; blend or process until smooth. Transfer to a small saucepan. Bring just to boiling; reduce heat. Simmer, uncovered, for 5 minutes, stirring the mixture occasionally.

Nutrition Facts per serving: **287 calories, 14 g total fat, 66 mg cholesterol, 677 mg sodium, 12 g carbohydrate, 31 g protein.**

- 4 **medium skinless, boneless chicken breast halves (about 1 pound total)**
- **Salt**
- **Pepper**
- 1 **14-ounce can chicken broth**
- 1 **recipe Warm Citrus Dressing**
- 6 **cups torn fresh spinach, watercress, and/or other salad greens**
- 2 **cups fresh strawberries, halved**
- ¼ **cup chopped walnuts, toasted**

# Three Corner Chicken Salad

*Offer a choice of salad dressings to drizzle over this simple salad that's served in bread bowls.*

**Prep:** 10 minutes  **Bake:** 15 minutes  **Makes:** 4 servings

1 10-ounce package
  refrigerated pizza dough
1 9- or 10-ounce package
  frozen cooked chicken
  strips
6 cups torn mixed salad
  greens
  Bottled salad dressing

**1.** Remove packaging and unroll refrigerated pizza dough on a cutting board. Shape into a 10-inch square; cut diagonally into 4 triangles. Drape triangles over well-greased, inverted 10-ounce custard cups. Place cups on a shallow baking pan. Bake in a 400° oven about 15 minutes or until deep golden brown. Remove from cups; cool.

**2.** Prepare chicken strips according to package directions. Divide mixed salad greens and the chicken among bread "bowls." Drizzle with salad dressing.

Nutrition Facts per serving: **419 calories, 21 g total fat, 43 mg cholesterol, 1,333 mg sodium, 37 g carbohydrate, 21 g protein.**

# Caesar Salad with Chicken

*If you prefer, broil or roast the chicken breasts yourself, rather than purchasing them already cooked. Just be sure to allow plenty of time to thoroughly chill them.*

**Start to Finish:** 15 minutes   **Makes:** 4 servings

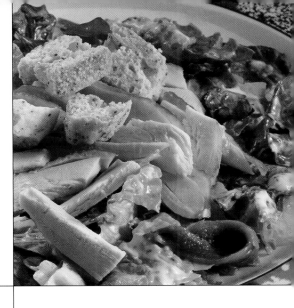

**1.** In a large bowl toss together salad greens and dressing. Divide evenly among 4 dinner plates. Arrange chicken strips on top. Sprinkle with croutons. If desired, top with anchovies. Sprinkle with Parmesan or Romano cheese.

Nutrition Facts per serving: 383 calories, 24 g total fat, 79 mg cholesterol, 259 mg sodium, 12 g carbohydrate, 28 g protein.

1 10-ounce package torn
  mixed salad greens
½ cup bottled Caesar or Italian
  salad dressing
4 purchased broiled or roasted
  chicken breast halves, cut
  into bite-size strips
1 cup garlic-seasoned croutons
1 2-ounce can anchovy fillets
  (optional)
2 tablespoons grated Parmesan
  or Romano cheese

# Grilled Chicken-Cilantro Salad

*This salad's cilantro-ginger sauce does triple duty—as a marinade, a basting sauce, and a dressing.*

**Prep:** 1 hour  **Marinate:** 2 hours  **Grill:** 12 minutes  **Makes:** 6 servings

½ cup dry vermouth

⅓ cup Cilantro Sauce

6 medium skinless, boneless chicken breast halves (about 1½ pounds total)

1 medium red sweet pepper, seeded and quartered

1 medium green sweet pepper, seeded and quartered

1 medium yellow or orange sweet pepper, seeded and quartered

1 tablespoon olive oil or cooking oil

1 cup brown basmati rice, cooked according to package directions

4 cups fresh spinach, stemmed and cut into ¼-inch-wide strips

1 15-ounce can pinto beans, rinsed and drained

½ cup frozen loose-pack whole kernel corn, cooked and drained

½ cup fat-free dairy sour cream

2 teaspoons fat-free milk

4 green onions, sliced

**1.** In a large bowl combine vermouth and 3 tablespoons of the Cilantro Sauce. Place chicken in bowl; turn to coat chicken. Cover and marinate in the refrigerator for 2 hours.

**2.** Drain the marinated chicken, reserving marinade. Grill chicken on the rack of an uncovered grill directly over medium coals for 12 to 15 minutes or until tender and no longer pink, turning and brushing once with reserved marinade halfway through grilling. Discard any remaining marinade. Meanwhile, brush peppers with oil. Place peppers on the grill rack next to the chicken; grill for 8 to 10 minutes or until tender, turning occasionally. Remove peppers and chicken from grill as each is done. Slice peppers and chicken breasts into ½-inch-wide strips.

**3.** To serve, arrange peppers, chicken, rice, spinach, pinto beans, and corn on 6 dinner plates. In a small bowl combine remainder of the ⅓ cup Cilantro Sauce, the sour cream, and milk; drizzle over salads. Sprinkle with green onions.

***Cilantro Sauce:*** In a blender container or food processor bowl combine 2 cups packed fresh cilantro, 3 tablespoons olive oil or salad oil, 1 tablespoon lime juice, 1 tablespoon ground cumin, 1 tablespoon grated fresh ginger, 1 tablespoon crushed garlic, ¼ teaspoon ground red pepper, and ¼ teaspoon salt. Cover and blend or process until nearly smooth. Store leftover sauce in the refrigerator for up to 5 days. Makes ⅔ cup.

Nutrition Facts per serving: 416 calories, 11 g total fat, 59 mg cholesterol, 499 mg sodium, 44 g carbohydrate, 31 g protein.

# Grilled California Chicken Salad

*If mango isn't available, carambola (star fruit), papaya, or peaches are a delicious substitute.*

**Prep:** 20 minutes  **Marinate:** 30 minutes  **Grill:** 12 minutes  **Makes:** 2 servings

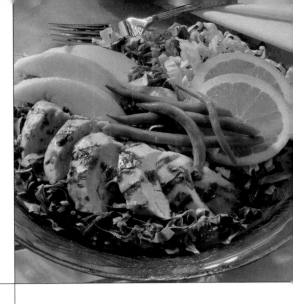

**1.** Set aside half of the Cilantro Vinaigrette for dressing. In a medium bowl combine remaining vinaigrette and chicken. Cover and marinate in the refrigerator for 30 minutes. Drain, reserving marinade.

**2.** Grill chicken on the rack of an uncovered grill directly over medium coals for 12 to 15 minutes or until tender and no longer pink, turning and brushing once with reserved marinade halfway through grilling. Discard any remaining marinade.

**3.** Meanwhile, in a small saucepan cook the green beans, uncovered, in a small amount of boiling water about 15 minutes or until crisp-tender. Drain beans.

**4.** To serve, divide the shredded greens among 2 dinner plates. Slice each chicken breast crosswise into 6 to 8 pieces. Reassemble chicken breasts on greens. Arrange cooked beans, orange slices, and mango slices on greens. Shake the reserved vinaigrette well; drizzle some over each serving. If desired, sprinkle with chopped peanuts or sesame seeds.

*Cilantro Vinaigrette:* In a screw-top jar combine ¼ cup papaya or apricot nectar, 3 tablespoons snipped fresh cilantro, 2 tablespoons olive oil or salad oil, 2 tablespoons rice wine vinegar or white wine vinegar, 1 teaspoon toasted sesame oil, ½ teaspoon ground ginger, and ⅛ to ¼ teaspoon ground red pepper. Cover and shake well. Store vinaigrette in the refrigerator for up to 2 weeks. Shake well before serving.

- 1 recipe Cilantro Vinaigrette
- 2 medium skinless, boneless chicken breast halves (about 8 ounces total)
- 1 cup fresh green beans
- 4 cups shredded mixed salad greens
- 1 orange, sliced
- 1 mango, seeded, peeled, and sliced
- Chopped peanuts or toasted sesame seeds (optional)

**Nutrition Facts per serving: 427 calories, 22 g total fat, 59 mg cholesterol, 78 mg sodium, 37 g carbohydrate, 25 g protein.**

# Dilled Chicken and Potato Salad

*Fresh dill and Dijon-style mustard add extra flavor and zip to bottled salad dressing in this hearty meal-on-a-plate.*

**Start to Finish:** 20 minutes  **Makes:** 4 servings

1 pound whole tiny new potatoes, quartered

12 ounces skinless, boneless chicken breasts, cut into bite-size strips

1 tablespoon olive oil or cooking oil

1 cup sliced celery

1 cup chopped green sweet pepper

½ cup bottled fat-free Italian salad dressing

2 tablespoons snipped fresh dill

1 tablespoon Dijon-style mustard

2 large tomatoes, halved and sliced

1 medium cucumber, thinly sliced

Fresh dill (optional)

**1.** In a covered medium saucepan cook the potatoes in a large amount of boiling salted water for 6 to 8 minutes or until tender; drain well.

**2.** In a large skillet cook chicken in hot oil over medium-high heat for 3 to 4 minutes or until tender and no longer pink.

**3.** In a large bowl place cooked potatoes, cooked chicken, celery, and sweet pepper. Toss gently. In a small bowl stir together salad dressing, the snipped dill, and the mustard. Drizzle over salad, tossing gently to coat.

**4.** Arrange sliced tomatoes and cucumber on 4 dinner plates. Spoon potato mixture over tomatoes and cucumber. If desired, garnish with additional fresh dill.

Nutrition Facts per serving: 283 calories, 7 g total fat, 45 mg cholesterol, 597 mg sodium, 36 g carbohydrate, 20 g protein.

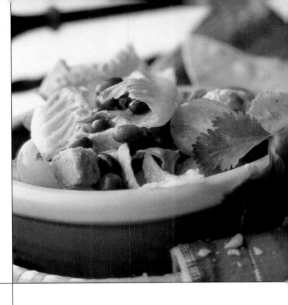

# Southwestern Chicken And Black Bean Salad

*A sprinkling of broken tortilla chips adds crunch.*

**Start to Finish:** 25 minutes   **Makes:** 4 servings

*1.* In a large bowl combine romaine, black beans, chicken or turkey, and tomatoes.

*2.* For dressing, in a small bowl whisk together salad dressing, chili powder, and cumin. Pour dressing over salad. Toss lightly to coat. Sprinkle with tortilla chips. If desired, garnish with cilantro or parsley.

Nutrition Facts per serving: **295 calories, 10 g total fat, 55 mg cholesterol, 913 mg sodium, 26 g carbohydrate, 27 g protein.**

10 cups torn romaine

1 15-ounce can black beans, rinsed and drained

1½ cups chopped cooked chicken or turkey (about 8 ounces)

1½ cups red and/or yellow cherry tomatoes, halved

½ cup bottled reduced-calorie Caesar salad dressing

2 teaspoons chili powder

½ teaspoon ground cumin

½ cup broken tortilla chips Fresh cilantro or parsley sprigs (optional)

# Parisian Chicken Salad

*This refreshing entrée is ideal for dinner on a hot summer evening.*

**Prep:** 25 minutes  **Marinate:** 6 to 8 hours  **Broil:** 12 minutes  **Makes:** 4 servings

4 medium skinless, boneless
  chicken breast halves
  (about 1 pound)
2 teaspoons finely shredded
  orange peel
⅓ cup orange juice
4 cloves garlic, minced
2 tablespoons honey
1½ teaspoons dried thyme,
  crushed
½ teaspoon salt
¼ teaspoon pepper
¼ cup olive oil
2 tablespoons white wine
  vinegar
2 tablespoons orange juice
2 cloves garlic, minced
1½ teaspoons finely chopped
  shallots
4 cups torn baby salad greens
1 medium yellow sweet
  pepper, thinly sliced
2 medium oranges, peeled
  and sectioned

*1.* Place chicken in a heavy, large self-sealing plastic bag set in a shallow dish. For marinade, in a bowl combine orange peel, the ⅓ cup orange juice, the 4 cloves garlic, the honey, and thyme. Pour over chicken. Seal bag; turn to coat chicken. Marinate in the refrigerator for at least 6 hours or up to 8 hours, turning bag occasionally.

*2.* Drain chicken, discarding marinade. Place chicken on unheated rack of a broiler pan. Season with half of the salt and half of the pepper. Broil 4 to 5 inches from heat for 12 to 15 minutes or until tender and no longer pink, turning once halfway through broiling.

*3.* Meanwhile, for dressing, in a screw-top jar combine olive oil, vinegar, the 2 tablespoons orange juice, the 2 cloves garlic, the shallots, the remaining salt, and the remaining pepper. Cover; shake well.

*4.* To serve, divide greens among 4 dinner plates. Top with yellow sweet pepper slices. Cut chicken into ½-inch-thick slices. Arrange chicken and orange sections on salads. Drizzle with the dressing.

Nutrition Facts per serving: 305 calories, 17 g total fat, 59 mg cholesterol, 261 mg sodium, 16 g carbohydrate, 23 g protein.

# Wild Rice-Chicken Salad

*To make decorative green onion curls, immerse the green onion strips in ice water and let stand for 20 minutes.*

**Prep:** 20 minutes  **Cook:** 40 minutes  **Chill:** 2 to 24 hours  **Makes:** 6 to 8 servings

**1.** In a large saucepan bring water to boiling. Add wild rice. Cover and simmer about 40 minutes or until most of the water is absorbed and wild rice is tender. Drain, if necessary.

**2.** Meanwhile, cook the rice pilaf mix according to the package directions.

**3.** In a large bowl combine the cooked wild rice, cooked rice pilaf, chicken, sweet pepper, and snow pea strips.

**4.** In a small bowl stir together dressings and black pepper. Pour over rice mixture. Stir gently to mix. Cover and chill in the refrigerator for at least 2 hours or up to 24 hours.

**5.** To serve, arrange green onions around the edges of 6 to 8 chilled dinner plates. Spoon rice mixture into center. If desired, garnish each plate with additional snow peas.

Nutrition Facts per serving: 530 calories, 28 g total fat, 81 mg cholesterol, 979 mg sodium, 48 g carbohydrate, 22 g protein.

3⅓ cups water

1⅔ cups wild rice, rinsed and drained

1 6¼-ounce package chicken-flavored rice pilaf mix

4½ cups coarsely chopped, cooked chicken (about 1½ pounds)

1 medium red sweet pepper, cut into thin, bite-size strips (about 1 cup)

8 ounces snow peas, ends and strings removed and cut into thin, bite-size strips

1 cup bottled lemon-pepper salad dressing or vinaigrette salad dressing

¼ cup bottled French salad dressing

⅛ teaspoon ground black pepper

2 bunches green onions (about 10 total), cut into thin strips

Snow peas (optional)

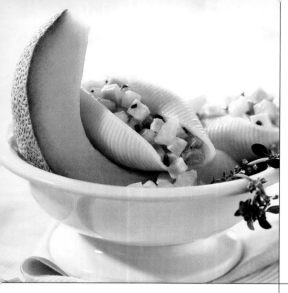

# Chicken-and-Melon-Stuffed Shells

*Next time you grill, cook an extra chicken breast and chill it to make this salad the following day.*

**Start to Finish:** 25 minutes   **Makes:** 4 servings

1 **medium cantaloupe, halved and seeded**

8 **dried jumbo shell macaroni**

1 **6- to 8-ounce chicken breast, grilled and cut into small pieces**

½ **cup finely diced honeydew melon**

¼ **cup plain lowfat yogurt**

1 **tablespoon snipped fresh chives**

2 **tablespoons lemon juice**

1 **teaspoon Dijon-style mustard**

**Fresh thyme sprigs (optional)**

*1.* Cut each cantaloupe half into thirds; cover 4 slices and refrigerate. Peel and dice remaining slices. Set aside.

*2.* Cook pasta shells according to package directions. Drain; rinse with cold water. Drain again; set aside.

*3.* In a large bowl combine diced cantaloupe, chicken, honeydew, yogurt, chives, lemon juice, and mustard. Spoon about ¼ cup of the mixture into each pasta shell. Arrange 2 filled shells and a chilled cantaloupe slice in each individual salad bowl. If desired, garnish with thyme sprigs.

Nutrition Facts per serving: **176 calories, 2 g total fat, 26 mg cholesterol, 55 mg sodium, 28 g carbohydrate, 14 g protein.**

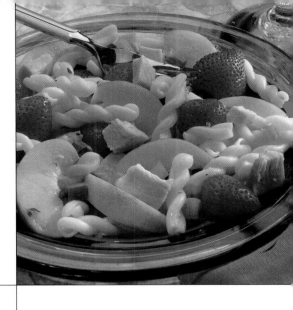

# Turkey and Fruit Pasta Salad

*For a slightly smoky flavor, use the turkey ham option.*

**Prep:** 25 minutes   **Chill:** 4 to 24 hours   **Makes:** 4 servings

*1.* Cook pasta according to package directions. Drain pasta; rinse with cold water. Drain again; set aside.

*2.* In a large bowl combine pasta; turkey, chicken, or turkey ham; and green onions. Toss to mix.

*3.* For dressing, in a screw-top jar combine lime or lemon juice, oil, honey, and thyme. Cover and shake well. Pour dressing over pasta mixture; toss to coat. Cover and chill in the refrigerator for at least 4 hours or up to 24 hours.

*4.* Just before serving, add the nectarines or plums and strawberries. Toss to mix.

Nutrition Facts per serving: **393 calories, 17 g total fat, 43 mg cholesterol, 42 mg sodium, 39 g carbohydrate, 21 g protein.**

1 cup dried rope macaroni (gemelli) or 1⅓ cups dried corkscrew macaroni (4 ounces)

1½ cups chopped cooked turkey or chicken or cooked turkey ham (about 8 ounces)

2 green onions, sliced

⅓ cup lime juice or lemon juice

¼ cup salad oil

1 tablespoon honey

2 teaspoons snipped fresh thyme or ½ teaspoon dried thyme, crushed

2 medium nectarines or large plums, sliced

1 cup halved fresh strawberries

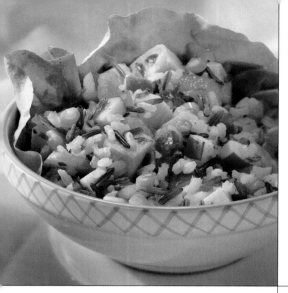

# Smoked Turkey and Wild Rice Salad

*The pairing of wild rice, brown rice, smoked turkey, and fruit makes a satisfying, yet refreshing, salad.*

**Prep:** 20 minutes   **Cook:** 45 minutes   **Stand:** 5 minutes   **Chill:** 2 to 6 hours
**Makes:** 4 servings

1¾ cups water
⅛ teaspoon salt
⅛ teaspoon pepper
½ cup brown rice
⅓ cup wild rice, rinsed
   and drained
8 ounces smoked turkey
   breast, cut into bite-size
   pieces (about 1½ cups)
½ cup thinly sliced celery
¼ cup sliced green onions
¼ cup pitted whole dates,
   snipped
2 medium pears or apples,
   cored and chopped
⅓ cup frozen apple juice
   concentrate, thawed
2 tablespoons cider vinegar
2 teaspoons snipped fresh
   tarragon or ½ teaspoon
   dried tarragon, crushed
   Lettuce leaves

**1.** In a medium saucepan bring the water, salt, and pepper to boiling. Stir in brown rice and wild rice. Return to boiling; reduce heat. Cover and simmer about 45 minutes or until rices are tender and liquid is absorbed. Let stand, covered, for 5 minutes. Stir in smoked turkey, celery, green onions, and dates. Cover and refrigerate for at least 2 hours or up to 6 hours.

**2.** Before serving, gently stir pears or apples into rice mixture. For dressing, in a small bowl stir together the apple juice concentrate, vinegar, and tarragon. Drizzle dressing over rice mixture. Toss to coat. Serve in 4 lettuce-lined bowls.

Nutrition Facts per serving: 313 calories, 2 g total fat, 24 mg cholesterol, 659 mg sodium, 60 g carbohydrate, 17 g protein.

# Curried Chicken and Pasta Salad

*Look for toasted sesame oil in the Asian food section of your supermarket or at an Asian food store. This golden brown oil adds a pleasant toasted nut flavor to salad dressings and stir-fries.*

**Start to Finish:** 40 minutes **Makes:** 4 servings

**1.** Cook pasta according to package directions. Drain pasta; rinse with cold water. Drain again.

**2.** Meanwhile, to prepare pineapple, remove crown. Wash and peel pineapple; remove eyes and core. Slice pineapple; cut slices into bite-size pieces. To prepare papaya, peel, halve, and scoop out seeds. Slice papaya.

**3.** In a large salad bowl combine cooked pasta, pineapple, papaya, romaine, and chicken. Toss lightly to mix. Divide salad among 4 dinner plates.

**4.** For dressing, in a small bowl stir together mayonnaise dressing or salad dressing, honey, rice vinegar, curry powder, sesame oil, and jalapeño peppers. Drizzle dressing over salads. If desired, sprinkle with cashew halves and pieces.

Nutrition Facts per serving: **411 calories, 18 g total fat, 51 mg cholesterol, 305 mg sodium, 42 g carbohydrate, 21 g protein.**

***Note:*** Because chile peppers, such as jalapeños, contain volatile oils that can burn your skin and eyes, avoid direct contact with them as much as possible. When working with chile peppers, wear plastic or rubber gloves. If your bare hands do touch the chile peppers, wash your hands and nails well with soap and warm water.

- 1 cup dried rope macaroni (gemelli) or rotini pasta
- 1 small pineapple
- 1 small papaya
- 5 cups shredded romaine
- 1½ cups cubed cooked chicken (about 8 ounces)
- ½ cup light mayonnaise dressing or salad dressing
- 1 tablespoon honey
- 1 tablespoon rice vinegar or white vinegar
- 1 teaspoon curry powder
- 1 teaspoon toasted sesame oil
- 1 to 2 fresh jalapeño peppers, seeded and chopped*
- 2 teaspoons cashew halves and pieces, toasted (optional)

# Chicken and Fruit Salad

*Leftover cooked chicken or turkey breast becomes an irresistible meal in a bowl with the addition of melon and grapes.*

**Prep:** 20 minutes   **Chill:** 2 to 4 hours   **Makes:** 6 servings

1 8-ounce carton lemon,
   peach, or pineapple low-fat
   yogurt
¼ cup fat-free mayonnaise
   dressing or salad dressing
½ teaspoon ground ginger
½ teaspoon finely shredded
   lemon peel
3 cups cubed cantaloupe,
   watermelon, and/or
   honeydew melon
2 cups cubed cooked chicken
   breast or turkey breast
   (about 10 ounces)
1 cup halved seedless
   red grapes
¾ cup sliced celery
   Lettuce and/or purple kale
   leaves

**1.** In a large bowl stir together yogurt, mayonnaise dressing or salad dressing, ginger, and lemon peel. Add melon, chicken, grapes, and celery. Toss until mixed.

**2.** Cover and chill in the refrigerator for at least 2 hours or up to 4 hours. Serve on 6 lettuce- and/or kale-lined dinner plates.

Nutrition Facts per serving: **195 calories, 5 g total fat, 47 mg cholesterol, 215 mg sodium, 22 g carbohydrate, 17 g protein.**

# Citrusy Chicken Salad

*Look for brown-skinned jicama, which tastes like a cross between a water chestnut and an apple, in the produce section of your supermarket or Mexican food shop.*

**Start to Finish:** 25 minutes **Makes:** 4 servings

**1.** For dressing, in a small bowl stir together orange juice concentrate, olive oil, vinegar, cumin, and ground red pepper. Set aside.

**2.** In a large bowl toss together salad greens, chicken or turkey, oranges, jicama, and sweet pepper. Pour dressing over salad; toss lightly to coat.

Nutrition Facts per serving: 348 calories, 20 g total fat, 68 mg cholesterol, 73 mg sodium, 20 g carbohydrate, 24 g protein.

⅓ cup frozen orange juice
   concentrate, thawed
¼ cup olive oil
2 to 3 tablespoons white wine
   vinegar or white vinegar
1 teaspoon ground cumin
⅛ teaspoon ground red pepper
4 cups torn mixed salad greens
10 ounces cooked chicken or
   turkey, cut into bite-size
   pieces (2 cups)
2 medium oranges, peeled
   and sectioned
1 cup jicama cut into thin,
   bite-size strips
1 medium red sweet pepper,
   cut into rings

# Curried Chicken and Apple Salad

*Mango chutney is readily available in large supermarkets, or look for other chutney flavors in specialty food stores.*

**Prep:** 20 minutes  **Chill:** 4 to 6 hours  **Makes:** 4 servings

1 8-ounce carton plain fat-free
  yogurt
¼ cup chutney
1 teaspoon curry powder
2 cups chopped cooked
  chicken or turkey
  (about 10 ounces)
1½ cups sliced celery
1 medium apple, cored
  and cut into chunks
¼ cup sliced green onions
  Purple kale and/or
  red-tipped leaf lettuce
  (optional)

**1.** In a large bowl stir together yogurt, chutney, and curry powder. Stir in chicken or turkey, celery, apple, and green onions. Cover and chill in the refrigerator for at least 4 hours or up to 6 hours.

**2.** Before serving, stir chicken mixture. If desired, serve on 4 kale- and/or lettuce-lined dinner plates.

Nutrition Facts per serving: **251 calories, 6 g total fat, 69 mg cholesterol, 157 mg sodium, 23 g carbohydrate, 26 g protein.**

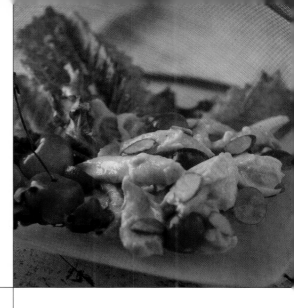

# Chutney-Chicken Salad

*Toasted almonds and an easy but exotic mango chutney dressing update the all-time favorite chicken salad.*

**Start to Finish:** 20 minutes  **Makes:** 4 servings

**1.** In a shallow baking pan spread almonds in a single layer. Bake in a 350° oven for 5 to 10 minutes or until nuts are a light golden brown, stirring once or twice to prevent overbrowning. Cool slightly.

**2.** Meanwhile, in a large bowl combine chutney, mayonnaise dressing or salad dressing, and curry powder. Add chicken, grapes, and toasted nuts; toss gently to coat. Serve on lettuce leaves. If desired, garnish with cherries.

Nutrition Facts per serving: 311 calories, 16 g total fat, 76 mg cholesterol, 118 mg sodium, 20 g carbohydrate, 21 g protein.

¼ **cup sliced or slivered almonds**
¼ **cup mango chutney, snipped**
 2 **tablespoons light mayonnaise dressing or salad dressing**
 1 **teaspoon curry powder**
 2 **cups shredded or chopped deli-roasted cooked chicken or turkey breast (about 10 ounces)**
 1 **cup seedless red grapes, halved**
   **Lettuce leaves**
   **Fresh Royal Ann or dark sweet cherries (optional)**

# Chicken, Pear, and Blue Cheese Salad

*Pick up cooked chicken breasts at your supermarket's deli, or the day before you want to serve the salad, broil or grill chicken breasts and chill them in the refrigerator.*

**Start to Finish:** 15 minutes  **Makes:** 4 servings

6 cups packaged torn mixed salad greens or mesclun (about 8 ounces)

10 to 12 ounces deli-roasted, broiled, or grilled chicken breasts, sliced

¾ cup bottled reduced-calorie or regular blue cheese salad dressing

2 pears, cored and sliced
Freshly ground black pepper (optional)

**1.** In a large bowl combine the salad greens, chicken, and salad dressing; toss gently to coat. Divide among 4 individual salad bowls or dinner plates. Arrange pear slices on top of salads. If desired, sprinkle with freshly ground pepper.

Nutrition Facts per serving: **208 calories, 6 g total fat, 72 mg cholesterol, 591 mg sodium, 18 g carbohydrate, 23 g protein.**

# Roasted Chicken Sandwiches with Red Pepper Mayonnaise

*Another time, use leftover grilled or broiled chicken instead of deli-roasted chicken.*

**Start to Finish:** 15 minutes  **Makes:** 4 servings

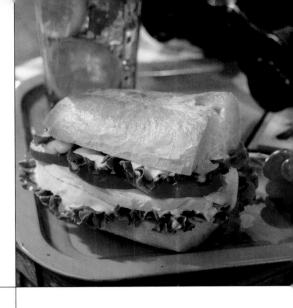

**1.** In a blender container or food processor bowl combine mayonnaise dressing or salad dressing, roasted red sweet peppers, mustard, and garlic. Cover and blend or process until smooth.

**2.** Slice the French rolls horizontally in half; spread cut sides with mayonnaise dressing mixture.

**3.** Layer lettuce, chicken, and tomato on bottom half of each roll. Top tomato with additional lettuce. Cover with roll tops.

Nutrition Facts per serving: 422 calories, 12 g total fat, 72 mg cholesterol, 676 mg sodium, 42 g carbohydrate, 34 g protein.

¼ cup light mayonnaise
　 dressing or salad dressing
2 tablespoons roasted red
　 sweet peppers (about ⅛ of
　 a 7-ounce jar)
1 teaspoon Dijon-style mustard
1 small clove garlic, peeled
4 individual French-style rolls
　 Lettuce leaves
12 ounces deli-roasted chicken
　 white meat, sliced
1 medium tomato, sliced

# Mad-Dash Dinner Salad

*After a quick stop at the store to pick up the ingredients, you can have this main-dish salad on the table in just 25 minutes. If your market has a salad bar, get pre-cut vegetables and cheese there.*

**Start to Finish:** 25 minutes  **Makes:** 6 servings

8 to 10 ounces lemon-herb or lemon-pepper marinated skinless, boneless chicken breast halves or
one 9-ounce package frozen cooked chicken breast strips

8 cups torn mixed salad greens

1 15-ounce can three-bean salad, drained, or 2 cups three-bean salad from deli, drained

1 medium cucumber, halved lengthwise and sliced

3 medium plum tomatoes, cored and cut into wedges (6 ounces)

4 ounces mozzarella cheese, cut into cubes (about 1 cup)

1 cup pitted green, kalamata, ripe black, or niçoise olives

1 small red onion, thinly sliced and separated into rings

⅓ cup bottled balsamic vinaigrette salad dressing or red wine vinaigrette salad dressing

**1.** If using marinated chicken breast halves, cook according to package directions. Drain and cut into strips. If using frozen chicken breast strips, heat according to package directions.

**2.** Divide salad greens among 6 individual salad bowls or dinner plates. Arrange chicken strips, three-bean salad, cucumber, tomatoes, mozzarella cheese, olives, and onion on salad greens. Drizzle salads with dressing.

Nutrition Facts per serving: 246 calories, 12 g total fat, 30 mg cholesterol, 840 mg sodium, 22 g carbohydrate, 15 g protein.

# Fabulous Focaccia Sandwiches

*On the next sunny day, fill your cooler with these sandwiches, some fresh fruit, and a beverage and take a picnic to the park.*

**Start to Finish:** 15 minutes   **Makes:** 4 servings

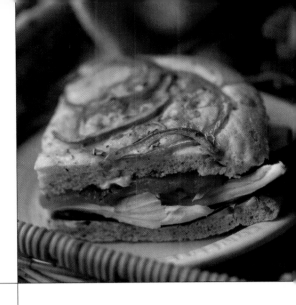

**1.** Using a long serrated knife, cut the bread in half horizontally. In a small bowl stir together mayonnaise dressing or salad dressing and basil. Spread cut sides of bread halves with dressing mixture.

**2.** Layer spinach, chicken, and roasted sweet peppers on bottom half of bread. Cover with top half of bread. Cut sandwich into quarters.

Nutrition Facts per serving: 370 calories, 11 g total fat, 51 mg cholesterol, 148 mg sodium, 43 g carbohydrate, 25 g protein.

1 8- to 10-inch tomato or onion Italian flatbread (focaccia) or 1 loaf sourdough bread

3 to 4 tablespoons light mayonnaise dressing or salad dressing

1 to 2 tablespoons shredded fresh basil

1½ cups packaged prewashed fresh spinach

1½ cups sliced or shredded deli-roasted chicken (about 8 ounces)

½ of a 7-ounce jar roasted red sweet peppers, drained and cut into strips (about ½ cup)

# Pulled Chicken Sandwiches

*This is definitely hands-on cooking. Use your fingers—or two forks—to pull the chicken meat into shreds.*

**Start to Finish:** 35 minutes  **Makes:** 6 sandwiches

1 1¾- to 2-pound deli-cooked
   rotisserie chicken
1 medium onion, cut into
   ¼-inch-thick slices
1 tablespoon olive oil
⅓ cup apple cider vinegar or
   white wine vinegar
½ cup tomato sauce
3 to 4 tablespoons finely
   chopped fresh red and/or
   green hot chili peppers*
2 tablespoons snipped
   fresh thyme
2 tablespoons molasses
2 tablespoons water
½ teaspoon salt
6 kaiser rolls or hamburger
   buns, split
   Bread-and-butter pickle
   slices

**1.** Pull the meat from the chicken, discarding skin (if desired) and bones. Use your fingers or 2 forks to pull meat into shreds. If desired, use a sharp knife to chop some of the seasoned skin and add it to the chicken.

**2.** In a large skillet cook onion in hot oil about 5 minutes or until tender, stirring occasionally to separate into rings. Add vinegar. Cook and stir for 1 minute more.

**3.** Stir in tomato sauce, hot peppers, thyme, molasses, water, and salt. Bring to boiling. Add the chicken; tossing gently to coat. Heat through. Serve on split rolls with pickle slices.

Nutrition Facts per serving: 532 calories, 13 g total fat, 84 mg cholesterol, 1,157 mg sodium, 67 g carbohydrate, 36 g protein.

***Note:*** Because chile peppers, such as jalapeños, contain volatile oils that can burn your skin and eyes, avoid direct contact with them as much as possible. When working with chile peppers, wear plastic or rubber gloves. If your bare hands do touch the chile peppers, wash your hands and nails well with soap and warm water.

# Thai Chicken Wraps

*Peanut butter, soy sauce, and garlic meld into a savory sauce for these mouthwatering wrap sandwiches.*

**Start to Finish:** 20 minutes  **Makes:** 6 servings

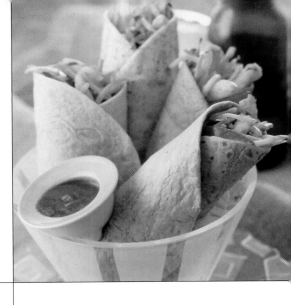

**1.** Wrap tortillas in foil. Heat in a 350° oven about 10 minutes to soften. Meanwhile, in a medium bowl combine garlic salt and pepper. Add chicken, tossing to coat evenly.

**2.** In a large skillet cook and stir seasoned chicken in hot oil over medium-high heat for 2 to 3 minutes or until no longer pink. Remove chicken from skillet; keep warm. Add broccoli, red onion, and ginger to skillet. Cook and stir for 2 to 3 minutes or until vegetables are crisp-tender. Remove from heat.

**3.** To assemble, spread each tortilla with about 1 tablespoon of the Peanut Sauce. Top with chicken strips and vegetable mixture. Roll up each tortilla, securing with a wooden toothpick. Serve immediately with remaining Peanut Sauce.

***Peanut Sauce:*** In a small saucepan combine ¼ cup sugar, ¼ cup creamy peanut butter, 3 tablespoons soy sauce, 3 tablespoons water, 2 tablespoons cooking oil, and 1 teaspoon bottled minced garlic. Heat until sugar is dissolved, stirring frequently.

Nutrition Facts per serving: **330 calories, 16 g total fat, 30 mg cholesterol, 911 mg sodium, 30 g carbohydrate, 17 g protein.**

- 6 8- to 10-inch green, red, and/or plain flour tortillas
- ½ teaspoon garlic salt
- ¼ to ½ teaspoon pepper
- 12 ounces skinless, boneless chicken breast strips for stir-frying
- 1 tablespoon cooking oil
- 4 cups packaged shredded broccoli (broccoli slaw mix)
- 1 medium red onion, cut into thin wedges
- 1 teaspoon grated fresh ginger
- 1 recipe Peanut Sauce

# Chicken and Feta Salad-Stuffed Pitas

*Starting with canned chunk-style chicken allows you to put these sandwiches together in a jiffy.*

**Start to Finish:** 15 minutes  **Makes:** 4 servings

2  **5-ounce cans or one 10-ounce can chunk-style chicken, drained and flaked**

½  **cup crumbled feta cheese (2 ounces)**

½  **cup loose-pack frozen peas**

1  **medium tomato, chopped**

1  **green onion, sliced**

⅓  **cup mayonnaise or salad dressing**

1  **teaspoon dried dillweed**

4  **white or wheat pita bread rounds, halved crosswise**

**Lettuce leaves**

**1.** In a medium bowl combine flaked chicken and feta cheese. Rinse peas in cold water until thawed; drain and pat dry with paper towels. Add peas to chicken mixture with tomato and green onion. Add mayonnaise or salad dressing and dillweed; toss to combine.

**2.** Line pita bread halves with lettuce. Spoon chicken mixture into pitas, dividing evenly. Serve immediately.

Nutrition Facts per serving: 462 calories, 28 g total fat, 78 mg cholesterol, 1,052 mg sodium, 27 g carbohydrate, 26 g protein.

# Chicken and Avocado Croissants

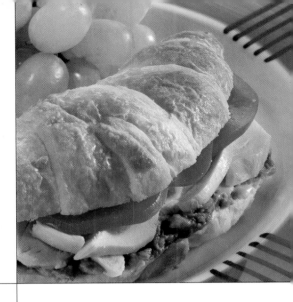

*To ensure that the avocado is ripe, choose one that feels soft but not mushy when you roll it between the palms of your hands.*

**Start to Finish:** 15 minutes  **Makes:** 4 servings

**1.** Remove and discard skin and bones from chicken breast halves; slice meat. In a small bowl mash avocado; stir in lemon juice and basil.

**2.** Spread bottom halves of croissants with Dijon-style mustard; spread with avocado mixture. Top with chicken and tomato slices. Sprinkle with seasoned salt. Add croissant tops.

Nutrition Facts per serving: 350 calories, 21 g total fat, 105 mg cholesterol, 361 mg sodium, 13 g carbohydrate, 28 g protein.

- 4 purchased broiled or roasted chicken breast halves
- 1 medium avocado, halved, seeded, and peeled
- 2 teaspoons lemon juice
- ¼ teaspoon dried basil, crushed
- 4 croissants, split
- 2 teaspoons Dijon-style mustard
- 1 small tomato, thinly sliced
- ¼ to ½ teaspoon seasoned salt

# Chicken Rolls Olé

*Shredded orange peel and orange juice add fresh flavor to these chicken and rice-filled wraps.*

**Prep:** 25 minutes  **Cook:** 35 minutes  **Makes:** 4 servings

⅔ **cup water**

⅓ **cup brown rice**

¼ **teaspoon salt**

2 **tablespoons light dairy**
   **sour cream**

2 **tablespoons fat-free**
   **mayonnaise dressing or**
   **salad dressing**

1 **small fresh jalapeño pepper,**
   **seeded and finely chopped\***

¼ **teaspoon finely shredded**
   **orange peel**

2 **teaspoons orange juice**

2 **9- to 10-inch flour tortillas**
   **Nonstick cooking spray**

6 **ounces skinless, boneless**
   **chicken breasts, cut into**
   **bite-size strips**

1 **cup torn mixed salad greens**

**1.** In a small saucepan combine water, brown rice, and salt. Bring to boiling; reduce heat. Cover and simmer about 35 minutes or until water is absorbed. Set aside.

**2.** Meanwhile, for sour cream sauce, in a small bowl stir together sour cream, mayonnaise dressing, jalapeño pepper, orange peel, and orange juice. Cover and chill in the refrigerator until serving time.

**3.** Wrap tortillas in foil. Heat in a 350° oven about 10 minutes to soften. Coat a medium skillet with nonstick cooking spray. Preheat over medium heat. Add chicken; stir-fry about 3 minutes or until no longer pink. Add cooked rice and sour cream sauce to the skillet; mix well.

**4.** To assemble, place tortillas on a cutting board. Spoon half of the rice-chicken mixture in a strip about 2 inches from one edge of each tortilla. Top with mixed greens. Fold the edge up over filling and fold the ends in; roll up. Using a serrated knife, diagonally cut the rolls into pieces.

Nutrition Facts per serving: **216 calories, 4 g total fat, 23 mg cholesterol, 396 mg sodium, 31 g carbohydrate, 12 g protein.**

**\*Note:** Because chile peppers, such as jalapeños, contain volatile oils that can burn your skin and eyes, avoid direct contact with them as much as possible. When working with chile peppers, wear plastic or rubber gloves. If your bare hands do touch the chile peppers, wash your hands and nails well with soap and warm water.

# Parmesan-Turkey Sandwiches

*These hearty sandwiches are fast enough for a weeknight family supper yet special enough for a casual dinner party.*

**Prep:** 15 minutes   **Cook:** 8 minutes   **Makes:** 4 servings

**1.** In a shallow dish stir together crushed cornflakes or crackers, Parmesan cheese, garlic powder, and pepper. In another shallow dish beat together egg and water. Dip turkey steaks into egg mixture. Coat with crumbs.

**2.** In a large skillet cook turkey in hot margarine or butter over medium heat for 8 to 10 minutes or until tender and no longer pink, turning once.

**3.** Place lettuce on bottom halves of hoagie buns. Top with turkey, salad dressing, and tomato slices. Add bun tops.

Nutrition Facts per serving: **686 calories, 21 g total fat, 112 mg cholesterol, 1,177 mg sodium, 83 g carbohydrate, 39 g protein.**

***Note:*** If you can't find turkey breast tenderloin steaks, buy two turkey breast tenderloins and split them in half lengthwise.

½ cup crushed cornflakes or crushed rich round crackers (about 12 crackers)

¼ cup grated Parmesan cheese (1 ounce)

⅛ teaspoon garlic powder

⅛ teaspoon pepper

1 beaten egg

1 tablespoon water

4 turkey breast tenderloin steaks* (about 1 pound total)

2 tablespoons margarine or butter

4 lettuce leaves

4 hoagie buns, split and toasted

¼ cup bottled creamy Parmesan or creamy buttermilk ranch salad dressing

2 tomatoes, thinly sliced

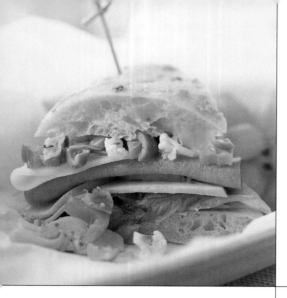

# Muffuletta

*Using reduced-fat meat and cheese in this adaptation of the classic New Orleans sandwich cuts the fat—but not the flavor.*

**Start to Finish:** 20 minutes **Makes:** 6 servings

1 12-inch Italian flat bread
   (focaccia)
   Lettuce leaves
6 ounces very thinly sliced
   mesquite-smoked turkey
   breast
4 ounces thinly sliced
   reduced-fat salami or sliced
   cooked turkey salami
5 ounces thinly sliced
   reduced-fat provolone or
   mozzarella cheese
⅓ cup giardiniera (pickled
   mixed vegetables) or
   pepperoncini salad
   peppers, drained and
   chopped
¼ cup chopped pitted
   green olives
¼ cup thinly sliced canned
   artichoke hearts
¼ cup bottled fat-free Italian
   salad dressing

*1.* Cut focaccia horizontally in half. Layer ingredients on bottom half of focaccia in the following order: lettuce, turkey, salami, and cheese.

*2.* In a small bowl combine giardiniera or pepperoncini, olives, artichoke hearts, and salad dressing; spoon evenly over cheese. Add the top half of focaccia.

Nutrition Facts per serving: **275 calories, 9 g total fat, 45 mg cholesterol, 1,262 mg sodium, 27 g carbohydrate, 21 g protein.**

# Turkey and Tomato Sandwiches

*Flavorful dried tomatoes make a terrific topping for broiled turkey breast tenderloin steaks.*

**Prep:** 15 minutes  **Broil:** 8 minutes  **Makes:** 4 servings

**1.** In a medium saucepan bring water to boiling; add dried tomatoes. Simmer about 5 minutes or until tomatoes are soft. Drain tomatoes and cut into thin slivers; set aside.

**2.** Coat the unheated rack of a broiler pan with nonstick cooking spray. Arrange turkey on rack.

**3.** In a small bowl combine red wine vinegar and pepper. Brush half of the mixture over turkey. Broil 4 to 5 inches from the heat for 4 minutes. Turn; brush with remaining vinegar mixture. Broil 4 to 6 minutes more or until turkey is tender and no longer pink.

**4.** Meanwhile, in a small bowl combine mayonnaise dressing or salad dressing and mustard. Line rolls with watercress, radicchio, or lettuce leaves. Place turkey on bottoms of rolls. Top turkey with mayonnaise dressing mixture and dried tomato pieces. Add tops of rolls. If desired, garnish with small tomatoes.

Nutrition Facts per serving: **252 calories, 4 g total fat, 50 mg cholesterol, 665 mg sodium, 26 g carbohydrate, 26 g protein.**

***Note:*** If you can't find turkey breast tenderloin steaks, buy two turkey breast tenderloins and split them in half lengthwise.

- 1 cup water
- 12 dried tomatoes (not oil-packed)
  Nonstick cooking spray
- 4 turkey breast tenderloin steaks*, cut ¼ inch thick (about 1 pound total)
- 1 tablespoon red wine vinegar
- ¼ teaspoon pepper
- 3 tablespoons fat-free mayonnaise dressing or salad dressing
- 1 tablespoon Dijon-style mustard
- 4 French-style or sourdough rolls, split and toasted
  Watercress sprigs, radicchio leaves, or lettuce leaves
  Small tomatoes (optional)

# Hot Turkey Sub Sandwiches

*A crisp tossed salad and these hefty sandwiches make a great warm weather lunch or supper.*

**Prep:** 15 minutes  **Bake:** 10 minutes  **Makes:** 4 servings

1 tablespoon olive oil

1 teaspoon dried basil, crushed

½ teaspoon bottled minced garlic or 1 clove garlic, minced, or ⅛ teaspoon garlic powder

1 8-ounce loaf or ½ of a 16-ounce loaf unsliced French bread

6 ounces sliced mozzarella cheese

4 ounces sliced smoked turkey

2 tablespoons sliced pitted ripe olives

2 tomatoes, thinly sliced

⅛ teaspoon coarsely ground black pepper

**1.** In a small bowl stir together the olive oil, basil, and garlic or garlic powder. Split the French bread lengthwise. Use a spoon to hollow out the top half, leaving a ¾-inch-thick shell. Brush the cut sides of both bread halves with the olive oil mixture.

**2.** On the bottom half of the French bread layer half of the mozzarella cheese, all of the smoked turkey, the olives, the remaining cheese, and the tomato slices. Sprinkle with pepper. Top with the bread top. Wrap in heavy-duty foil.

**3.** Bake in a 375° oven about 10 minutes or until heated through. Cut into pieces.

Nutrition Facts per serving: 335 calories, 13 g total fat, 36 mg cholesterol, 849 mg sodium, 33 g carbohydrate, 22 g protein.

# Smoked Turkey Salad Sandwiches

*Round out the meal with some fresh fruit and a relish tray filled with assorted pickles (try some pickled watermelon for a change), crisp cucumber slices, and olives.*

**Start to Finish:** 15 minutes  **Makes:** 4 servings

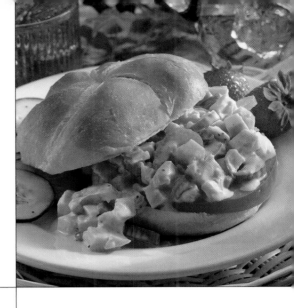

**1.** For dressing, in a small bowl stir together mayonnaise dressing and yogurt. Stir in corn relish.

**2.** In a large bowl combine turkey and celery. Add dressing; toss gently to coat. Serve on rolls with tomato slices.

Nutrition Facts per serving: **314 calories, 5 g total fat, 37 mg cholesterol, 1,251 mg sodium, 46 g carbohydrate, 21 g protein.**

¼ **cup fat-free mayonnaise dressing or regular mayonnaise or salad dressing**

¼ **cup plain fat-free yogurt**

½ **cup corn relish**

2 **cups chopped smoked turkey**

1 **stalk celery, thinly sliced**

4 **kaiser rolls, split**

1 **medium tomato, sliced**

# Veggie-Topped Turkey Burgers

*Sautéed carrots and bean sprouts top these extraordinary burgers.*

**Prep:** 15 minutes  **Cook:** 12 minutes  **Makes:** 4 servings

½ cup fine dry bread crumbs

3 green onions, finely chopped (⅓ cup)

1 tablespoon soy sauce

¼ teaspoon ground ginger

¼ teaspoon garlic powder

¼ teaspoon bottled hot pepper sauce

1 pound uncooked ground turkey or ground chicken

1 tablespoon cooking oil

1 medium carrot, shredded

1 cup fresh bean sprouts

1 tablespoon margarine or butter

Soy sauce (optional)

Honey mustard (optional)

4 hamburger buns, split and toasted

**1.** In a large bowl combine bread crumbs, green onions, the 1 tablespoon soy sauce, the ginger, garlic powder, and hot pepper sauce. Add ground turkey or chicken; mix well. Shape into 4 patties, each ¾ inch thick.

**2.** In a 10- or 12-inch skillet cook patties in hot oil over medium heat for 10 to 12 minutes or until done (165°),* turning once. Remove from skillet. Keep warm.

**3.** Add shredded carrot, bean sprouts, and margarine or butter to skillet. Cook and stir for 2 to 3 minutes or until carrot is crisp-tender. If desired, season vegetables with a few drops soy sauce. If desired, spread honey mustard on bun tops. Place burgers on bun bottoms. Top with cooked vegetables. Cover with bun tops.

Nutrition Facts per serving: **385 calories, 17 g total fat, 42 mg cholesterol, 682 mg sodium, 35 g carbohydrate, 21 g protein.**

***Note:*** The internal color of a ground poultry patty is not a reliable doneness indicator. A turkey or chicken patty cooked to 165°, regardless of color, is safe. Use an instant-read thermometer to check the internal temperature. To measure the doneness of a patty, insert an instant-read thermometer through the side of the patty to a depth of 2 to 3 inches.

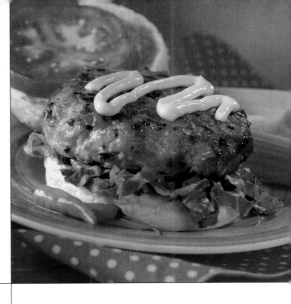

# Thai-Style Burgers

*Lemongrass adds a touch of the exotic to these juicy burgers.*

**Prep:** 15 minutes  **Broil:** 11 minutes  **Makes:** 2 servings

*1.* In a large bowl combine ground turkey, bread crumbs, green onion, lemongrass, basil, soy sauce, egg white, and garlic. Mix well. Shape meat mixture into 2 patties, each ½ inch thick.

*2.* Meanwhile, stir together mayonnaise dressing or salad dressing and hot chili sauce. Cover and chill in the refrigerator until serving time.

*3.* Place patties on the unheated rack of a broiler pan. Broil 4 to 5 inches from the heat for 11 to 13 minutes or until done (165°),** turning once halfway through broiling time.

*4.* To serve, if desired, cover bottom halves of buns with lettuce. Place cooked patties on top. Top patties with mayonnaise mixture, tomato slices (if desired), and top halves of the buns.

**Nutrition Facts per serving: 322 calories, 10 g total fat, 50 mg cholesterol, 791 mg sodium, 28 g carbohydrate, 28 g protein.**

*\*Note:* Look for fresh lemongrass in Asian markets. For light, lemony flavor, chop only the inner portions of the white bulb. If unavailable, use 1 teaspoon grated lemon peel.

*\*\*Note:* The internal color of a ground poultry patty is not a reliable doneness indicator. A turkey or chicken patty cooked to 165°, regardless of color, is safe. Use an instant-read thermometer to check the internal temperature. To measure the doneness of a patty, insert an instant-read thermometer through the side of the patty to a depth of 2 to 3 inches.

**8 ounces uncooked ground turkey breast**

**2 tablespoons fine dry bread crumbs**

**1 green onion, finely chopped**

**2 tablespoons finely minced lemongrass\***

**1 tablespoon snipped fresh basil**

**2 teaspoons soy sauce**

**1 egg white**

**1 clove garlic, minced**

**2 tablespoons light mayonnaise dressing or salad dressing**

**½ teaspoon hot chili sauce**

**2 sesame seed hamburger buns, split and toasted**

**Shredded lettuce (optional)**

**Tomato slices (optional)**

# carving a roasted bird

## *With these tips, you can carve a whole turkey or chicken without a hitch.*

**You don't have to be a chef** to serve attractive slices of turkey or chicken from a whole bird. All you need are a sharp carving knife, a long-tined meat fork, and a few simple hints. Here's what you need to know.

**The key to** a perfectly roasted bird is to make sure the bird is done. Before roasting, insert an oven-going meat thermometer into the the center of an inside thigh muscle. Then before taking the bird from the oven, check the thermometer. It should register 180°. Also check to see that the drumsticks move easily in their sockets and that the thickest parts feel soft when you press them. Finally, the juices from the thigh should run clear. When the bird is done, remove it from the oven. And if you have cooked a stuffing in the bird, use an instant-read thermometer to check the stuffing temperature. It needs to register at least 165°.

**1.** Loosely cover the bird with foil and let it stand for 15 to 20 minutes before carving. During standing, the internal temperature of the bird will rise 5° to 10°. Standing gives time for the bird's flesh to firm up, which helps the carved slices hold together.

**2.** To begin carving the bird, place it on a carving board. (If carving is new to you, take the pressure off by carving the bird in the kitchen instead of in front of your guests.) Remove the stuffing, placing it in a serving bowl. Make the first cut by grasping the end of a drumstick and pulling it away from the body. Cut through the skin and meat between the thigh and the body (see photo above). With the tip of the knife, separate the thighbone from the carcass by cutting through the joint. Repeat with the remaining drumstick and thigh.

**Above:** To separate the thigh and drumstick from the bird, pull the leg away from the body and cut through the skin and meat as shown.

**3.** Separate the thighs from the drumsticks by cutting through the joints where the drumstick bones and thighbones meet.

**4.** To carve the meat from the drumsticks, hold each drumstick vertically by the tip with the large end resting on the cutting board. Slice the meat parallel to the bone, working under any tendons to free the meat and turning the drumstick to get even slices. Slice the thigh meat by holding each thigh at one end and slicing the meat parallel to the bone, turning the piece as you slice.

**5.** Next carve the breast meat. Make a deep horizontal cut into the breast above each wing (see photo at top right). This cut will be the bottom of the breast slices. Beginning at the outer top edge of one side of the bird, cut the slices from the top down until you reach the horizontal cut (see photo at bottom right). Cut the final smaller slices following the curve of the breastbone. Repeat on the other side.

**6.** Finally, remove the wings by cutting through the joints where the wing bones and back meet.

**For safety's sake,** do not allow the meat to remain at room temperature for more than 2 hours. Store the leftovers in the refrigerator as soon as possible. If you plan to freeze some of the turkey or chicken, chill the meat completely in the refrigerator before freezing. Refrigerating the meat decreases the chance of harmful bacteria growing. It also allows the meat to freeze faster, preventing the formation of large ice crystals that can ruin the meat's texture. Later, divide the turkey or chicken into serving-size portions (avoid stacking the slices any more than 2 inches thick) and package the meat in freezer bags. Freeze the bags in a single layer. (This allows cold air to circulate around the packages, freezing them faster.) Once frozen, you can stack the bags.

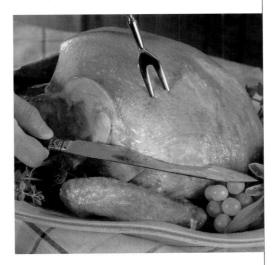

With one hand, use a long-tined meat fork to steady the bird, and with the knife in the other hand, make a deep horizontal cut into the breast above the wing.

Working from the top down, cut the meat into thin slices, stopping when you reach the deep horizontal cut. For the final smaller slices, cut along the curve of the breastbone.

# Poultry Cooking Charts

## Roasting Poultry

**To prepare a bird for roasting, follow these steps. Because birds vary in size and shape, use the times as general guides.**

**1.** If desired, rinse whole bird thoroughly on outside as well as inside body and neck cavities. Pat dry with paper towels. If desired, sprinkle inside of the body cavity with salt.

**2.** For an unstuffed bird, if desired, place quartered onions and celery in body cavity. Pull neck skin to back and fasten with a skewer. If a band of skin crosses tail, tuck drumsticks under band. If there is no band, tie drumsticks to tail. Twist wing tips under the back. To stuff a bird (do not stuff duckling or goose), just before cooking spoon some stuffing loosely into the neck and body cavities. Fasten neck skin and secure the drumsticks and wings as for an unstuffed bird.

**3.** Place bird, breast side up, on a rack in a shallow roasting pan; brush with cooking oil and, if desired, sprinkle with a crushed dried herb, such as thyme or oregano. (When cooking a domestic duckling or goose, use a fork to prick skin generously all over and omit cooking oil.) For large birds, insert an oven-going meat thermometer into center of one of the inside thigh muscles. The thermometer should not touch the bone.

**4.** Cover Cornish game hen, pheasant, squab, and whole turkey with foil, leaving air space between bird and foil. Lightly press the foil to the ends of drumsticks and neck to enclose bird. Leave all other types of poultry uncovered.

**5.** Roast in an uncovered pan. Two-thirds through roasting time, cut band of skin or string between drumsticks. Uncover bird the last 45 minutes of roasting for larger birds or the last 30 minutes of roasting for smaller birds. Continue roasting until the meat thermometer registers 180°F in thigh muscle (check temperature of thigh in several places) or until drumsticks move easily in their sockets and juices run clear. Center of stuffing should register 165°F. (For a whole or half turkey breast, thermometer should register 170°F.) Remove bird from oven; cover. Allow whole birds and turkey portions to stand for 15 minutes before carving.

| Type of Bird | Weight | Oven Temperature | Roasting Time |
|---|---|---|---|
| **Chicken** | | | |
| **Capon** | 5 to 7 pounds | 325°F | 1¾ to 2½ hours |
| **Meaty pieces** (breast halves, drumsticks, and thighs with bone) | 2½ to 3 pounds total | 375°F | 45 to 55 minutes |
| **Whole** | 2½ to 3 pounds | 375°F | 1 to 1¼ hours |
| | 3 to 3½ pounds | 375°F | 1¼ to 1½ hours |
| | 3½ to 4 pounds | 375°F | 1¼ to 1¾ hours |
| | 4½ to 5 pounds | 375°F | 1½ to 2 hours |
| **Game** | | | |
| **Cornish game hen** | 1¼ to 1½ pounds | 375°F | 1 to 1¼ hours |
| **Duckling, domestic** | 4 to 6 pounds | 350°F | 1½ to 2 hours |
| **Goose, domestic** | 7 to 8 pounds | 350°F | 2 to 2½ hours |
| | 8 to 10 pounds | 350°F | 2½ to 3 hours |
| **Pheasant** | 2 to 3 pounds | 350°F | 1¼ to 1½ hours |
| **Squab, domestic** | 12 to 16 ounces | 375°F | 45 to 60 minutes |
| **Turkey** | | | |
| **Boneless whole** | 2½ to 3½ pounds | 325°F | 2 to 2½ hours |
| | 4 to 6 pounds | 325°F | 2½ to 3½ hours |
| **Breast, whole** | 4 to 6 pounds | 325°F | 1½ to 2¼ hours |
| | 6 to 8 pounds | 325°F | 2¼ to 3¼ hours |

**Roasting Poultry** *(continued)*

| Type of Bird | Weight | Oven Temperature | Roasting Time |
|---|---|---|---|
| **Turkey** *(continued)* | | | |
| **Drumstick** | 1 to 1½ pounds | 325°F | 1¼ to 1¾ hours |
| **Thigh** | 1½ to 1¾ pounds | 325°F | 1¼ to 1¾ hours |
| **Whole (unstuffed)\*** | 8 to 12 pounds | 325°F | 2¾ to 3 hours |
| | 12 to 14 pounds | 325°F | 3 to 3¾ hours |
| | 14 to 18 pounds | 325°F | 3¾ to 4¼ hours |
| | 18 to 20 pounds | 325°F | 4¼ to 4½ hours |
| | 20 to 24 pounds | 325°F | 4½ to 5 hours |

\*Stuffed birds generally require 15 to 45 minutes more roasting time than unstuffed birds. Always verify doneness of poultry and stuffing with a meat thermometer.

# Broiling Poultry

If desired, remove the skin from the poultry; sprinkle with salt and black pepper. Remove broiler pan from the oven and preheat the broiler for 5 to 10 minutes. Arrange the poultry on the unheated rack of the broiler pan with the bone side up. If desired, brush poultry with cooking oil. Place the pan under the broiler so the surface of the poultry is 4 to 5 inches from the heat; chicken and Cornish game hen halves should be 5 to 6 inches from the heat. Turn the pieces over when browned on one side, usually after half of the broiling time. Chicken halves and quarters and meaty pieces should be turned after 20 minutes. Brush again with oil. The poultry is done when the meat is no longer pink and the juices run clear. If desired, brush with a sauce the last 5 minutes of cooking.

| Type of Bird | Thickness/Weight | Broiling Time |
|---|---|---|
| **Chicken** | | |
| **Broiler-fryer, half** | 1¼ to 1½ pounds each | 28 to 32 minutes |
| **Broiler-fryer, quarter** | 10 to 12 ounces | 28 to 32 minutes |
| **Kabobs** (boneless breast, cut into 2×½-inch strips and threaded loosely onto skewers) | | 8 to 10 minutes |
| **Meaty pieces** (breast halves, drumsticks, and thighs with bone) | 2½ to 3 pounds total | 25 to 35 minutes |
| **Skinless, boneless breast halves** | 4 to 5 ounces | 12 to 15 minutes |
| **Game** | | |
| **Cornish game hen, half** | 10 to 12 ounces | 25 to 35 minutes |
| **Turkey** | | |
| **Breast steak or slice** | 2 ounces | 6 to 8 minutes |
| **Breast tenderloin steak** | 4 to 6 ounces | 8 to 10 minutes |
| **Patties** (ground raw turkey) | ¾ inch thick | 14 to 18 minutes |
| | ½ inch thick | 11 to 13 minutes |

# Direct-Grilling Poultry

If desired, remove skin from poultry. For a charcoal grill, place poultry on grill rack, bone side up, directly over medium coals. Grill, uncovered, for the time given below or until the proper temperature is reached and meat is no longer pink, turning once halfway through grilling. (For a gas grill, preheat grill. Reduce heat to medium. Place poultry on grill rack, bone side down, over heat. Cover and grill as above.)

Test for doneness using a meat thermometer (use an instant-read thermometer to test smaller portions). Thermometer should register 180°F, except in breast meat when thermometer should register 170°F. Poultry should be tender and no longer pink. If desired, during the last 5 to 10 minutes of grilling, brush often with a sauce.

| Type of Bird | Weight | Grilling Temperature | Approximate Direct-Grilling Time | Doneness |
|---|---|---|---|---|
| **Chicken** | | | | |
| **Chicken, broiler-fryer,** half or quarters | 1½- to 1¾-pound half or 12- to 14-ounce quarters | Medium | 40 to 50 minutes | 180°F |
| **Chicken breast half,** skinned and boned | 4 to 5 ounces | Medium | 12 to 15 minutes | 170°F |
| **Chicken thigh,** skinned and boned | 4 to 5 ounces | Medium | 12 to 15 minutes | 180°F |
| **Meaty chicken pieces** (breast halves, thighs, and drumsticks) | 2½ to 3 pounds total | Medium | 35 to 45 minutes | 180°F |
| **Turkey** | | | | |
| **Turkey breast** tenderloin steak | 4 to 6 ounces | Medium | 12 to 15 minutes | 170°F |

All cooking times are based on poultry removed directly from refrigerator.

# Indirect-Grilling Poultry

If desired, remove skin from poultry. Rinse whole birds; pat dry. For a charcoal grill, arrange medium-hot coals around a drip pan. Test for medium heat above the pan. Place unstuffed poultry, breast side up, on grill rack over drip pan. Cover and grill for the time given below or until the proper temperature is reached and meat is no longer pink, adding more charcoal to maintain heat as necessary. (For a gas grill, preheat grill. Reduce heat to medium. Adjust for indirect cooking. Grill as above.) For large poultry cuts and whole birds, we suggest placing the poultry on a rack in a roasting pan and omitting the drip pan.

Test for doneness using a meat thermometer (use an instant-read thermometer to test smaller portions). For whole birds, insert thermometer into the center of the inside thigh muscle, not touching bone. Thermometer should register 180°F, except in breast meat when thermometer should register 170°F. Poultry should be tender and no longer pink. (Note: Birds vary in size and shape. Use these times as general guides.)

| Type of Bird | Weight | Grilling Temperature | Approximate Indirect-Grilling Time | Doneness |
|---|---|---|---|---|
| **Chicken** | | | | |
| **Chicken**, whole | 2½ to 3 pounds | Medium | 1 to 1¼ hours | 180°F |
| | 3½ to 4 pounds | Medium | 1¼ to 1¾ hours | 180°F |
| | 4½ to 5 pounds | Medium | 1¾ to 2 hours | 180°F |
| **Chicken breast half**, skinned and boned | 4 to 5 ounces | Medium | 15 to 18 minutes | 170°F |
| **Chicken, broiler-fryer**, half | 1½ to 1¾ pounds | Medium | 1 to 1¼ hours | 180°F |
| **Chicken, broiler-fryer**, quarters | 12 to 14 ounces each | Medium | 50 to 60 minutes | 180°F |
| **Chicken thigh**, skinned and boned | 4 to 5 ounces | Medium | 15 to 18 minutes | 180°F |
| **Meaty chicken pieces** (breast halves, thighs, and drumsticks) | 2½ to 3 pounds total | Medium | 50 to 60 minutes | 180°F |
| **Game** | | | | |
| **Cornish game hen**, whole | 1¼ to 1½ pounds | Medium | 50 to 60 minutes | 180°F |
| **Pheasant**, whole | 2 to 3 pounds | Medium | 1 to 1½ hours | 180°F |
| **Quail**, semiboneless | 3 to 4 ounces | Medium | 15 to 20 minutes | 180°F |
| **Squab** | 12 to 16 ounces | Medium | ¾ to 1 hour | 180°F |
| **Turkey** | | | | |
| **Turkey**, whole | 6 to 8 pounds | Medium | 1¾ to 2¼ hours | 180°F |
| | 8 to 12 pounds | Medium | 2½ to 3½ hours | 180°F |
| | 12 to 16 pounds | Medium | 3 to 4 hours | 180°F |
| **Turkey breast**, half | 2 to 2½ pounds | Medium | 1¼ to 2 hours | 170°F |
| **Turkey breast**, whole | 4 to 6 pounds | Medium | 1¾ to 2¼ hours | 170°F |
| | 6 to 8 pounds | Medium | 2½ to 3½ hours | 170°F |
| **Turkey breast tenderloin steak** | 4 to 6 ounces | Medium | 15 to 18 minutes | 170°F |
| **Turkey drumstick** | ½ to 1 pound | Medium | ¾ to 1¼ hours | 180°F |
| **Turkey tenderloin** | 8 to 10 ounces (¾ to 1 inch thick) | Medium | 25 to 30 minutes | 170°F |
| **Turkey thigh** | 1 to 1½ pounds | Medium | 50 to 60 minutes | 180°F |

# Index

# S-Z

# Metric Information

The charts on this page provide a guide for converting measurements from the U.S. customary system, which is used throughout this book, to the metric system.

## Product Differences

Most of the ingredients called for in the recipes in this book are available in most countries. However, some are known by different names. Here are some common American ingredients and their possible counterparts:

■ Sugar (white) is granulated, fine granulated, or castor sugar.

■ Powdered sugar is icing sugar.

■ All-purpose flour is enriched, bleached or unbleached, white household flour. When self-rising flour is used in place of all-purpose flour in a recipe that calls for leavening, omit the leavening agent (baking soda or baking powder) and salt.

■ Light-colored corn syrup is golden syrup.

■ Cornstarch is cornflour.

■ Baking soda is bicarbonate of soda.

■ Vanilla or vanilla extract is vanilla essence.

■ Green, red, or yellow sweet peppers are capsicums or bell peppers.

■ Golden raisins are sultanas.

## Volume and Weight

The United States traditionally uses cup measures for liquid and solid ingredients. The chart below shows the approximate imperial and metric equivalents. If you are accustomed to weighing solid ingredients, the following approximate equivalents will be helpful.

■ 1 cup butter, castor sugar, or rice = 8 ounces = ½ pound = 250 grams

■ 1 cup flour = 4 ounces = ¼ pound = 125 grams

■ 1 cup icing sugar = 5 ounces = 150 grams

Canadian and U.S. volume for a cup measure is 8 fluid ounces (237 ml), but the standard metric equivalent is 250 ml.

1 British imperial cup is 10 fluid ounces.

In Australia, 1 tablespoon equals 20 ml, and there are 4 teaspoons in the Australian tablespoon.

Spoon measures are used for smaller amounts of ingredients. Although the size of the tablespoon varies slightly in different countries, for practical purposes and for recipes in this book, a straight substitution is all that's necessary. Measurements made using cups or spoons always should be level unless stated otherwise.

## Common Weight Range Replacements

| Imperial / U.S. | Metric |
| --- | --- |
| ½ ounce | 15 g |
| 1 ounce | 25 g or 30 g |
| 4 ounces (¼ pound) | 115 g or 125 g |
| 8 ounces (½ pound) | 225 g or 250 g |
| 16 ounces (1 pound) | 450 g or 500 g |
| 1¼ pounds | 625 g |
| 1½ pounds | 750 g |
| 2 pounds or 2¼ pounds | 1,000 g or 1 Kg |

## Oven Temperature Equivalents

| Fahrenheit Setting | Celsius Setting* | Gas Setting |
| --- | --- | --- |
| 300°F | 150°C | Gas Mark 2 (very low) |
| 325°F | 160°C | Gas Mark 3 (low) |
| 350°F | 180°C | Gas Mark 4 (moderate) |
| 375°F | 190°C | Gas Mark 5 (moderate) |
| 400°F | 200°C | Gas Mark 6 (hot) |
| 425°F | 220°C | Gas Mark 7 (hot) |
| 450°F | 230°C | Gas Mark 8 (very hot) |
| 475°F | 240°C | Gas Mark 9 (very hot) |
| 500°F | 260°C | Gas Mark 10 (extremely hot) |
| Broil | Broil | Grill |

*Electric and gas ovens may be calibrated using celsius. However, for an electric oven, increase celsius setting 10 to 20 degrees when cooking above 160°C. For convection or forced air ovens (gas or electric), lower the temperature setting 25°F/10°C when cooking at all heat levels.

## Baking Pan Sizes

| Imperial / U.S. | Metric |
| --- | --- |
| 9×1½-inch round cake pan | 22- or 23×4-cm (1.5 L) |
| 9×1½-inch pie plate | 22- or 23×4-cm (1 L) |
| 8×8×2-inch square cake pan | 20×5-cm (2 L) |
| 9×9×2-inch square cake pan | 22- or 23×4.5-cm (2.5 L) |
| 11×7×1½-inch baking pan | 28×17×4-cm (2 L) |
| 2-quart rectangular baking pan | 30×19×4.5-cm (3 L) |
| 13×9×2-inch baking pan | 34×22×4.5-cm (3.5 L) |
| 15×10×1-inch jelly roll pan | 40×25×2-cm |
| 9×5×3-inch loaf pan | 23×13×8-cm (2 L) |
| 2-quart casserole | 2 L |

## U.S./Standard Metric Equivalents

⅛ teaspoon = 0.5 ml

¼ teaspoon = 1 ml

½ teaspoon = 2 ml

1 teaspoon = 5 ml

1 tablespoon = 15 ml

2 tablespoons = 25 ml

¼ cup = 2 fluid ounces = 50 ml

⅓ cup = 3 fluid ounces = 75 ml

½ cup = 4 fluid ounces = 125 ml

⅔ cup = 5 fluid ounces = 150 ml

¾ cup = 6 fluid ounces = 175 ml

1 cup = 8 fluid ounces = 250 ml

2 cups = 1 pint = 500 ml

1 quart = 1 litre